LINCOLN'S
Constitution

Daniel Farber

LINCOLN'S
Constitution

THE

UNIVERSITY

OF CHICAGO

PRESS

CHICAGO &

LONDON

The University of Chicago Press, Chicago 60637
The University of Chicago Press, Ltd., London
© 2003 by The University of Chicago
All rights reserved. Published 2003
Printed in the United States of America

12 11 10 09 08 07   3 4 5

ISBN: 0-226-23793-1 (cloth)
ISBN: 0-226-23796-6 (paperback)

Library of Congress Cataloging-in-Publication Data

Farber, Daniel A., 1950–
    Lincoln's Constitution / Daniel Farber.
      p. cm.
    Includes bibliographical references (p.) and index.
    ISBN 0-226-23793-1 (alk. paper)
        1. Lincoln, Abraham, 1809–1865—Views on the
    Constitution.   2. United States—Politics and gov-
    ernment—1861–1865.   3. Constitutional history—
    United States.   I. Title.
    E457.2. F216 2003
    342.73'029—dc21

                                        2002151576

To the late Gerry Gunther—
in gratitude for his friendship and support

Contents

Acknowledgments *ix*

Introduction *1*

CHAPTER 1: The Secession Crisis *7*

CHAPTER 2: Sovereignty *26*

CHAPTER 3: The Supreme Law of the Land *45*

CHAPTER 4: The Union Forever? *70*

CHAPTER 5: The Legitimacy of Coercion *92*

CHAPTER 6: Presidential Power *115*

CHAPTER 7: Individual Rights *144*

CHAPTER 8: The Rule of Law in Dark Times *176*

Afterword: The Lessons of History *196*

Notes *201*

Index *235*

Acknowledgments

Writing this book would have been impossible if I had not been able to build on the extraordinary efforts of James G. Randall, Don E. Fehrenbacher, and more recent Lincoln scholars. I owe an equally large debt to historians of the antebellum era and the Civil War, such as David Potter, Allan Nevins, and their successors. I also owe special thanks to David Currie, David McGowan, and an anonymous reader for the University of Chicago Press for their extensive comments on the entire manuscript. Additional thanks are due to Brian Bix, Guy Charles, Jim Chen, Dianne Farber, Miranda McGowan, and Jeff Powell for comments on individual chapters. I am much indebted to my research assistants, Jaime Driggs, Mike Mergens, Katie Moerke, Bill Preston, Andrew Schoenthal, and Andrew Young. Sonia Farber corrected numerous errors in the final manuscript. John Tryneski was a source of wise counsel and moral support. I would be especially remiss, however, if I did not say something about the stimulating experience of co-teaching a seminar on Lincoln and the Constitution with Mike Paulsen. Fortunately, the students enjoyed our vigorous debates as much as we did, as well as providing useful insights of their own. My seminar students at the University of Chicago also contributed greatly to the development of my thinking. The staff of the University of Minnesota law library was energetic and resourceful in tracking down sources. As always, Laurie Newbauer handled many rounds of revisions with impeccable skill. None of the aforementioned, of course, is responsible for any errors or inaccuracies.

Introduction

Did the South have the right to secede? During the war, did Lincoln usurp the powers of Congress and the courts? Did he trample on the Bill of Rights and the rule of law?

For anyone interested in the Civil War era, these questions seem pressing even today. We not only want to know what happened during that era, we want to know how to assess those events. Our judgments about their actions can make no difference to Lincoln or Grant or Lee. Professional historians may consider such value judgments irrelevant or distracting. Still, given the continuing importance of the Civil War in the American consciousness, we cannot resist making them. Almost a century and a half later, we remain fascinated with Abraham Lincoln and the great national ordeal of the Civil War.

To call the Civil War a constitutional crisis is almost a misuse of words, like calling Pearl Harbor a military setback. In the Civil War, the Constitution was placed under pressure that it had never seen before and has not seen since. Engineers test materials to destruction to probe their structure. In the same way, the Civil War experience illuminates the deepest, most critical constitutional issues. The extraordinary circumstances of the war have never been repeated. But American history has time and again raised questions about state sovereignty versus national power, executive authority versus congressional prerogatives, and individual rights versus national security. The Civil War gives us the opportunity to probe these issues where they were presented most starkly.

Conversely, constitutional analysis may help provide a perspective on the historical events. Intense constitutional debates permeated the Civil War era. Unlike geometry problems, these questions can never be answered with absolute certainty. There are no theorems in constitutional law. But some answers are more plausible than others. The tools of constitutional analysis are the language of the document, its historical context, judicial precedents, and the lessons of our nation's history. These tools can provide reasonable confidence about the better reading of the Constitution, even if complete proof is impossible.

We obviously owe it to Lincoln (and ourselves) to try to understand him in his own historical and legal context. But, I believe, this need not be the full extent of our thinking about Lincoln and his presidency. Secretary of War Edwin M. Stanton, standing nearby when Lincoln died, said, "Now he belongs to the ages." That means us. We are interested in Lincoln not only because he was an important figure in nineteenth-century history, but because he still speaks powerfully to us today. Thus, besides considering him in his context, we are also called upon to consider him in our own. Moreover, he was in many respects the first modern president, fighting what was arguably the world's first modern war. We have had far more time to ponder such actions than the people of Lincoln's day. It is useful to consider how his actions stack up against later, more fully matured views about these issues. It is also useful to consider whether our ideas, based in part on later, less extreme crises, stand up to the test of the Civil War era. In short, we can use Lincoln as a test of modern constitutional doctrine, and use modern doctrine as a medium for assessing Lincoln's actions.

If we are concerned about whether Lincoln's actions were dictatorial, it makes sense to compare them with our modern conception of the presidency. Likewise, if we are concerned about whether modern conceptions of the presidency are adequate during an extreme threat to national security, we can use the Civil War as a test case. Similar considerations hold with respect to Lincoln's opponents. Knowing that the views of Calhoun, the South's great constitutional philosopher, have echoes in the jurisprudence of modern conservative justices may lead us to take his ideas more seriously. His views also provide a broader context for current federalism debates. In short, we need to try to comprehend the history of the period in and of itself, but we should also feel free to go beyond that where a contemporary perspective is illuminating.

The constitutional dimensions of the war are complex (even putting aside the constitutional puzzles of Reconstruction, which are not covered in this volume). Civil War constitutional issues fall into two broad categories. The first relates to federalism. Breaking up the Union was supposedly justified on the basis of states' rights. Secession was not a sudden Southern inspiration. The Southern view of states' rights claimed the authority of Madison and Jefferson, based on the Virginia and Kentucky Resolutions. Those resolutions themselves had relied on earlier constitutional history. Thus, to evaluate secession, we need to look to a time well before Lincoln's election. We need first to go back to the formation of the states and the federal government. Then we need to trace the later debate over states' rights and national power waged by men such as John Marshall, John Calhoun, and the aging James Madison. With this history in mind, we can analyze Southern arguments for secession and Lincoln's response to those arguments, both of which were rooted in those earlier constitutional debates. We must also consider the related problem of whether the federal government was entitled to use force to keep the South in the Union.

An overview of the secession crisis is presented in chapter 1. The next four chapters address this first cluster of constitutional issues. In chapter 2, I will show how disputes over the nature of state sovereignty can be traced back to the beginning of the struggle for independence. Chapter 3 examines the fight over federal supremacy from early battles between Federalists and Jeffersonians through the nullification crisis. As we will see, an integral part of this dispute involved the jurisdiction of the federal courts over state judges and other officials. Chapter 4 directly confronts the constitutionality of secession. Although the constitutional issue is more complex than modern readers sometimes assume, the bottom line is not surprising: secession was indeed unconstitutional. I round out the discussion of this first set of issues by asking whether the federal government had the power to resist secession by force. Chapter 5 concludes that military resistance to secession was not only constitutional but also morally justified.

Once the Confederacy opened fire on Fort Sumter, a second set of problems was presented. Lincoln's use of executive authority was extraordinary in its breadth. Since Washington's administration, controversy has raged over the scope of presidential authority. Throughout our history, we have struggled to accommodate the needs for executive initiative and for checks and balances. We have also struggled to reconcile national security and individual rights. Lincoln's actions raise grave questions about the status of individual rights during national emergencies, another issue that has become unexpectedly germane today. Finally, Lincoln's stormy relationship with Chief Justice Taney raises broader questions. To what extent can presidential authority to interpret and execute the laws be independent of the judiciary without imperiling the rule of law?

The second half of the book is dedicated to these wartime issues. Chapter 6 considers the separation-of-powers question. Lincoln remains the paramount example of unilateral presidential initiative, but we have now had another 140 years of debate over executive power. This provides us with a fuller perspective on Lincoln's actions than his contemporaries enjoyed. Chapters 7 and 8 consider the most troubling aspects of the war record—Lincoln's extraordinary use of military authority at the expense of traditional civil liberties and the conflict between some of his actions and the conventional conception of the rule of law.

The lessons to be learned from comparison with modern constitutional doctrine vary, depending on the topic. In terms of federalism, the most striking insight concerns the parallels between antebellum Southern constitutional thought and current theories about states' rights held by some members of the Supreme Court. I hope the comparison will make readers take the antebellum theories more seriously; it may also make them more skeptical of the current judicial revival of states' rights. In terms of the issues about separation of powers and individual rights, the main point is that most of Lincoln's actions (contrary to common belief) were generally in line with our current view of executive authority. On the one hand, this helps eliminate the "Lincoln as dictator" myth. On the other hand, it suggests that Lincoln's example does not support current advocates of further expansion of presidential power.

I have been stressing the book's references to modern constitutional doctrine because they are probably its most distinctive feature. But these references do not dominate the discussion. Before we can even think about comparing Lincoln's actions with modern constitutional thought, we need to understand exactly what Lincoln did, what arguments he made in defense of those actions, and how his words and deeds fit into the context of the times. Thus, most of the book is purely historical. The discussions of modern law are intended to enrich our understanding of Lincoln and his era, not merely to exploit that era for its present-day relevance.

Lincoln and his contemporaries, along with modern scholars, would agree on the importance of relating his actions to the text of the Constitution and the understandings of its framers. Indeed, if the first half of the book has a hero, that hero is as much James Madison as Abraham Lincoln. Among antebellum thinkers, it was Madison who provided the most cogent constitutional vision of the Union. It is no coincidence that Madison, often known as the father of the Constitution, was also an outspoken opponent of nullification and secession.

There has been no systematic evaluation of constitutional problems under Lincoln in the decades since the publication of James Randall's admirable work.[1] Randall's book remains a wonderful resource for constitutional scholars, but it is also technical, difficult to obtain, and in some respects outmoded. In the intervening decades, much has changed in terms of our historical understanding of the Framers, and even more in terms of our understanding of the Civil War and Reconstruction. Randall wrote in an era when Reconstruction was considered a tragic interlude before the reestablishment of white supremacy in the South; needless to say, the perspective of current historians is much different. Moreover, several generations of Lincoln scholars have greatly deepened our understanding of the man and his era. It is surely time for a fresh look at the constitutional issues.

The Civil War raised the most profound questions about our constitutional order. Accordingly, this book concerns the largest of constitutional questions: the nature of the Union and of the states, the breadth of the president's independent power to pursue the national interest, the scope of civil liberties during national emergencies, and the collision between the imperatives of national survival and the rule of law. I do not expect that my answers to these questions will satisfy every reader; I have not always been sure whether they fully satisfied me either. Every chapter of this book could well be the subject of a book of its own, and I have no illusion that I have written the last word about any of them. I will be content, however, if I have moved the debate about these issues forward a step or two.

CHAPTER 1

The Secession Crisis

The Civil War began in the chilly morning hours of April 12, 1861, when a Confederate battery opened fire on Fort Sumter. Major Robert Anderson, the U.S. Army commander in Charleston, South Carolina, had moved his forces to Sumter from a more vulnerable position at nearby Fort Moultrie. In the next two days, a thousand shots were fired by the fort and three thousand by the attackers. After being battered for thirty-three hours, Anderson gave in to the inevitable. The American flag came down on the afternoon of April 14. Despite the ferocious crossfire, not a single soldier was killed in the battle itself. At the surrender ceremony, however, one of the guns used to salute the flag went off prematurely, killing Private Daniel Hough.[1]

Despite initial expectations on both sides, the war was neither short nor easy. Fort Sumter opened the bloodiest war in American history. It was four years to the day after the Fort's surrender when Major Anderson ran the U.S. flag back up at Sumter. In the meantime, the world had forever changed. "By then," in the words of a leading historian, "[s]lavery was dead; secession was dead; and six hundred thousand men were dead." "That," he added, "was the basic balance sheet of the sectional conflict."[2]

Later that same day, April 14, 1865, yet another price was added to that balance sheet. As the war had begun with the death of a single individual, so it would end. That evening, just about the time Major Anderson toasted the president of the United States, John Wilkes Booth entered the presidential box at Ford's Theater. By the next morning, Lincoln was dead.[3]

Thus, the first modern war—a war in which death had virtually become an item of mass production—was bracketed by the deaths of a single private and a president. Many wondered during the conflict whether the Constitution would also be a casualty of war. Lincoln had said that the Constitution was on trial—that the issue was whether "government of the people, by the people, and for the people, would perish from the earth."

Others must have questioned whether the Constitution would survive Lincoln's own efforts to save it. Like modern-day chemotherapy, the cure seemed nearly as dangerous as the disease. Without direction from Congress, Lincoln had taken the nation to war. He had curtailed individual liberties by suspending habeas corpus and instituting military trials. Lincoln himself had asked, "Must a government, of necessity, be too *strong* for the liberties of its own people, or too *weak* to maintain its own existence?" It was not irrational to fear that those liberties might also be casualties of war.[4]

The constitutional issues of Lincoln's time are not important purely for historical reasons. The Civil War was a unique epoch in American history. But questions about state sovereignty, federal authority, presidential power, and civil liberties have recurred again and again. Even today, the Supreme Court wrestles with these issues. Lincoln has been something of a paradigm for later presidents, and the Civil War was a defining moment for modern federalism. Legal theories about these constitutional issues need to be tested against the events of that period. At times, the relevance of these issues may seem to recede. But as recent events have shown, we can never take for granted the nation's power to maintain its security while upholding the rule of law.

Before addressing the constitutional issues, we need some historical context. We will return to some of the history in more detail in connection with specific legal issues. Even so, the historical descriptions in this book do not pretend to be a substitute for the extensive treatments by experts on the period. Building on the work of those scholars, the historical discussions are intended only to provide background for understanding the constitutional issues. Our main focus is on the constitutional analysis.

In constitutional terms, Fort Sumter was both the end of one era and the beginning of another. It ended a long political struggle over slavery and states' rights. These constitutional disputes had bedeviled the nation since the beginning. Sumter also began a military struggle that raised constitutional issues of its own. Our emphasis will be on the legal issues rather than on history for its own sake, but readers who are not immersed in the history are entitled to some orientation. We begin, then, with the issue that eventually divided the nation to the point of civil war.

A HOUSE DIVIDED

Where to start? Perhaps with a sultry night in Washington in 1846, when a previously unknown representative named Wilmot proposed that any territory acquired from Mexico be kept free from slavery. But of course, the slavery issue already had a long history. By 1820, Missouri's effort to join the Union had led to a crisis, ending with the compromise solution of limiting future expansion of slavery north of a line drawn at thirty-six degrees, thirty minutes. The battle over the extension of slavery to new territories was reignited by the war with Mexico. Some, like Wilmot, argued that Congress had the power to forbid slavery in the territories, as had been done in the old Northwest Ordinance before the Constitution was even adopted. Led by John C. Calhoun, some Southerners responded that the territories were held in trust by the federal government on behalf of all the states, and that discriminating against the institutions of the slave states would be unconstitutional. By 1849, some Southern states were threatening secession if the Wilmot Proviso were adopted. But the crisis was defused by the Compromise of 1850, designed by Henry Clay but actually pushed through Congress by Stephen A. Douglas. By assembling separate coalitions on different parts of the compromise, Douglas obtained passage of a package that included something for each side. For the North, the compromise admitted California as a free state and abolished the slave trade in the District of Columbia. For the South, it strengthened the Fugitive Slave Act and created the New Mexico and Utah territories without the Wilmot Proviso. The slavery issue had been safely settled.[5]

Or so it seemed. The story of the 1850s is in large part the saga of how this apparent settlement of the slavery issue came unglued. In the process, the conflict destroyed the Democratic party as a national institution, taking Stephen Douglas along with it. It also created the Republicans as a sectional party, ultimately leading to Lincoln's election. The combined effect was to produce Lincoln's election and the secession crisis. The process was incredibly complicated, but we can focus on three major contributing factors.[6]

First, enforcement of the Fugitive Slave Act horrified Northerners. The spectacle of escaped slaves being dragged away in manacles roused public opinion against slavery. The number of slaves who escaped to the North was quite small, and few who did were ever returned under the act. The South paid a heavy price in Northern anger and resentment for a statute whose value to slave owners was largely symbolic.[7]

Second, Douglas unwittingly reignited the issue of slavery in the territories with his Kansas-Nebraska Act. Douglas was eager to organize these territories in order to pave the way for settlement and a transcontinental railroad. By adopting "popular sovereignty," thereby leaving control of slavery to the territorial legislature, Douglas hoped to finesse the slavery issue and keep it off the national agenda. His tactic backfired. Northerners were appalled by the repeal of the Missouri Compromise. Implementation of the statute was also a disaster. Kansas became the scene of bloodshed as rival groups of Northerners and Southerners vied for control. Worse, the Buchanan administration broke its pledges and endorsed the fraudulent, proslavery Lecompton constitution for Kansas. This was intolerable to Douglas, who broke with the administration. When Buchanan threatened to destroy him politically, reminding him that Jackson had destroyed his own opponents within the Democratic party, Douglas was not impressed. "Mr. President," he replied, "I wish you to remember that General Jackson is dead." But despite this bravado, Douglas had to fight for his political life against Buchanan. The schism between the two men badly damaged the Democratic party in the North, thereby strengthening the emerging Republican party.[8]

Third, the Supreme Court made its own disastrous miscalculation in the *Dred Scott* case. *Dred Scott v. Sandford* began as a relatively simple dispute over Scott's status, but developed into a complex legal snarl.[9] Scott brought suit in Missouri, where he was held as a slave, arguing that he had become free as a result of his former residence with his master in Illinois and in the Minnesota territory. The Supreme Court was initially ready to dispose of the case on relatively narrow grounds. For reasons that are still disputed, however, the majority decided instead to take on the slavery issue once and for all. Chief Justice Taney's opinion for the Court had two major holdings. First, blacks could never become citizens of the United States (nor, for federal constitutional purposes, of the states where they lived). Second, Congress lacked the power to ban slavery in the territories. The case was a true trainwreck. Taney's opinion is widely agreed to be an intellectual disgrace. Because several concurring opinions were filed, historians still dispute just what parts of Taney's opinion had the support of a majority of the justices. As it turned out, Buchanan had not only been informed about the opinion prior to its release but played an active role in bringing one key justice into the majority. Despite the Court's hopes of finally putting the vexing issue of slavery to rest, its opinion had the opposite effect.[10]

Douglas was typical of those who wished to keep the slavery issue off the national political agenda. On both sides of the Mason-Dixon line, however, significant and vocal groups wanted more. An increasingly outspoken group of Southerners insisted that federal neutrality on the slavery issue was not enough. They called for active federal support, taking the form of a federal slave code for the territories. Unlike earlier generations of Southerners, typified by Jefferson, they viewed slavery not as a necessary evil but rather as a positive good. It provided the foundation for a gracious and proud white society, they argued, while benefiting blacks who would otherwise live in savagery. They viewed Northern "agitation" on the slavery issue as an intolerable insult, as was Northern resistance to the Fugitive Slave Act. Fearful that Northern agitation would appeal to nonslaveholding Southerners and perhaps even goad the slaves to revolt, they demanded that the North silence all antislavery voices. Their fears and their anger were heightened by John Brown's raid on Harpers Ferry, particularly since prominent antislavery figures had given Brown some support. Threats of secession, if their demands were not met, became increasingly common.[11]

On the other side were both abolitionists and less zealous antislavery men like Lincoln. Lincoln, speaking for the loose coalition that was drawn into the Republican party, explained their obstinacy on the slavery issue. Despite pleas that the agitation about slavery should be ended, Lincoln did not believe this would be possible "until a *crisis* shall have been reached, and passed." For, he observed, a "house divided against itself cannot stand." The government could not endure permanently half slave and half free. Ultimately, it "will become *all* one thing, or *all* the other." Either its opponents would "arrest the further spread of it, and place it where the public mind shall rest in the belief that it is in course of ultimate extinction," or its advocates would succeed in foisting it on the whole nation.[12]

In his debates with Douglas, Lincoln made his moral condemnation of slavery clear. He did not contend for complete social or even legal equality for blacks. Nevertheless, he held that blacks were "entitled to all the natural rights enumerated in the Declaration of Independence, the right to life, liberty, and the pursuit of happiness." Though blacks might not be the equals of whites, slavery was morally wrong. Less racist than most around him, he nevertheless did not repudiate racism in terms that we would demand today. Lincoln acknowledged that a black man "is not my equal in many respects—certainly not in color, perhaps not in moral or intellectual endowment." "But," he continued, "in the right to eat the bread, without leave of anybody else, which his own hand earns, *he is my equal and the equal of Judge Douglas, and the equal of every living man.*" When Douglas invited the people of a territory to adopt slavery if they desired, Lincoln declared, "[H]e is in my judgment penetrating the human soul and eradicating the light of reason and the love of liberty in this American people."[13]

Earlier, Lincoln had addressed the constitutional status of slavery. The

Framers, he claimed, regarded it as a necessary evil. "They found the institution existing among us, which they could not help." But the Constitution carefully avoided even using the word *slavery,* resorting instead to circumlocutions like a "PERSON held to service or labor." With this language, Lincoln said, "[T]he thing is hid away, in the constitution, just as an afflicted man hides away a wen or a cancer, which he dares not cut out at once, lest he bleed to death." Less than this the Framers "COULD not do; and [MORE] they WOULD not do." And the earliest Congresses took the same view of slavery: "They hedged and hemmed it in to the narrowest limits of necessity." Thus, Lincoln said, existing rights to slaves had to be respected, but no extension of slavery could be tolerated.[14]

The end of the 1850s found the nation poised on the brink of disaster. The Democratic party was shattered by Southern demands that the party repudiate popular sovereignty and endorse a slave code. The Republicans had a strong base of support in the North. By nominating a moderate "westerner" like Lincoln, they could pick up Illinois and other swing states in the North. By the time it was actually held, the election of 1860 was almost a foregone conclusion. Although Lincoln was outvoted nationally by supporters of Douglas and other candidates, the Republicans' strength in the North gave them the electoral college and the presidency. Key figures in the South had already announced that living under a Republican president was utterly unacceptable to them.[15]

This account has stressed the slavery dispute as a cause of the Civil War. Slavery was not, of course, the only source of division between North and South. The South differed in many ways from the North. It was far more agrarian, giving it strikingly different interests in connection with such issues as the tariff. It was more intellectually isolated, with a weak educational system, a sparse publishing industry, and a largely parochial view of the world. The white population was more ethnically homogenous. The South also aspired to a kind of aristocratic grace and nobility, with a strong emphasis on personal honor, foreign to the more commercial North. All of these differences were real and would have caused trouble, slavery or no slavery. But modern historians seem agreed that the slavery issue was critical to the ultimate breakdown of the Republic.[16]

THE ROAD TO CIVIL WAR

In the Deep South, the reaction to Lincoln's election was immediate. Even before the results were in, Southern fire-eaters had warned that Lincoln's election would dissolve the Union. The governor of South Carolina had opened correspondence in October with other Southern governors about ways and means of pursuing secession. Within three weeks of the election, conventions to consider secession were called in South Carolina, Alabama, Mississippi, Florida, and Georgia. In the early afternoon of December 20, the South Carolina convention voted to secede. Georgia, Mississippi, Florida, Alabama, Louisiana, and Texas followed by the end of January. Within another week or so, delegates from these states had met in convention, adopted a constitution closely modeled after that of the United States, and elected Jefferson Davis as provisional president. All this was accomplished well before Lincoln was scheduled to take office in March.[17]

The North's initial response to secession was hampered by the weakness of the Buchanan administration. Buchanan had never been much of a president. He was a good administrator and might have made a good judge, but he was too timid, indecisive, and intellectually inflexible to take decisive initiative in a crisis. Though he was from Pennsylvania, he had also hewed closely to the Southern line throughout his political career. Rather than providing leadership, he was often managed by his cabinet, which was dominated by Southerners. When outvoted in the cabinet, he would give way. He was further hampered by his lame-duck status during the secession crisis.[18]

Buchanan's view was that secession was unconstitutional, but that the federal government could not constitutionally coerce states to remain in the Union. At most, the federal government could use force only to protect its own property. If an immediate explosion could be prevented, he hoped that he could eventually defuse the crisis. These views were not well received by Northerners, who considered them spineless. Yet they also irritated Southerners who considered secession to be a constitutional right.[19]

Between the election and Lincoln's inauguration, the two sides moved toward a collision. On December 26, finding his position at Fort Moultrie untenable, Major Anderson shifted his forces during the night to Sumter. Southerners were outraged at this initiative. The federal government also inched toward a firmer position. Buchanan's cabinet was reshuffled, resulting for the first time in control by supporters of the Union. Buchanan apparently was open to the idea of negotiating with commissioners sent by South Carolina, but he was beaten down by the opposition of two key cabinet members. Efforts to reach a compromise in Congress with the South petered out. Led by Kentucky senator Crittenden, a select committee proposed constitutional amendments shielding slavery from congressional interference. Congress approved an amendment that would forbid any future interference with slavery in the states. Northerners such as Lincoln were willing to go along with this amendment because they thought it did little more than restate the existing limit on congressional power. But Lincoln and his allies would not give way on the issue of slavery in the territories, which was the central tenet of their party. The compromise effort foundered as a result.[20]

As the Buchanan administration ended, Major Anderson was in Sumter, compromise efforts had failed, and the federal government had yet to take a strong stance. Because of a possible assassination attempt, Lincoln entered Washington incognito. Buchanan was sufficiently worried about the capital's security that he ordered special protective measures during Lincoln's inaugural. Riflemen were posted on rooftops, streets crossing Pennsylvania Avenue were guarded, and troops paraded. In a day when the Secret Service had not been invented and presidents customarily met the public informally, these were extraordinary security measures.[21]

In his inaugural address, Lincoln took a firm but conciliatory tone. Later chapters will consider in detail Lincoln's specific arguments in this speech. For now, what is important is his effort to uphold unionism without further inflaming the South. Lincoln denied that secession was authorized by the Constitution or that the South had any moral right to revolt. He pledged to enforce existing federal laws, including the Fugitive Slave Act. But he pledged to hold all government property such as Sumter and to collect tariffs, using force if necessary. He would also continue to deliver the mail if possible. Apart from these minimal measures, he promised not to use force and not to impose new federal appointees on the South. Thus, "[T]here needs to be no bloodshed or violence; and there shall be none, unless it be forced upon the national authority." It was the concluding portion of the speech, however, that became most famous. "I am loth to close," Lincoln said. "We are not enemies, but friends. We must not be enemies." And at the end, a sentence hopeful for reconciliation: "The mystic chords of memory, stretching from every battle-field, and patriot grave, to every living heart and hearthstone, all over this broad land, will yet swell the chorus of the Union, when again touched, as surely they will be, by the better angels of our nature."[22]

Despite what seems now to be its measured tone, the speech was not well received in the South. It was denounced as a call to arms against the

South. It was variously considered a "war message," the equivalent of a declaration of war, a "silly production," and a sign of Lincoln's "insolence" and "brutality." Although there was approval in some quarters even in the South, it was muted by comparison. The better angels of our nature were apparently slumbering.[23]

The government and its leadership were ill prepared for the crisis. When Lincoln took office, he was the head of a new and untested party. He led a cabinet containing several men of greater national stature than his own. Lincoln had no experience as an administrator and only two years of experience in Washington as a member of the House. He was facing the greatest crisis in the nation's history. Not surprisingly, the administration's first few weeks were uninspiring, marred by jostling for control by cabinet members, indecision, and general confusion. In the end, Lincoln decided to send more supplies to Fort Sumter, which was rapidly running out of food, but not to provide reinforcements or take any aggressive action, unless the fort or the relief fleet was attacked. He probably knew that even this action would spark a violent response from the South. When the guns opened fire on April 12, the days of indecision were over, and the war had begun.[24]

The Confederacy had not taken this step blindly. The Confederate cabinet had earnestly debated the issue on the morning of the ninth. The secretary of war was concerned about the Confederacy's general lack of military preparedness. Robert Toombs feared that the action would backfire. "Mr. President," he said, "at this time it is suicide, murder, and will lose us every friend at the North. You will wantonly strike a hornet's nest which extends from mountain to ocean, and legions now quiet will swarm out and sting us to death." But other members of the cabinet demanded action. Public sentiment in the South favored taking the initiative and striking a bold blow. There was also some risk that South Carolina would act on its own. Striking against Sumter would help bring Virginia into the Confederacy, put Northern resolve to the test, and prove the South's own resolve to nations such as Britain and France. Beyond all that, it was intolerable to suffer the insolent presence of a federal fort in the heart of the Confederacy. So the fatal step was taken.[25]

AFTER SUMTER

The day after Sumter surrendered, Lincoln issued a proclamation calling on the states to supply seventy-five thousand militiamen and calling a special session of Congress on July 4. Response in the North was enthusiastic.

In the upper South, which had been wavering, Lincoln's call for federal "coercion"—as Southerners saw it—promptly led Virginia, Tennessee, North Carolina, and Arkansas to leave the Union.[26]

Seventy-five thousand men were not nearly enough, but the government could barely handle that number. Small arms were supposedly available but in reality they were hard to locate and often in poor repair. The government had no foundry for cannons. Uniforms, tents, and medical equipment were inadequate. Some troops were half starved; though an ample amount of food existed, no one knew how to distribute it. Troops were stuffed into any available building because barracks and camps were lacking. When New York mustered six hundred troops, a third had to be left behind because they had no muskets. As each New Yorker was enrolled, a blanket was thrown over him, his hat was snatched away and replaced with a military cap, and a plate and silverware were thrust into his hands. These were the troops who were supposed to put down the rebellion.[27]

When Virginia seceded, the situation in the remaining border states was critical, nowhere more so than in Maryland. The Confederate secretary of war had boasted, even before Sumter fell, that the Confederate flag would "float over the dome of the old Capitol at Washington before the first of May." Washington was defended only by eight army companies, two hundred marines, and the city's militia. If Maryland seceded, the city would become an island in Confederate territory. As the situation in Maryland deteriorated, Washington panicked. Deeply depressed, Lincoln feared that he had been cut off from the North entirely. Families packed their belongings, and women and children left the city. Theaters were closed, and buildings were barricaded.[28]

The situation in Maryland was bad. The legislature was pro-Southern, as were most city officers in Baltimore except the mayor. On April 19, a train arrived in Baltimore with volunteers from Massachusetts. The troops had to march across town to another station to reach Washington. En route, they were attacked by a mob. By the time the city police restored order, four soldiers and several rioters were dead. The Massachusetts troops did finally reach Washington, but troops from Pennsylvania had to be sent home. After four days of rioting, the pro-Union governor gave in. He telegraphed Lincoln to send no more troops—and much worse, he allowed the destruction of the railroad bridges and telegraph lines linking Baltimore with the North. Hundreds of Union supporters were driven out of Baltimore.

Lincoln called the governor and mayor to Washington, where he was able to negotiate safe transit around the city. The North did not have the military strength to force local authorities to provide access to Baltimore itself. After some anxious days, troop strength in Washington finally reached the point in early May where Maryland could be brought under control.[29]

On April 27, in an effort to restore order, Lincoln authorized the suspension of habeas corpus anywhere necessary between Philadelphia and Washington. The order became the subject of a famous opinion by Chief Justice Taney, prompted by an arrest about a month later. After the worst part of the crisis was over, troops charged with protecting the railroad line to Washington entered the home of John Merryman and arrested him for helping to destroy railroad bridges after the Baltimore riots. He contacted his lawyer, who filed a writ of habeas corpus with Taney. The writ was addressed to General Cadwalader, who was in charge of the military district. When Taney took his place on the bench the next day, Cadwalader did not appear, instead sending an aide-de-camp to present his regrets to the Court. The aide informed Taney that Merryman was being held subject to Lincoln's suspension of the writ. Taney thereupon denounced Cadwalader for failing to produce Merryman in court as ordered and issued an arrest warrant. Not surprisingly, the arrest effort was unsuccessful; the marshal was turned back at the gate of the fort. Taney then upbraided the general and announced that he would file a written opinion. (Technically, he did not issue it in his capacity as a judge "on circuit" but rather as an "in chambers" opinion of the chief justice.) Taney argued that only Congress had the power to suspend the writ of habeas corpus. He portrayed the president as little more than an errand boy for Congress and the courts. Taney directed his clerk to send a copy to the president, whom Taney tartly reminded of his duty to "take care that the laws be faithfully executed." According to a leading constitutional historian, Taney's opinion "had the impact of a military victory for the South and was hailed with delight by enemies of the Administration."[30]

Suspending habeas was not Lincoln's only dramatic initiative in those early weeks of the war. He imposed a blockade on Southern ports, implying as a matter of international law that a state of war existed between the United States and the Confederacy. He also closed the U.S. mails to "disloyal" publications, expanded the regular military, and pledged the government's credit for millions of dollars. He required all army officers to renew their oaths of allegiance to the United States. He summoned an additional forty-two thousand volunteers for the U.S. military. Navy vessels were as-signed to protect ships carrying gold from California; other ships were pur-chased and fitted with arms to protect Washington. In addition, Lincoln paid private citizens two million dollars to help with recruiting. Lincoln's authority to do any of these things on his own was, to say the least, unclear. Under the Constitution, Congress rather than the president has the au-thority to declare war and to control the mails, the military, and the purse.[31]

Still, Lincoln did not act without restraint. He was under pressure to pre-vent the Maryland legislature from meeting at the end of April, for fear that they might pass a secession ordinance. Lincoln concluded that arresting the members of the legislature was not justifiable. First, he said, "[T]hey have a clearly legal right to assemble; and, we can not know in advance, that their action will not be lawful, and peaceful." Arresting them after the fact would be pointless in terms of maintaining control of Maryland. Second, arrests would be ineffectual. "If we arrest them, we can not long hold them as prisoners; and when liberated, they will immediately re-assemble, and take their action." The same result would follow if they were dispersed rather than arrested; they would simply reassemble somewhere else. The only thing to do, he concluded, was to wait and see what they did—and if they did secede, bring them back into the Union using whatever means were necessary.[32]

When Congress finally came into session, Lincoln was ready with a ma-jor address defending his actions. Again, we will defer until later chapters any detailed analysis of his arguments. Lincoln described his actions at Sumter as purely defensive, casting the blame for starting the war on the South. Given the unprovoked attack and the threat to legal authority, he said, "[N]o choice was left but to call out the war power of the Govern-ment." Sadly, when the government defended itself, the people of Virginia "allowed this giant insurrection to make its nest within her borders," again leaving the government no choice but to respond accordingly. Lincoln summarized and defended his actions since Sumter. Some, he said, were "strictly legal." Others may have required congressional authorization, which he hoped would be forthcoming after the fact. Lincoln then devoted some effort to defending his power to suspend habeas corpus, responding to Taney without naming him. The Constitution did not clearly vest this power solely in Congress, he maintained. And even if his suspension of habeas *was* illegal, he argued, that action would still have been imperative to save the Union: "[A]re all the laws, *but one,* to go unexecuted, and the government itself go to pieces, lest that one be violated?" Lincoln also attacked the idea that secession was a legitimate exercise of state sovereignty. "Much is said about the 'sovereignty' of the States," he observed, "but the word, even, is not in the national Constitution." In reality, according to Lincoln, the "Union is older than any of the States; and, in fact, it created them as States."[33]

For Lincoln, the war was "essentially a People's contest." On the Union side, it was a "struggle for maintaining in the world" a form of government based on individual freedom—"whose leading object is, to elevate the condition of men" and to "afford all, an unfettered start, and a fair chance, in the race of life." Yielding only to "partial, and temporary departures, from necessity," this was the goal of the national government. And so, he concluded, "having thus chosen our course, without guile, and with pure purpose, let us renew our trust in God, and go forward without fear, and with manly hearts."[34]

Although Lincoln spoke of "partial, and temporary departures, from necessity," away from American ideals, some observers then and since have accused him of stepping over the line into dictatorship. Even in the early days of the war, he alone had made fundamental decisions defining the nation's future course. He, rather than Congress, had made the critical determinations that secession was illegal and that the North would use force if necessary to defend federal property. He had called up the militia en masse and had instituted the blockade, in effect taking upon himself the responsibility for declaring the existence of a state of war. And he had sharply curtailed individual liberty by suspending habeas corpus, again without congressional participation. This seemed more like autocracy than constitutional democracy.

Lincoln's formidable exercise of executive power did not end when Congress came back into session. It continued throughout the war. In terms of unilateral action, the most dramatic example was the Emancipation Proclamation, freeing millions of slaves by presidential fiat. Lincoln also imposed unprecedented limits on civil liberties. Thousands of civilians, North and South, were arrested and held without trial—just how many thousands is difficult to determine, even today. Many of these arrests were justifiable, but glaring instances of abuse are not hard to find.[35]

A few examples will illustrate the lengths to which some of the arrests went. A Missourian was arrested by General Halleck for saying he "wouldn't wipe [his] ass with the stars and stripes." A drunken Baltimore hotel operator was arrested for saying he would be the first man to hang Lincoln. It turned out he was also the writer of a famous patriotic song, *Columbia, Gem of the Ocean*. The editor of the *Dubuque Herald* was arrested for publications allegedly discouraging enlistments; like the Maryland songwriter, it turned out his patriotism was irreproachable: he had helped raise a Union regiment in Iowa. Secretary of State William H. Seward even came close to arresting former president Franklin Pierce, a Democratic critic of the administration. Apparently, a U.S. marshal in Illinois was particularly quick on the draw, arresting one doctor because of an unconfirmed report that he had made disloyal remarks at a meeting of an antiwar group. As it turned out, the doctor actually was trying to get an army commission and had been busy tending a sick child on the day in question. When the doctor's case reached Lincoln's desk, he ordered the man released—but the doctor was lucky in having gained the president's attention. Others were not so lucky.[36]

After September 24, 1862, suspects were not merely detained without legal process, they were also tried by military tribunals. The jurisdiction of these tribunals extended to "all Rebels and Insurgents, their aiders and abettors within the United States, and all persons discouraging volunteer enlistments, resisting militia drafts, or guilty of any disloyal practice, affording aid and comfort to Rebels against the authority of the United States." What authoritarian government could have asked for a broader charter?[37]

Thus, it is understandable that Lincoln should have been accused of dictatorship. Nevertheless, these charges were exaggerated. According to the most careful study of the arrests, very few were politically motivated. Far from being an authoritarian ruler, Lincoln was sorely beset by the leaders of his own party in Congress, by the opposition party, and by public opinion. Most importantly, he always faced the possible wrath of the electorate. Although Lincoln's reelection was in grave doubt, no thought was given to suspending the democratic process. If it had not been for some crucial military victories by the North, Lincoln would have lost to George McClellan in 1864.[38]

Although Lincoln cannot fairly be accused of dictatorship, he did stretch the power of the presidency to its outer reaches. He also authorized unprecedented exercises of government power over individuals: arrest and detention without military process, trial by military tribunals, and wholesale destruction of individual property (most famously in Sherman's march through Georgia). After decades in which nearly everyone had agreed that slavery in the South was beyond the reach of federal power, he ordered the freeing of millions of slaves with a stroke of the presidential pen. It is little wonder that the constitutionality of his actions has been hotly disputed since almost the day he took office.

THE CRISIS OF THE UNION AND THE RULE OF LAW

This book will cover a wide range of constitutional issues. Beginning with the initial separation from England, we will trace the struggle to define the relationship between the states and the Union. This struggle took various forms: the contested location of sovereignty, the disputed constitutional authority of the federal courts over state courts, the nullification crisis, the long and bitter debate over secession, and finally the contentious issue of federal coercion of the errant states. After Sumter the focus changed as Lincoln struggled to meet the emergency. Now the questions were the president's power to go beyond enforcing statutory commands and take the initiative on his own, the limits of civil liberties such as the right to jury trial or free speech in wartime, the authority of the military over civilians, and the president's right to violate court orders or even constitutional provisions in the national interest.

Despite the range of these constitutional issues, they had a common thread. The Civil War put the rule of law to its greatest test. In a broad sense, a major goal of the Civil War was to establish the power of legal institutions to authoritatively resolve fundamental social disputes. Lincoln, as we saw earlier, said that the basic issue was whether bullets could supplant ballots as a way to decide national policy. Since 1800, Southerners had been arguing that the states had the ultimate sovereign right to interpret the Constitution. The final resolution of constitutional disputes would have to depend on negotiation with dissenting states. Nationalists had said that it was up to the federal government, in particular the federal courts, to determine the meaning of the Constitution. Thus, the war was in part about whether the Constitution provided a system of authoritative dispute resolution or merely a forum for negotiation between contesting sovereignties.

In the next four chapters, we will explore the Southern claim that the states were the ultimate judges of the meaning of the Constitution and of the justice of their own cause. Although this claim appeared under various rubrics such as state sovereignty, nullification, and secession, the fundamental argument was always that the federal government lacked the ulti-

mate authority to settle constitutional disputes. Against these claims, James
Madison and others argued that a key purpose of the Constitution was to
provide an authoritative legal mechanism for resolving disputes between
states. Thus, despite his collaboration with Jefferson (whose states' rights
views were more pronounced), Madison viewed Congress and the federal
courts as the ultimate arbiters of constitutional disputes. The states themselves were subject to the rule of law, like everyone else within the constitutional system.

One goal of the war, then, was to establish the primacy of the rule of
law. This evocative phrase has served as a rallying cry for centuries, though
it lacks any clear-cut definition. Rather, the ideal of the rule of law involves
a cluster of concepts: (1) the existence of understandable legal rules governing individual conduct, so that they are not at the mercy of arbitrary executive or judicial authority; (2) the legal system's ability to maintain social
control, so that disputes are settled through orderly procedures rather than
force; (3) the supremacy of legal authority, so that officials as well as citizens are governed by law; and (4) the availability of impartial legal forums
to enforce the law, replacing the "rule of men" with the "rule of law." In a
democratic society, disputes over policy are settled through the political
system, rather than by negotiation between disputing power centers. In a
constitutional democracy, the courts stand ready to ensure that the political
actors comply with fundamental constitutional standards. That, at least, is
the theory. Whether our system complies with the ideal, or whether any
system of government actually could comply with the ideal, is another
question.[39]

Events put various aspects of the rule of law at issue. The South's constitutional theory was that ultimate authority over constitutional issues did
not reside in the Supreme Court or in the process for constitutional
amendments, but in the sovereign people in each state. This theory (and its
attempted implementation at Sumter) put into question the idea that written constitutional rules, interpreted through an authoritative tribunal,
could really govern the country. Instead, Southern constitutional theory
pointed toward a basically political process of negotiating conflicting state
viewpoints. But when the war came, the rule of law was placed under other
stresses. The question then became the scope of executive initiative at the
apparent expense of preexisting legislative directives and constitutional restraints. In trying to save the rule of law as the key principle of constitu-

tional order, Lincoln seemed to be tearing gaping holes in it, leaving theory and practice in terrible tension.

The complex relationship between war and the rule of law can be seen in the thought of General Sherman, who at least in popular imagination still epitomizes the brutality of war. One side of Sherman's thought does place the use of force above legalities. Sherman's reputation is exaggerated, but he was not timid about the use of military authority. Sherman's view was that "[w]hen one nation is at war with another, all the People of the one are enemies of the other. Then the Rules are plain and Easy of understanding." These rules overrode the normal rights of citizens. "Being at war we have a right to Seize the property of Rebels"—"we can & do take corn, mules, horses, wagons and all the materials of transportation & subsistence." Speedy, rough justice was needed in war: "Spies and guerrillas, murderers under the assumed title of Confederate soldiers, deserters on leave, should be hung quick"—though this should be done only "after a trial" (so as to eliminate the growing practice of "losing prisoners in the swamp" rather than risking their escape during lengthy detention). In Sherman's view, "Agitators and theorists have got us into this scrape, and only practical men and Fighting men can extricate us."[40]

Yet Sherman wanted his nephew to become a lawyer rather than a soldier. The dignity of the legal profession, he said, "must be enhanced by this war for I contend we are fighting for the supremacy of *Written* Law, as against the Rule of mere party & popular prejudice." Only the rule of law could assure peace: "Until all the People are willing to refer all questions even of the greatest magnitude to our Courts, instead of to mere Party Cabals, or the dread chances of war there can be no real Peace." Ultimately, the sacrifices of the war "are to enhance the dignity of the Profession of Law, rather than the influence of the Military class which is too costly to be endured long." At the end of the war, he still continued to maintain that the "People of this Country are subject to the Constitution, and Even they Cannot disregard it without Revolution, the very thing we have been fighting against."[41]

Sherman's statements reflect the practical tensions within the ideal of the rule of law. If the rule of law is to be more than a pious hope, the legal system must have the power to enforce compliance, even in the face of violent resistance. But the use of force cannot be fully controlled by legal niceties, by predefined regulations and legal adjudications. Even in less extreme circumstances, we must ensure both that the executive is bound by law, and also that the executive has the strength and discretion necessary to deal with crises. The great question leading up to the Civil War was whether the federal government did have the power to enforce compliance with its legal determinations, either legislative or judicial. The great question during the war was whether the rule of law itself could survive the effort to defend it.

The final chapters of the book investigate the pressures on the rule of law during the war. As we will see, the Constitution itself allows deviations from ordinary legal rules in wars and other emergencies. As discussed in chapter 6, the president can call upon a broad, though not unlimited, power to protect the federal government and its operations. In the theater of war, the Constitution contemplates replacement of the normal legal regime by the laws of war and expanded military authority even over civilians. And deference to the courts has its limits, particularly after the power to suspend habeas corpus is invoked. Still, in the end, some of what Lincoln and his subordinates did exceed their constitutional authority. What prevented these unauthorized executive actions from becoming a threat to the entire constitutional order was Lincoln's willingness to seek congressional ratification and face the legal consequences if it was not forthcoming.

At the very beginning, in his July 4, 1861, special address to Congress after Sumter, Lincoln tried to put the war in a larger perspective. He said that the issue of secession "embraces more than the fate of these United States." Rather, "It presents to the whole family of man, the question, whether a constitutional republic, or a democracy—a government of the people, by the same people—can, or cannot, maintain its territorial integrity, against its own domestic foes." Could "discontented individuals, too few in numbers to control administration," on any pretext they chose, "break up their Government, and thus practically put an end to free government upon the earth." He phrased the critical question as this: "Must a government, of necessity, be too *strong* for the liberties of its own people, or too *weak* to maintain its own existence?" So, too, the question was whether the rule of law could maintain its grip on even the most violent social conflicts, without itself being distorted beyond recognition. As we will see, despite some important missteps, Lincoln was successful on the whole in negotiating this treacherous terrain. It remains to be seen if we will be equally successful today in maintaining the rule of law in the face of violence.[42]

In that July 4 speech, Lincoln spoke of the government maintaining its territorial integrity. But Southerners would have challenged Lincoln's very premise. Did the Constitution establish a true government, or merely a compact between sovereign states? Who had the final word over interpreting the Constitution, the federal courts or the states? Did a disgruntled state have the right to leave the Union and make its own way? It is with these questions that we will begin.

CHAPTER 2 *Sovereignty*

The idea of state sovereignty has exercised great appeal in American history, perhaps never so much as in the antebellum South. It was this "sublime moral principle" that was said to justify secession. It behooves us, then, to begin our analysis of secession by exploring the debate over state and federal sovereignty, a debate that predated the Constitution itself.[1]

This chapter, like the one that follows it, may seem a bit abstruse. But to understand the Civil War, we must understand the contrasting constitutional visions of the North and the South. The conceptual differences ran deep and had many legal ramifications. Unless we take a serious look at the conception of state sovereignty embraced by the South, the constitutional debate about secession is incomprehensible.

In examining the question of state sovereignty, the starting point must be the status of the states before the Constitution. Next comes the question of how the Constitution affected sovereignty. The Framers did not have a clear consensus about this as a matter of political theory. As a practical matter, however, the Constitution's expansion of federal powers clearly made major incursions into state autonomy. Indeed, if there is anything at all that is clear about the intent of the Framers, it is their desire to strengthen federal power.

THE SOVEREIGNTY DEBATE IN PERSPECTIVE

The term *sovereignty* has several meanings. Political scientists distinguish four types of sovereignty: domestic sovereignty (meaning internal control); interdependence sovereignty (the power to control what crosses the border); international legal sovereignty (diplomatic recognition by foreign nations); and Westphalian sovereignty (independence from foreign political control). For our purposes, domestic sovereignty is the crucial concept.

When Americans debated sovereignty before the Civil War, they were debating the ultimate locus of political authority.[2]

Secession is dead, but not the dispute over state sovereignty. As recently as 1995, the Supreme Court found occasion to debate again the nature of the Union. Pre–Civil War conceptions of the Constitution made an unexpected reappearance in the Supreme Court's decision in the *Term Limits* case, which involved a state's power to set term limits for members of Congress.[3] Although the subject of term limits may seem far removed from the issue of sovereignty, the case prompted a spirited debate about the fundamental nature of the Union. This modern debate provides a contemporary window into the historical dispute over sovereignty.

The majority view in *Term Limits* was that control over federal legislators pertained solely to the new government created by the Constitution rather than to any preexisting state authority, and hence was not "reserved" by the Tenth Amendment. Justice Stevens's majority opinion lays out the conventional modern view of state and federal sovereignty. Under the Articles of Confederation, Stevens said, "[T]he States retained most of their sovereignty, like independent nations bound together only by treaties." The new Constitution "reject[ed] the notion that the Nation was a collection of States, and instead creat[ed] a direct link between the National Government and the people of the United States." For this reason, federal legislators "are as much officers of the entire Union as is the President." A patchwork of local qualifications for federal office, Justice Stevens stated, would "sever the direct link that the Framers found so critical between the National Government and the people of the United States." Stevens's view harkened back to Daniel Webster's assertion that "[t]he people of the United States are one people."[4]

Justice Thomas's dissent, joined by Rehnquist, Scalia, and O'Connor, squarely rejected this vision of national sovereignty. "Because the majority fundamentally misunderstands the notion of 'reserved' powers," he said, "I start with some first principles." The most basic of those first principles, according to Justice Thomas, was this: "The ultimate source of the Constitution's authority is the consent of the people of each individual State, not the consent of the undifferentiated people of the Nation as a whole." Justice Thomas argued that under the Constitution "the people of each State retained their separate political identities."[5]

Even in language others have seen as nationalist, Thomas found a reaffirmation of states' rights. The Preamble refers to "We the People of the

United States," but Justice Thomas observed that the Constitution consistently treats "the United States" as a plural noun. An earlier draft of the Preamble actually listed the states separately, and the current phrasing may have simply reflected uncertainty about which states would ratify. (If Thomas is right, perhaps the Framers would have made their meaning clearer if they had referred to "We the Peoples of the United States.")[6]

In any event, Justice Thomas said, the concept of popular sovereignty underlying the Constitution "tracks" rather than erases state lines. It would make no sense to interpret the Tenth Amendment as reserving powers to the "undifferentiated people of the Nation as a whole, because the Constitution does not contemplate that those people will either exercise power or delegate it. The Constitution simply does not recognize any mechanism for action by the undifferentiated people of the Nation." Some observers viewed these remarks as little more than a rhetorical flourish. Others saw an ironic echo of John Calhoun.[7]

Justice Kennedy refused to go along with Thomas's view of state sovereignty in *Term Limits*. In his view, the basis of the federal government's legitimacy is "that it owes its existence to the act of the whole people who created it." Although the Framers were "solicitous of the prerogatives of the States," the states cannot be allowed to interfere with the exercise of federal powers or with "the most basic relation between the National Government and its citizens, the selection of legislative representatives." Kennedy denied that "the sole political identity of an American is with the State of his or her residence." He disputed the view that "the people of the United States do not have a political identity as well, one independent of, though consistent with, their identity as citizens of the State of their residence." Like the states, Kennedy concluded, the national government is "republican in essence and in theory," drawing its power from the People.[8]

More recently, however, in *Alden v. Maine*,[9] Justice Kennedy joined the four *Term Limits* dissenters in proclaiming that the states retain "a residuary and inviolable sovereignty" or at least, as he quickly added, "the dignity, though not the full authority, of sovereignty."[10] Apparently, the sovereignty issue remains unsettled, even today. Of course, the stakes today are much smaller. Secession is no longer an issue. But within a narrower compass, the debate goes on.

As we review the current dispute among the justices and the earlier quarrels of the eighteenth and nineteenth centuries, it is tempting to ask who was right about the *true* location of sovereignty. But this is the wrong question to ask. If, as Blackstone said, sovereignty resides in a society's "supreme, irresistible, absolute, uncontrolled authority," no government in America since 1789 has ever fit this description. All units of government are subject to the Constitution. Thus, for domestic purposes (as opposed to its use in international law), sovereignty does not describe an operational feature of our political system.[11]

In the American context, sovereignty often seems to function as an almost metaphysical concept—some secret essence of legal potency that cannot be detected directly, but only as a kind of normative aura. One hotly debated question, for example, is whether the populations of the various states existed (or still exist) as separate entities acting together as a conglomeration, or rather as a single entity acting through the agency of multiple subgroups. This is reminiscent of medieval disputes about the nature of the Trinity. It is not in any real sense a question of fact or even one of law.

This is not to say that the concept of sovereignty is completely vacuous. In international law, it makes perfect sense to say that China is a sovereign nation and that California is not. In the law of federal jurisdiction, it is clear that Wyoming has sovereign immunity from suit in federal court under the Eleventh Amendment and that New York City does not. Thus, American states are "sovereign" governments for some purposes but not for others. The federal government is clearly sovereign in some respects, most obviously in foreign relations, but it lacks unlimited power within its own territory, since states do have some independent powers and rights of their own. As we will see, when we turn to the historical record and ask what people in 1776 or 1787 thought about sovereignty, the answers are equally ambiguous. In the end, there is no clear historical answer to the precise locus of American sovereignty.

Sovereignty is thus not unlike the concept of ownership. In a naive view, every tract of land must have a single identifiable "owner." In the Middle Ages, lawyers used the concept of "seisin" to refer to the person who truly "owned" the land, as opposed to others who had various other rights regarding the land. With the end of feudalism, seisin became something of a metaphysical idea and lost any utility as an operational concept. Instead, we now think of ownership as a "bundle of sticks"—a collection of different kinds of authority over property, potentially distributed among many different people. Similarly, lawmaking authority is distributed among different sets of officials.[12]

Thus, the concept of sovereignty (whether state or federal) has modest intellectual content. It is at best an organizing concept, providing a framework for debating other issues. But the gap between the sovereignty concept and American governmental realities has not made the concept politically irrelevant. On the contrary, as the conflicting opinions in *Term Limits* illustrate, sovereignty has served a powerful rhetorical function in arguments about national and state power. Ideas about sovereignty may also color the understanding of particular constitutional issues. Thus, while it may not be useful to ask who *really* had sovereignty in 1776 or 1789, it is potentially useful to ask who was *believed* to have sovereignty then. As it turns out, however, the historical record does not supply a clear answer to the latter question either.

CONFLICTING VISIONS OF THE UNION

Three major views of domestic sovereignty have figured in American thought. The most nationalistic view was that of Lincoln. According to Lincoln, the colonies declared independence as a collective body, which thereby succeeded to the sovereignty formerly held by the king. This national sovereignty remained with the federal government during the Articles of Confederation and then under the Constitution.

The Union, Lincoln said in his most frequently cited statement on the subject, "is older than any of the States; and, in fact, it created them as States"—for before they formed the Union and collectively declared independence, they were mere "dependent colonies." "Not one of them," Lincoln pointed out, "ever had a State constitution, independent of the Union." In this view, only the nation ever enjoyed sovereign status. If sovereignty requires "[a] political community, without a political superior," Lincoln argued, then none of the states except Texas had ever enjoyed such an independent existence (and Texas only briefly).[13]

A second view is that the adoption of the Constitution transformed the nature of sovereignty in America. Under this transformational view of sovereignty, the states retained their separate sovereignty until the adoption of the Constitution, which created a new national sovereign (*E pluribus unum*). The transformational view posits that the Constitution was a new social compact among the American people as a whole. This view is supported by the Preamble and by references in the *Federalist Papers* to "the People" as the source of national political authority. Federalist 22 speaks of the need to lay the "foundation[ ] of our national government . . . on the solid basis of THE CONSENT OF THE PEOPLE," the "pure, original fountain of all legitimate authority." Similarly, in discussing conflicts between the states and the federal government, Federalist 46 speaks of both as representing "the whole body of their common constituents," and refers to the states as "subordinate governments." According to this theory, once the individual states ratified the Constitution, they transferred their sovereignty—in whole or in part—to the people of the nation.[14]

The transformation theory fits nicely with the Constitution's approach to constitutional change. When the Constitution itself was adopted, states were bound only if they individually consented. But under the amendment process, an individual state can be bound without its consent by the agreement of Congress and a sufficient number of other state legislatures, suggesting a movement of sovereignty toward the national populace.

The final view of sovereignty was Calhoun's. According to Calhoun, the people of each state separately became sovereign when they became independent of England. When they adopted the Constitution, they retained their separate political existences, but each state's populace delegated some of their powers to the national government and some to the state government. "I go on the ground," Calhoun said, "that [the] constitution was made by the States; that it is a federal union of the States, in which the several States still retain their sovereignty." In adopting the Constitution, the states' populaces had appointed the federal government to act as their agent to undertake certain functions. This did not transfer sovereignty to the federal government. Rather, Calhoun thought, the people of each state retained the power to nullify the agency relationship by action of a state convention. On the whole, the Articles of Confederation would probably have been more to Calhoun's liking than the Constitution.[15]

According to Calhoun, the "government is a federal, in contradistinction to a national government—a government formed by the States; ordained and established by the States, and for the States—without any participation or agency whatever, on the part of the people, regarded in the aggregate as forming a nation." (Note the contrast with Lincoln's famous "of the people, by the people, and for the people.") There is, Calhoun continued, "indeed, no such community, *politically* speaking, as the people of the United States, regarded in the light of, and as constituting one people or nation." In "all its parts—including the federal as well as the separate State governments, it emanated from the same source—the people of the several States." After reviewing some of the same features of the Constitution that Justice Thomas would later stress, Calhoun concluded: "[I]t is apparent that the States, regarded in their corporate character, and the population of the States . . . are the two elements, of which the government is exclusively composed." In short, the Constitution established "the government of a community of States, and not the government of a single State or nation."[16]

The differences between these theories are somewhat subtle and can easily be misunderstood, in part because of the confusing vocabulary of the debate. One source of confusion involves the term *state*. The claim that the United States is a confederacy of sovereign states sounds as if the Constitution is an agreement between state governments, just as an international treaty is between national governments. But this was not Calhoun's claim (or Justice Thomas's, for that matter). The Framers of the Constitution went to some trouble to insure that the Constitution would derive its authority directly from the people, rather than from the state governments. This was the reason for requiring it to be ratified in state conventions rather than by state legislatures. So in this setting, the term *state* refers to the state's populace, not to its government. It is easy to confuse this point, and states' rights advocates have been known to take advantage of the confusion to further the claims of state governments.[17]

Thus, the key issue is how to characterize "We the People of the United States"—as fifty state peoples tied together in one Union or one American people divided among fifty states. This is a rather elusive distinction, which is further obscured by another terminological problem. The term *compact* is used by all of the theories but in different ways. A contract between the peoples of the separate states might well be termed a compact. The critical question was whether a national social compact arose at some point, binding all Americans together into one people, or whether the only real social compacts were at the state level, with those political societies then forming a second-level compact. The "compact theory" of sovereignty refers to this second-level compact, which is considered to have a less fundamental status than the social compacts establishing each state. If this all seems rather aridly metaphysical, that's because it is.

Asking whether the state populaces or the national one "really" had sovereignty in 1776 or 1789 is somewhat like asking whether Lady Macbeth really had children. In both cases the available textual material supports conflicting inferences, and perhaps one set of inferences is a bit stronger than the other. (No children are mentioned, and Lady M. does not seem the maternal type; yet she has dynastic ambitions that would necessitate children.) Still, like Lady Macbeth's children, popular sovereignty lacks any physical existence. We might politely call it a theoretical construct or less politely call it a useful fiction. We should not be surprised if its location is sometimes impossible to pin down.

SOVEREIGNTY BEFORE THE CONSTITUTION

The concept of sovereignty had great resonance for the Framers' generation and has elicited a corresponding amount of interest on the part of historians. Unraveling the meaning of the historical records is quite difficult. Invocations of sovereignty were often driven by immediate political interests, which gave the participants an incentive to distort whatever their true understandings of sovereignty might have been. In addition, various senses of the word *sovereignty* were not carefully distinguished. As one historian observed, the Framers were "politically multilingual," using a variety of political theories whenever it suited their purposes. In the end, it is difficult to identify a single dominant theoretical understanding. As the dispute in the *Term Limits* case illustrates, there is no consensus today about which theory was the dominant understanding of the framing period.[18]

The dispute over the nature of the Union is in part an argument about whether we existed as a nation before the Constitution was adopted in 1789, and in part an argument about the effect of the Constitution itself. When they proposed the Constitution, the Framers themselves did not have a clear idea of how to characterize the existing situation. Even during the Constitutional Convention itself, the status of the states had been a matter of dispute. Luther Martin argued that separation from England had placed the former colonies "in a state of nature towards each other" and only then had these "separate sovereignties" formed a federal government. James Wilson responded in Lincolnesque terms that the states became independent only through their combined action: "[T]hey were independent, not *Individually* but *Unitedly*." The leading legal theorists of the time also disagreed about the extent to which a confederation would partake of some degree of sovereignty. The German legal writer Pufendorf took the view that in a perpetual union, sovereignty was ceded to the federation, while Vattel thought it remained wholly with the member states.[19]

In short, the understanding of sovereignty in the late eighteenth century was far from settled. Today, for every scholar who espouses the state compact reading of the record, there is one with a nationalist reading. One difficulty is that sovereignty claims were deployed strategically. For example, one issue was whether the colonies declared independence collectively, so that sovereignty at least momentarily reposed in the Continental Congress, or severally, so that it resided in the states at the time of independence. This seemingly esoteric question had legal implications regarding title to vast disputed areas of land. Under the theory of a collective declaration of independence, western land claimed by Virginia had instead reverted to the Continental Congress at the time of independence. Naturally, this had an effect on the views of sovereignty expressed by some Virginians. It is little wonder that even in 1787, confusion existed about the sovereignty issue.[20]

True, it is possible to impose some sort of order on the record, and advocates on both sides can tell a plausible enough historical tale. The advocate of states' rights can present one story about the evolution of sovereignty in America. This story begins with the colonies, which are said to have had "thirteen real compacts in the form of charters that gave them existence as political societies." When they each declared their separate independence in a joint declaration, sovereignty was transferred from the king to each of the thirteen, or in the cases of Massachusetts and New Hampshire, to individual towns. As an agent for the states, the Continental Congress conducted the war, but the states retained the sovereign power. Then, the sovereign peoples of the thirteen states entered into a mutual agreement to create a federal government, all the while retaining their separate sovereignty.[21]

We can imagine a historical record in which this story could pass as plainly descriptive, just as we can imagine finding a draft of the play in which Lady Macbeth's maternal status is unambiguous. Imagine that when unhappiness with English rule reached a pitch, representatives in each colony had decided to pursue independence and had drafted a new constitution for that colony, which was ratified by the people. Acting under the new constitutions, state governments then sent delegates to form a league with the similar new governments in the other former colonies. When the initial arrangement proved unsatisfactory, their delegates proposed giving greater power to the league management. The new arrangements were approved by the peoples of each separate state, who each retained a veto over any future changes in the arrangement. On these facts, we would say that the state compact theory was no more than an accurate recounting of events.

On the other hand, we can imagine a historical record embodying the nationalist vision as expressed by Lincoln and others. In this story, the un-happy colonists send representatives to decide on independence and to form a national government. The new central government in turn autho-rizes autonomous action by local subdivisions, which become the equiva-lent of cities with home rule in today's states. When changes are proposed to strengthen the government, they go into effect nationwide after being approved by a majority of the population (meeting in local conventions). These events would have made Lincoln's nationalist version of the found-ing unimpeachable history.

Alas, the realities were much messier and more complex than either Lin-coln's account or the states' rights story about sovereignty and indepen-dence. From the beginning, the key historical actors seemed to be of two minds. In early 1776, John Adams had proposed to Patrick Henry "for all the colonies to confederate and define the limits of the continental Consti-tution; then to declare the colonies a sovereign state, or a number of sover-eign states." As we will see, events left it a little unclear just which course was followed.

Begin with independence. The Declaration speaks in the plural, declar-ing the colonies to be "Free and Independent States" and says that "they" have the full powers of independent states. On the other hand, no colony declared independence before being authorized to do so by Congress. Even before independence, the Continental Congress was already func-tioning as an informal government. Rather than being lawfully selected by the existing colonial legislatures, the representatives at the First Continen-tal Congress were chosen in a variety of extralegal ways, including revolu-tionary committees and impromptu elections. Thus, they were not delegates of the existing local governments, but had a direct (if informal) mandate from the people. Furthermore, no state government gave itself a constitu-tion before being invited to do so by Congress. (Congress had actually issued such an invitation two months before formally declaring indepen-dence. The resolution's preamble suggests that the "invitation" was in fact mandatory, requiring that "the exercise of every kind of authority . . . un-der the Crown . . . be totally suppressed and all the powers of government exerted under the authority of the people of the colonies.") Thus, in this early period, "Power and legitimacy . . . flowed reciprocally" between na-tional and local leaders.[22]

In practice, the states often deferred to national decisions during the Revolution: "[L]ocal revolutionaries always preferred to commit treason with the explicit sanction of Congress." From the start, the states accepted the primacy of Congress in foreign relations. The states looked for national assistance in resolving boundary disputes and combating local separatist movements. Still—confounding any purely nationalist account—the Articles of Confederation (while purportedly perpetual) explicitly recognized the "sovereignty, freedom and independence" of each state. In form, the Articles were more like a present-day interstate compact than a constitution: "The said states hereby severally enter into a firm league of friendship with each other."[23]

Not everyone agreed, however, with the Articles' endorsement of state sovereignty. National sovereignty was championed by the men who would later play critical roles under the new Constitution, such as John Adams, James Wilson, and Alexander Hamilton.[24] In listing the vices of the Articles of Confederation, James Madison complained of the Union being regarded "as a league of sovereign powers, and not as a political Constitution by virtue of which they are become one sovereign power." Presciently, he lamented that such a concept of sovereignty would imply a power of individual states "of dissolving the Union altogether" if they believed their rights had been violated.[25]

FEDERATION OR NATION?

Before 1787, the center of gravity had hovered between the states and Congress, with the states scoring a theoretical victory in the language of the Articles and a practical victory with the increasing weakness of Congress after the war ended. Key movers in the adoption of the new Constitution favored a more nationalistic conception. Even so, the precise nature of sovereignty under the new Constitution was never quite specified.

The key problems facing the country were practical, not theoretical. These problems involved the division of powers between the state and federal governments. The sovereignty issue involved the question of whether the population of America should be considered a single group forming a national government, thirteen separate groups agreeing on joint government but entirely maintaining their own distinct group identities, or thirteen separate groups agreeing to merge their identities and form a unified group for some purposes but retaining their individual identities for others. Whatever else might be said about this dispute, it provided little guidance in designing the federal government.

As a leading historian explains, "[N]o single vector neatly charted the course the framers took in allocating power between the Union and the states." Rather, as Madison stressed in Federalist 37, experience and practical exigencies rather than abstract theory shaped the Constitution. As we have seen, at the time the Constitution was drafted, the Framers did not agree on the prior status of sovereignty. They were similarly unclear about whether the Constitution formed a new, national social compact, or was a compact between distinct state peoples.[26]

Some features of the Constitution (such as its grammatical treatment of *United States* as a plural) support the state compact theory. (Keep in mind, however, that in British usage, collective nouns such as *Parliament* or *the Court of Appeals* are always treated as plural.) On the other hand, the reference to "We the People of the United States" clearly points in the other direction, toward the existence of the United States as in some sense a preexisting entity. As Justice Thomas noted, this choice of language may have resulted partly from uncertainty over which states would ratify. But the words that follow—"do ordain and establish this Constitution of the United States of America"—are emphatically nationalistic. Justice Story observed that similar language was contained in the state instruments ratifying the Constitution. As Story pointed out, the language about the people ordaining a constitution stands in sharp contrast with that of the Articles of Confederation: "The said states hereby severally enter into a firm league of friendship with each other for their common defence . . . binding themselves to assist each other."[27]

Somewhat more light is shed on the views of the convention by the other document it unanimously adopted, an official letter to Congress, signed by George Washington on behalf of the convention. This letter was the only official, public explanation that the convention ever gave about the meaning of the Constitution. Unlike other ratification documents such as the *Federalist Papers,* the letter spoke for all the signers of the Constitution. It was also available to ratifiers in every state.[28]

The Washington letter invokes the language of social compact rather than treaty: "It is obviously impracticable in the federal government of these states, to secure all rights of independent sovereignty to each, and yet provide for the interest and safety of all: Individuals entering into society, must give up a share of liberty to preserve the rest." The implications of this analogy to the social compact would later be discussed in the *Federalist Papers.* In Federalist 33, Hamilton observes that when "individuals enter into a state of society, the laws of that society must be the supreme regulator of their conduct." Similarly, Hamilton continues, when "a number of political societies enter into a larger political society, the laws which the latter may enact, pursuant to the powers intrusted to it by its constitution, must necessarily be supreme over those societies and the individuals of whom they are composed." Otherwise, the larger political society would be "a mere treaty, dependent on the good faith of the parties, and not a government." This language seems to contemplate a kind of merger of pre-existing populations.[29]

Clearly, the Constitution was supposed to establish something more solid than a mere league. The Washington letter speaks of the "consolidation of our Union" as perfecting "the general government of the Union," which seems to contemplate a degree of political unity, rather than a mere league between entities retaining their own sovereign identities. Other language indicates that some merger might have taken place even prior to the adoption of the Constitution. The letter warns that the "consolidation" of the Union involves "our prosperity, felicity, safety, perhaps our national existence." The implication is that in some sense there was already a "*national* existence" capable of being at risk, which is to say that the United States under the Articles of Confederation was already a nation of sorts rather than a league.[30]

On balance, the Washington letter seems to support at least the transformation, if not the pure nationalism, theory of sovereignty. Thus, it provides support for the views expressed by Justice Kennedy when he broke rank with the other conservative justices in the *Term Limits* case. He argued that the national government "owes its existence to the act of the whole people who created it" and insisted that "the people of the United States . . . have a political identity as well, one independent of, though consistent with, their identity as citizens of the State of their residence." The Philadelphia convention seems to have had some leanings in that direction as well.[31]

Still, it would be a mistake to view the Framers as purely nationalistic. During ratification, the most direct discussion of the source of the Constitution's legitimacy was in Federalist 39. Inquiring into the formation of the new Constitution, Madison explained that ratification takes place by the authority of the people—"not as individuals composing one entire nation, but as composing the distinct and independent States to which they respectively belong." Madison went on to call ratification a "federal and not a national act," that is, "the act of the people, as forming so many independent States, not as forming one aggregate nation."[32] This passage seems at odds with Lincoln's theory, but leaves open the possibility that ratification resulted in the creation of a unified American people.

The sovereignty issue remained unclear even after the Constitution went into effect. For example, this issue was touched upon by Chief Justice Marshall in *McCulloch v. Maryland*.[33] Marshall was anxious to rebut the argument that the Constitution was a compact between the state governments. Admittedly, the Constitutional Convention had been called into being by Congress, and its members were selected by the states. But the Constitution was only a proposal and had no legal force until it was ratified by the People, meeting in state conventions. Thus, he said, "The government of the Union . . . is emphatically and truly, a government of the people." True, in adopting the Constitution, the people assembled in "their several states"—but where else, asked Marshall, could they have assembled? "No political dreamer was ever wild enough to think of breaking down the lines which separate the states, and of compounding the American people into one common mass. Of consequence, when they act, they act in their states." In the next chapter, we will consider the views of federalism held by Marshall and others during the half-century after ratification.[34]

The Framers themselves had no established orthodoxy on this point, and the muddled political developments of their times confound efforts to identify the "true" location of sovereignty after the fact. In Federalist 39, which refers to the origins of the Constitution in the "federal" action of the peoples of the various states, Madison concludes by speaking of the untidy, mixed nature of the new government. "The proposed Constitution," he said, "is, in strictness, neither a national nor a federal Constitution, but a composition of both." It combines some features of each. "In its foundation," he said, "it is federal, not national." But "in the sources from which the ordinary powers of the government are drawn, it is partly federal and partly national; in the operation of these powers, it is national, not federal; in the extent of them, again, it is federal, not national." Finally, according to Madison, the amendment process "is neither wholly federal nor wholly national." Thus, if there was a simple answer about the location of sovereignty after ratification, the Framers themselves apparently didn't know it. As a leading historian of the framing period says, after 1789, "[S]overeignty itself would remain diffused—which is to say, it would exist everywhere and nowhere."[35]

A QUESTION OF POWER

A recent historian refers to the convention as a "rally of nationalists." Another observes that the anti-Federalists "had no doubt that it was precisely an absorption of all the states under one unified government that the

Constitution intended, and they therefore offered this prospect of an inevitable consolidation as the strongest and most scientifically based objection to the new system." Clearly, the central purpose of the Constitution was to strengthen the weak government created by the Articles of Confederation; the question is how far down the road to centralized government the Framers intended to go.[36]

If we take the words of the Philadelphia convention at face value, the answer is that the Framers were quite serious about creating a powerful national government. The discussion of governmental powers in Washington's letter has a strongly nationalistic bent. It emphasizes the imperative of "consolidation of our Union" in the interests of prosperity and security. It also portrays the goal of "fully and effectually vesting" key powers in the national government, in particular those relating to foreign affairs, taxation, and commerce. These powers are portrayed as dangerously strong— too important to trust to any single body of men, thus requiring the division of power among the president and two houses of Congress. A desire to preserve state sovereignty does not figure in the letter.

Unless its language has strong unspoken qualifications, the Constitution appears to contain a formidable list of national powers. The federal government was given an impressive array of economic powers, extending deeply into the financial sector, national and international trade, and even production. The power to regulate interstate and foreign commerce is the best known, but it did not stand alone. A perusal of Article I shows that the federal government had broad control over monetary policy and credit, via the bankruptcy power (contrasted with the contract clause limitation on the states), the exclusive power to coin money, and the power to issue debt. The patent power also clearly intruded on the manufacturing sector, as did the power to establish a national system of standards. Madison thought it was clear that the encouragement of manufacture was one of the purposes of the commerce clause.[37]

Beyond these economic powers, the government has complete control of foreign affairs and national security. It can also intervene to provide each state "a Republican Form of Government," to control most aspects of the militia, and to block cooperative agreements between state governments. The jurisdiction of the federal government was not unlimited, but the Constitution's goal was, after all, to "promote the general Welfare," and this required a formidable arsenal of power.

It is understandable that the anti-Federalists were alarmed by the assignment of these powers to Congress. To see how important those powers were, imagine a proposal to give the United Nations the following powers: the power to tax and spend money for global welfare, exclusive power to issue currency, control of international commerce, jurisdiction over all cases involving the UN charter and even over all litigation involving members of more than one country—and then add the proviso that the UN's rule will be the "supreme law of the planet, binding judges notwithstanding the provisions of their own national constitutions." If even that is not enough, add to that a power to guarantee each member a democratic form of government, a power to take over national armies to execute UN law, and a general power to make any law "necessary and proper" for carrying out these other powers. How much would truly be left of U.S. sovereignty?

To continue with our example of a worldwide government, we might not be sure exactly what to say about the sovereignty of the United Nations, but we would be clear that a major power shift had taken place. In one sense, this is a limited set of powers, which might leave some matters of purely local concern like family law to the national legislatures. In another sense, these powers are extraordinarily broad. It would be quite understandable if today's equivalents to the anti-Federalists thought that almost everything of importance had been lost. Quite likely, the full sweep of these powers would not be realized for decades, but no one would doubt that the potential for a tremendous reallocation of power was present. This is not to say that the UN's powers would be unlimited, or that the UN courts would or would not be justified in attempting to draw some limits in construing those powers. Actual exercise of these powers might be restrained by structural protections, giving individual governments a voice in decisions. But the charter would represent a shift of the most profound kind away from national governments. It would also be seen as a serious, although not complete, loss of national sovereignty in favor of a supranational organization.

The same kind of power shift was seemingly contemplated by the Constitution. It is true that the powers of the federal government are "few and defined." But the anti-Federalists were right to demur from the conclusion that, as a present-day commentator puts it, "[t]his is not the stuff of which Leviathan is made." If given their full scope, the anti-Federalists realized, these powers might well eclipse any real sovereignty on the part of the states. Of the various federal powers, the tax power may have been the most significant. In the eighteenth century, taxation was a key attribute of sovereignty. (Thus, "no taxation without representation," as opposed to "no regulation without representation.") Giving Congress the tax power was thus a signal of its increased sovereignty.[38]

Historians may underestimate the extent of this constitutional power shift for two reasons. First, for political reasons, many of the new federal powers were not used to their full extent for many years—sometimes not until the Civil War era or even later. So we tend to overlook the extent of the unexercised legal authority Congress had in the early days. Second, although the Constitution rendered the federal government exponentially more potent than it had been previously, we tend to look forward rather than backward in making comparisons. Rather than comparing the First Congress under the Constitution with the last Congress under the Articles of Confederation, we tend to compare federal power under George Washington with federal power under Lyndon Johnson or Franklin Roosevelt. The federal government is far more powerful today than it was two centuries ago. Blinded by the glaring transformation from 1800 to, say, 2000, we overlook the extent of the earlier change between 1780 and 1800.

The point is not that the states were utterly submerged when the Constitution was ratified, or that the federal government was suddenly omnipotent, as in the worst of the anti-Federalist nightmares. But the Constitution gave the federal government the core powers normally associated with a sovereign nation—the power to make war, raise its own armies, enter treaties, tax its citizens, regulate internal and foreign trade, decide legal issues at the expense of subnational courts, and so forth. These are far more sweeping powers than those enjoyed by the European Union today, and indeed, far more sweeping powers than have ever been enjoyed by any league of sovereign nations.

On its face, if sovereignty is a matter of governmental powers, the Constitution *seemed* to transfer a great deal of sovereignty to the national government. Of course, it might be possible to construe the national powers very narrowly or to view states' rights as a trump over those powers. This was the basic Jeffersonian view, in response to Hamilton's reliance on the broad grants of power in the document.

Jefferson's problem was how to implement this idea of implicit limitations and make it effective. Jeffersonian arguments might sometimes prevail in Congress, but the South's political influence, as great as it was in the early nineteenth century, did not prove sufficient to block unfavorable legislation such as protective tariffs. The federal courts also could not be counted on to protect state sovereignty. In *McCulloch,* Chief Justice Marshall held that "the government of the Union, though limited in its powers, is supreme within its sphere of action." He also emphasized Congress's discretion in choosing the means to implement its constitutional powers, and he rebuffed state efforts to impede the accomplishment of federal policy. According to Marshall, "[T]he sound construction of the constitution must allow to the national legislature that discretion . . . which will enable that body to perform the high duties assigned to it, in the manner most beneficial to the people." Marshall also emphasized that state sovereignty does not include any control whatsoever over the programs enacted by Congress.[39]

Clearly, the Supreme Court could not be completely relied upon to defend the Southern vision of state sovereignty, nor could Congress. If the compact theory of the Constitution (and the accompanying visions of state sovereignty and limited federal power) were to be fully vindicated, some more reliable forum had to be found. Advocates of the compact theory of the Constitution were naturally drawn to empower the states as interpreters of the Constitution. Hence, they disfavored national enforcement mechanisms in favor of a mediating role by the states. If state sovereignty was going to mean anything, it had to include the state's ability to interpose itself between the federal government and the citizenry. As we will see, in the first half of the nineteenth century, states' rights advocates turned to nullification and resistance to federal coercion as the only way to revive true state sovereignty.

What are we to make of the historical record regarding the sovereignty issue at the time of ratification? As we have seen, each of the three positions regarding sovereignty can find some support in the historical record. State sovereignty language is not hard to find—most notably, in the Articles of Confederation—as well as indications that state sovereignty retained significance in political theory and practice. Lincoln's view of the preexisting nation also has some support, especially in the early days of the Revolution and in the nationalistic sentiments of some of the Framers. On the whole, the transformation theory probably has stronger support than either of the other two theories, although the convention records and ratification debates are admittedly ambiguous.

Although it really adds nothing of substance, the Tenth Amendment further muddied the waters by emphasizing the significance of the powers retained by the "states respectively" and by "the people." But are "the people" all Americans as a collectivity, or all Americans as members of state populations? This question, which was one subject of debate between

Justices Stevens and Thomas in *Term Limits,* is no more susceptible to a clear answer than is the question whether society is *really* composed of individuals or families.

Since the Constitution never expressly invokes the concept of sovereignty, it is only indirectly relevant to constitutional interpretation. If the Framers had had a clear consensus about the application of political theories of sovereignty, these background assumptions might be useful in understanding specific portions of the text—for example, by establishing a default role in favor of federal or state power. If the evidence were crystal clear that the Framers regarded the federal government as merely a servant of the states, for example, we might adopt a strong presumption of narrowly construing federal powers when they conflict with state policy. The absence of a clear consensus on sovereignty simply means that constitutional interpretation must proceed without whatever assistance such background assumptions might supply.

Consequently, the ambiguity of the historical record is more of a problem for staunch states' rights advocates like Jefferson and Calhoun than for nationalists like Hamilton and Lincoln. The Constitution on its face gives the federal government sweeping powers. Nationalists had to do little more than take the document at its word, with some added support from the *Federalist Papers* and from the early decisions of the Supreme Court. It was the states' rights advocates who needed to argue for strong implicit limitations on federal power, and to support this argument, they needed a solid demonstration of the dominance of state sovereignty. The record, taken as a whole, does not provide this kind of support.

In practical terms, then, the key issue was not sovereignty but power. The Constitution had been adopted in a relatively nationalistic period. Consequently, its history and text, along with early practice in the hands of men such as Alexander Hamilton, were also nationalistic. But after the turn of the nineteenth century, first Jefferson's followers and then Jackson's succeeded in paring federal activities to a bare minimum, in a triumph of the ideology of states' rights. Yet this political victory for states' rights was necessarily incomplete, dependent on any shift in the political winds. Hence, an increasingly threatened South was anxious to find a constitutional basis for limiting federal power. As we will see in the next chapter, this quest led to the effort to limit federal enforcement powers, so that the states themselves could become the judges of their own rights.[40]

CHAPTER 3

The Supreme Law of the Land

Giving Congress such extensive powers may have seemed a little risky, even to the Constitution's supporters. These broad powers must have seemed more palatable, however, when assumed to be in friendly hands. But it was not long before rifts between the Framers made this assumption untenable. During Washington's presidency, the first signs of what would later become the two-party system began to emerge with the split between Jefferson and Hamilton. Because organized political parties were an unfamiliar concept, each group saw the other as a subversive threat to republican government.[1]

The Jeffersonians, having less success in the federal government during the early years, began to cast about for methods of resistance. The vague theoretical underpinnings of the Constitution, with its uncertain assignment of sovereignty, provided an attractive opening. If the Constitution was a compact among sovereign states, then the states might block abuses of federal power. Furthermore, compact theory might provide a basis for limiting federal powers in order to maintain the sovereignty of the states.

Later the compact theory proved especially appealing to Southerners like Calhoun, who were in search of a way of protecting the South and its "peculiar institution" from national interference. In the meantime, however, the Supreme Court had developed a series of doctrines to reinforce national supremacy. These doctrines in turn became focal points of criticism by Calhoun, who was in his own turn challenged by none other than the aged James Madison. Eventually, the immediate crisis caused by South Carolina's effort to nullify federal law was defused, but the greatest threat to national supremacy lay ahead.

THE JEFFERSONIAN CHALLENGE

George Washington took office as the uncontested leader of the American people. The new government included a triad of luminaries—Alexander Hamilton and Thomas Jefferson in the cabinet, and James Madison in Congress. Divisions soon developed, however, between the two Virginians and the more nationalist Hamilton, who with Washington's support was anxious to establish a strong federal government. The turning point was the debate between Hamilton and Jefferson over the new government's financial policies. They sharply disagreed over the constitutionality of the Bank of the United States, hotly debating whether federal powers should be narrowly construed. These disputes led to the creation of two proto-parties, later to become the Federalists and the Democratic Republicans. Unfortunately, the Framers had no conception of political parties as a normal part of democracy. Instead, they had a horror of "factions," and each group viewed the other with intense suspicion. Lacking the idea of a "loyal opposition," they could only see their opponents, as they had once seen the British, as conspirators against republican government and liberty.[2]

Combined with rising international tensions, these fears led to the passage of the notorious Alien and Sedition Acts. The narrowest of the statutes authorized the president to arrest citizens of an enemy power during wartime. Since war with France did not erupt as feared, this statute never took effect. The other statutes were more sweeping. The Alien Act allowed the president to expel any noncitizen he considered "dangerous to the peace and safety of the United States," without any hearing or explanation. The Sedition Act attempted to suppress criticism of the government. This law made it a crime to print "any false, scandalous, and malicious writing or writings against the Government of the United States, or either House of the Congress of the United States, with intent to defame . . . or to bring them . . . into contempt or disrepute."[3]

Having lost the struggle in Congress, and with no prospect of help from the Federalist-dominated courts, the Republicans turned to the states, seeking to use them as a forum in which to oppose these statutes. As early as 1791, Madison had warned that Hamilton's programs were leading to a consolidation of national power. He had pointed to the states as a possible check on federal power and as a resource for mobilizing public opinion.[4]

These ideas bore fruit in 1798. As Jefferson later recalled, the leading congressional Republicans, finding themselves "of no use there," resolved to "retire from that field, take a stand in their state legislatures, and endeavor there to arrest" the Federalist usurpation. Jefferson's draft of what became the Kentucky Resolutions called upon the states to join "in declaring these acts void, and of no force," and in taking steps to insure that "neither these acts, nor any others of the General Government not plainly and intentionally authorized by the Constitution, shall be exercised within their respective territories." Jefferson's involvement was kept secret, however. His draft was considerably watered down by his "front man," John Breckinridge, so as to better suit public opinion in Kentucky. When Jefferson's original draft was finally published in 1832, however, it was greeted with jubilation by John C. Calhoun and other Southern foes of national authority. They particularly liked the language that "every state has a natural right . . . to nullify of their own authority all assumptions of power by others within their limits," and likewise to "take measures of its own" to ensure that unconstitutional federal authority was not "exercized within their respective territories." This was music to the ears of Calhoun and company—not to mention Jefferson's closing statement that nullification "is the rightful remedy."[5]

As enacted by the legislature, the Kentucky Resolutions were less radical than Jefferson's draft. They began with a strong affirmation of the compact theory. The "several states" had "constituted a general government for special purposes," reserving to each state all remaining power. "[T]o this compact, each State acceded as a State." Federal action in excess of this delegated authority was "unauthoritative, void and of no force." The resolutions maintained that "this government, created by this compact, was not made the exclusive or final judge of the extent of the powers delegated to itself." Instead, "[A]s in all other cases of compact among parties having no common judge, each party has an equal right to judge for itself, as well of infractions as of the mode and measure of redress." But in the end, after a tremendous states' rights windup, the actual remedy in the public version of the resolutions fell a bit flat. Kentucky merely asked the other states to "concur in declaring these [acts] void and of no force" and in "requesting their repeal at the next session of Congress."[6]

The Virginia Resolutions were somewhat tamer. Madison's original draft merely called upon the other states to "cooperate in the annulment" of the Alien and Sedition Acts, but Jefferson pushed for stronger language like Kentucky's. Madison—always the more careful thinker of the two—remained concerned that Jefferson had not "considered thoroughly the distinction between the power of the *State* and that of the *Legislature,* on questions relating to the federal pact." Madison was more cautious than Jefferson about giving state legislatures any power to block federal legislation. Since the Constitution was ratified by a convention rather than by the legislature, Madison viewed the state legislature's role in the compact as unclear.[7]

Like the Kentucky Resolutions, Virginia's spoke of the Constitution as a "compact to which the states are parties." Rather than focusing on individual states, however, the Virginia Resolutions spoke of the states as a collectivity. In the event of a "deliberate, palpable and dangerous exercise of other powers not granted by the said compact, the states who are parties thereto have the right, and are in duty bound, to interpose for arresting the progress of the evil, and for maintaining, within their respective limits, the authorities, rights and liberties appertaining to them." But what such "interposition" might mean in practice was unclear. The resolutions merely requested other states to "concur with this Commonwealth in declaring, as it does hereby declare, that the acts aforesaid are unconstitutional, and that the necessary and proper measures will be taken by each for cooperating with this State, in maintaining unimpaired the authorities, rights, and liberties, reserved to the States respectively, or to the people." The phrase "necessary and proper" was taken from the Constitution itself, where Madison had been arguing for a narrow interpretation. Perhaps the implication was that the state's power was similarly limited. Nevertheless, the mood was dangerously tense. Steps were apparently taken to arm the state against possible federal intervention. "The situation, as the frog said when the carriage rolled over him, was a little taut over the eyeballs," remarks a modern constitutional historian.[8]

The Virginia and Kentucky Resolutions were not well received elsewhere. Other states either ignored the resolutions or savaged them. The Vermont legislature declared that the resolutions were "dangerous in their tendency" and "unconstitutional in their nature." Rhode Island argued that Article III of the Constitution "vests in the Federal Courts, exclusively, and in the Supreme Court of the United States, ultimately, the authority of deciding on the constitutionality of any act or law of the Congress of the United States." For any state legislature to take such action would violate the separation of powers by blending legislative and judicial power. It would also risk "an interruption of the peace of the states by civil discord, in case of a diversity of opinions among the state legislatures; each state having, in that case, no resort, for vindicating its own opinions, but the strength of its own arm."[9]

In response to this criticism from other states, Madison authored a "Report on the Alien and Sedition Acts." The report was more careful to distinguish between various usages of the term *state*. The term "sometimes means the separate sections of territory occupied by the political societies within each; sometimes the particular governments, established by those societies; sometimes those societies as organized into those particular governments; and lastly, it means the people composing those political societies, in their highest sovereign capacity." The Constitution was a compact between the states at least in the last sense (of sovereign peoples). Consequently, "[T]here can be no tribunal above their authority, to decide in the last resort, whether the compact made by them be violated." Although the federal judiciary "is, in all questions submitted to it by the forms of the constitution, to decide in the last resort, this resort must necessarily be deemed the last in relation to the authorities of the other departments of the government; not in relation to the rights of the parties to the constitutional compact, from which the judicial as well as the other departments hold their delegated trusts."[10]

But the resolutions did not imply a legislative power to annul the judgments of the courts, according to Madison. Such state declarations do not intrude on the judicial power because they are merely "statements of opinion, unaccompanied with any other effect, than what they may produce on opinion, by exciting reflection." In contrast, judicial decrees "are carried into immediate effect by force." How could there be anything wrong with one state legislature merely communicating its views to other legislatures? After all, Madison observed, the Constitution clearly allows legislatures to communicate with each other for other purposes: to call for a constitutional convention or to negotiate over interstate compacts.[11]

The Kentucky legislature also responded to its critics. Although the response used the term *nullification,* it also asserted that Kentucky would "bow to the laws of the Union." Jefferson had flirted with the idea of secession as an ultimate remedy, but Madison talked him out of using such extreme language. At Madison's urging, Jefferson eliminated language reading, "But determined, were we to be disappointed in this [the reaction of the American people], to sever ourselves from that union we so much value, rather than give up the rights of self government which we have reserved, & in which alone we see liberty, safety & happiness." It should not be forgotten that Madison was one of the main drafters of the Constitution, while Jefferson had been out of the country and a halfhearted supporter. Understandably, Madison was more reluctant to contemplate even a hint of destroying the constitutional order.[12]

Helped in no small measure by public reaction to abuses under the Alien and Sedition Acts, the Republicans were swept into power by the 1800 election, and the Federalists were effectively destroyed as a political party. But the Virginia and Kentucky Resolutions had a life that extended beyond the immediate occasion. Their vitality also exceeded, at least in Madison's case, the intention of the author. The resolutions became known as the "Principles of '98" and "would for decades be regarded as almost sacred to the adherents of the states' rights faith." To quote a modern scholar, "If you were wondering where John C. Calhoun and Ross Barnett got their weird notions about disobedience of federal law, you can stop looking." For much of the early nineteenth century the political heirs of Jefferson and Madison viewed the Virginia and Kentucky Resolutions as a courageous rescue of American democracy from the nefarious schemes of Federalists like Hamilton.[13]

THE JUDICIARY STRIKES BACK

While Jefferson and Madison had assigned some role to the states as interpreters of the Constitution, the federal courts increasingly emphasized national supremacy. The key decisions were handed down by the Marshall Court in the decade between 1815 and 1825. The Marshall Court's opinions have a distinctive intellectual style. As a leading constitutional historian explains, Marshall generally began by articulating an "unassailable principle of American government," then analyzed specific constitutional language with that principle in mind, and finally applied the analysis to the case at hand. Of course, this was not an impartial exercise in political science. Rather, the "brilliance—and the legerdemain—of Marshall's interpretations was the partisan gloss he was able to put on the principles he extracted." In part, however, this approach also served another function, by reconnecting Americans with their past. This approach also sometimes marked the opinions of other justices such as Story.[14]

The Marshall Court found itself embroiled in a series of disputes about whether state courts had independent authority to interpret the Constitution. These disputes are familiar to modern lawyers. What may be less familiar is the way these disputes fit into the overall debate about states' rights. Men like Madison and Calhoun saw a tight connection between these issues and the more dramatic questions of secession and nullification.

The Virginia Supreme Court's 1814 decision in *Hunter v. Martin*[15] was the most notable challenge to federal judicial supremacy. In a previous stage of the same litigation, the U.S. Supreme Court had reversed the Virginia court, holding that certain Virginia laws violated the treaty of peace with Britain by confiscating a huge tract of property owned by Lord Fairfax. The Supreme Court had vacated the Virginia court's decision and remanded the case with the curt instruction to enter judgment in favor of the defendant. (Today, the Supreme Court more politely remands decisions to state courts for "further proceedings not inconsistent with this opinion.") On remand, however, the Virginia court held that the Supreme Court had no authority to review its decisions. The Virginia court argued that it was exempt from the U.S. Supreme Court's appellate jurisdiction, and that section 25 of the Judiciary Act, which purported to convey such jurisdiction, was unconstitutional. Thus, the U.S. Supreme Court had no authority to issue a writ of error to the Virginia court.[16]

The lead opinion in the Virginia court was written by Judge Cabell. He viewed the two governments as parallel and independent, though both were bound by the Constitution. "The two governments, therefore, possessing, each, its portion of the divided sovereignty, although embracing the same territory, and operating on the same persons and frequently on the same subjects, are nevertheless separate from, and independent of, each other." Consequently, "[E]ach government must act by *its own* organs: from no other can it expect, command, or enforce obedience, even as to objects coming within the range of its powers." True, state courts were bound by the supremacy clause. But this only required them to apply the Constitution in cases coming before them "according to their own judgments, and upon their own responsibility." The Supreme Court could not have appellate jurisdiction over a state court, because this would imply "superiority" over a separate sovereign.[17]

The concurring opinions are also interesting. Judge Brooke relied on the Virginia Resolutions as authority for the proposition that the states are "the guardians of the people's and their own rights." He also stressed that under the Articles of Confederation, Congress had had to rely on the states to enforce federal law. The whole point of the Constitution was to avoid such commandeering of state government. "To have relied on the state authorities, as the means of exercising its most essential powers, would have totally changed the character of the national government, and reduced it to a state of imbecility little short of that of the former confederation." After all, the "great and radical vice" of government under the Articles was its dependence on the cooperation of the states. Judge Roane also relied on the Virginia Resolutions and Madison's subsequent report. He stressed that the Constitution adopted a new scheme by which "the general government acted directly upon the people," with no need for cooperation by the state governments except in electing the president and senators. Indeed, he said, if state judges were considered to be arms of the federal judiciary, they could be forced to hear so many federal cases as to "actually drive them out of office!"[18]

Some of the language used by these Virginia judges in 1814 will strike modern constitutional scholars as familiar. In 1992, the Supreme Court used similar arguments on the way to a five-to-four holding that prohibited Congress from requiring state legislators to implement federal law. The majority emphasized the transition from the Articles' system of demanding state governmental assistance to the Constitution's system of acting directly on individuals. But unlike the Virginia judges in 1814, the modern Court has been unwilling to follow the logic of this argument when it comes to judicial power. Instead, the Court now distinguishes between commandeering state courts and commandeering state legislatures. According to the Court, "Federal statutes enforceable in state courts do, in a sense, direct state judges to enforce them, but this sort of federal 'direction' of state judges is mandated by the text of the Supremacy Clause." Thus, the Court has fulfilled Judge Roane's fear that Congress might force state trial courts to hear federal cases. So well settled is the issue of appellate review now, that it never occurred to later justices that their own authority over state courts might be considered an invasion of state sovereignty.[19]

Today, no one questions the holding in Justice Story's 1816 opinion for the Supreme Court in *Martin v. Hunter's Lessee,* which reaffirmed the Court's jurisdiction over state courts. Story began his analysis by clarifying the relationship between the state and federal governments. The Constitution was ordained, in his view, "not by the states in their sovereign capacities, but emphatically . . . by 'the people of the United States.'" Thus, federal powers were not carved out of existing state sovereignties, but both were derived from the people. Federal powers were defined in broad terms because the Constitution "was not intended to provide merely for the exigencies of a few years, but was to endure through a long lapse of ages, the events of which were locked up in the inscrutable purposes of Providence." The language of Article III, conveying the judicial power, was "the voice of the whole American people solemnly declared, in establishing one great department of that government which was, in many respects, national, and in all, supreme." The Constitution acts "not merely upon individuals, but upon states," and deprives them "altogether of the exercise of some powers of sovereignty" while restraining them in others. After this nationalist prologue, Story argued that the Framers had anticipated that cases within the federal judicial power might also arise in the state courts. When "the states are stripped of some of the highest attributes of sovereignty . . . it is certainly difficult to support the argument that the appellate power over the decisions of state courts is contrary to the genius of our institutions." Since the federal courts clearly had the power to set aside unconstitutional actions of the state legislators and governors, why not those of the state courts?[20]

Five years after *Martin v. Hunter's Lessee,* the Court was faced with another challenge to its appellate jurisdiction. *Cohens v. Virginia*[21] involved the application of a Virginia ban on lotteries to the sale of a ticket for a District of Columbia lottery. The defendants took the state judgment to the Supreme Court. The state resisted on the basis of sovereign immunity. Issuing a writ of error would force the state, which had brought the criminal case, into federal court. The state challenged this exercise of federal jurisdiction under the Eleventh Amendment, which bars suits in federal court against any state by citizens of another state.

Although the lottery law itself had no great importance, Virginians were already alarmed by the power of the federal courts. (They may also have been concerned about the extraterritorial effect of Congress's broad powers over the District of Columbia, which might also have been used to permanently free any slave who entered the district.) The federal courts seemed to be insidiously expanding federal powers. Jefferson, for example, had lamented in 1820 that "[t]he steady tenor of the Courts of the United States is to break down the constitutional barriers between the coordinate powers of the States and the Union." In 1821, he had written to Judge Roane, author of one of the concurrences in *Martin,* saying that his greatest fear was the federal judiciary, a body which was "like gravity, ever acting, with noiseless foot, and unalarming advance, gaining ground step by step, and holding what it gains," thus "engulfing insidiously" the states into the federal government.[22]

Marshall rejected the state immunity argument, largely on the basis of his general vision of the Union. "The American States," he said, "as well as the American people, have believed a close and firm Union to be essential to their liberty and to their happiness." Such a Union "would be a mere shadow, that must disappoint all their hopes, unless invested with large portions of that sovereignty which belongs to independent States." Without Supreme Court review of state criminal convictions, federal power could be frustrated by any hostile state government, for federal officials who were convicted of violating unconstitutional state laws would have no federal recourse. True, state judges were generally entitled to public confidence, but collisions between state and federal government could sometimes take place. The Constitution had to be construed with bad times as well as good ones in mind. "[A] constitution is framed for ages to come." It is "exposed to storms and tempests," and no government could be "so defective in its organization, as not to contain within itself the means of securing the execution of its own laws." State governments, said Marshall, had no right to interfere with the constitutional scheme. While the people made and could unmake the Constitution, "this supreme and irresistible power to make or to unmake, resides only in the whole body of the people; not in any subdivision of them." Any effort by a subdivision to interfere with the federal Constitution "is usurpation, and ought to be repelled by those to whom the people have delegated their power of repelling it."[23]

Cohens also gave Chief Justice Marshall, who had not sat in *Martin* because of a conflict of interest, the opportunity to address the Court's relationship with state courts. Again, Marshall took a strongly nationalistic stance. "That the United States form, for many, and for most important purposes, a single nation, has not yet been denied." "[W]e are one people" in war and peace, and in "all commercial regulations." Rather than being independent sovereigns, Marshall said, the states are "constituent parts of the United States"—"members of one great empire—for some purposes sovereign, for some purposes subordinate." Logically, then, the federal government's judicial organ should be supreme in interpreting federal law. Nothing but "contradiction and confusion" could result from independent interpretations by every state supreme court in the land. Furthermore, the exercise of such appellate jurisdiction was explicitly condoned by the *Federalist,* a source that "has always been considered as of great authority." Finally, Marshall observed, this interpretation of Article III was endorsed by the First Congress when it passed the Judiciary Act, and had been accepted by all but one of the state courts that had been reversed.[24]

Republican newspapers were aghast at the decision. The *Richmond En-*

quirer feared that "the Judiciary power, with a foot as noiseless as time and a spirit as greedy as the grave, is sweeping to their destruction the rights of the State." But the reaction was not limited to the South. An Ohio paper proclaimed the "alarming progress of the Supreme Court in subverting the Federalist principles of the Constitution and introducing on their ruins a mighty consolidated empire fitted for the sceptre of a great monarch." Judge Roane tried unsuccessfully to get James Madison to write an attack on the Court's opinion. To Roane's frustration, Madison said that the "sounder policy" was that federal decisions should prevail when in collision with state courts. So Roane undertook the task himself, calling the Court's ruling a "most monstrous and unexampled decision," which could only be explained by the "love of power which all history informs us infects and corrupts all who possess it." Jefferson also continued to bemoan the federal judiciary, calling it "[t]he engine of consolidation" and advocating congressional action to reverse the *Cohens* decision.[25]

In two other significant cases, the Marshall Court also limited the ability of states to operate as checks on the federal government, implicitly repudiating the idea of state interposition. *Osborn v. Bank of the United States*[26] was one round in the long struggle over the constitutionality of the bank. Opposition to the bank was strong in Ohio, where the Court's earlier decision upholding the constitutionality of the bank was bitterly criticized. (One paper's editorial on the subject had been titled, "The United States Bank— Everything! The Sovereignty of the States—Nothing!") Ohio passed a law imposing a fifty-thousand-dollar tax on each of the bank's branches. Pursuant to this law, the state auditor, Ralph Osborn, decided to seize the funds from the bank. The bank obtained a federal injunction against collection of the tax, but state officials went ahead anyway. After being refused payment of the tax, Osborn's assistant entered the bank's vault and took everything he could find, to the tune of $120,000. The lower federal court issued an order directing the return of the funds to the bank.[27]

Today, *Osborn* is mostly known only to experts in the law of federal jurisdiction, primarily because of the Court's holding that a federal court could hear any suit brought by the bank as a federal instrumentality. For present purposes, however, the more important point was the injunction against the state officers. Marshall repudiated the claim that the suit was barred by the state's sovereign immunity. The state officers claimed that the true defendant in the injunction action was the state itself, because the suit was an effort to "restrain the officers of the State from executing the [state] law." Marshall admitted that "[t]he full pressure of this argument is felt, and the difficulties it presents are acknowledged," given that the state clearly had a direct interest in the case. Nevertheless, he unhesitatingly rejected it.[28]

Marshall stressed the possible impact of a contrary holding on federal supremacy. State officers could "arrest the execution of any law in the United States." If a state administrator imposed a fine or penalty on a federal official, the official would be unable to obtain an injunction. The postman, the tax collector, the U.S. marshal, the military recruiter, would all be at risk of ruinous penalties like those assessed against the bank. In short, Marshall said, a state would be "capable, at its will, of attacking the nation, of arresting its progress at every step, of acting vigorously and effectually in the execution of its designs, while the nation stands naked, stripped of its defensive armour."[29]

In a fourth case, the Court also acted to prevent state interference with federal activities. The plaintiff in *McClung v. Silliman*[30] contended that the federal land registrar had illegally failed to register his claim. He sought a writ of mandamus against the registrar from two separate courts. (Mandamus is a legal writ to compel a government official to perform his or her duty.) The federal court rejected the suit on the ground that it had no power to review the actions of the registrar. The state court held that it did have such jurisdiction but rejected the claim on the merits. Both rulings were appealed to the Supreme Court. Justice Johnson began his opinion with the observation that the cases presented "a striking specimen of the involutions which ingenuity may cast about legal rights, and an instance of the growing pretensions of some of the State Courts over the exercise of the powers of the general government." Having found that the lower federal court was correct to reject the federal lawsuit, Johnson said that it was "not easy to conceive on what legal ground a State tribunal can, in any instance, exercise the power of issuing a mandamus to the register." When it withheld mandamus authority from its own courts, Johnson said, the inference was clear that Congress meant to preclude the state courts as well.[31]

Taken together, these decisions undermined any effort to use state sovereignty as a shield against perceived federal excesses. Rather than being allowed to exercise independent judgment about constitutional issues, the state courts were subordinated to the Supreme Court. Their power to control the actions of federal officers was limited. If the state legislature, disagreeing with the Supreme Court, considered a federal statute unconstitutional, its officials could be enjoined by a federal court from obeying the state law and would be liable for damages as well.

These decisions reflected Marshall's vision of the federal judiciary's role in the constitutional scheme. He made this vision even more explicit in a series of anonymous pamphlets defending the Court from attacks by leading Virginia states' rights advocates. Writing as "A Friend of the Constitution," Marshall challenged the compact theory and proclaimed the existence of a collective American people. "Have we no national existence?" he asked. "We were charged by the late emperor of France with having no national character, or actual existence as a nation; but not even he denied our theoretical or constitutional existence." The "United States is a nation; but a nation composed of states in many, though not in all, respects, sovereign. The people of these states are also the people of the United States." In short, "Our constitution is not a compact. It is the act of a single party. It is the act of the people of the United States, assembling in their respective states, and adopting a government for the whole nation." Hence, "All arguments founded on leagues and compacts, must be fallacious when applied to a government like this." Marshall rejected the argument that the federal judiciary, as part of the national government, could not settle the meaning of the so-called compact between it and the states. Rather, the "whole owes to its parts the peaceful decision of every controversy which may arise among its members." For settling such disputes is "one of the great duties of government, one of the great objects for which it is instituted."[32] This was a ringing affirmation of federal supremacy. Marshall's vision, however, did not go unchallenged.

THE NULLIFICATION CRISIS

The Supreme Court was far from being the only forum in which issues of national supremacy were debated. Congress was another important setting. One famous debate took place on the floor of the Senate in 1830. The occasion was a dispute about public lands policy, but the specifics of the dispute were soon left behind. Senator Hayne of South Carolina argued that the lands should be given to the states containing them as soon the national debt had been paid off. Easterners instead favored sale of the lands, with the proceeds being distributed to all the states to support education and public improvements. Hayne vigorously attacked this proposal on states' rights grounds. While waiting to argue a case before the Supreme Court, which then met in the Capitol building, Daniel Webster dropped by the Senate and overheard Hayne. (Webster was a leading appellate lawyer and has been called "the most famous, the most controversial, and perhaps the most charismatic of all the leading Marshall Court advocates.") He delivered a response the next day. Hayne in turn delivered a two-day reply, aided by suggestions from Vice President Calhoun.[33]

The next day, the "Godlike Daniel"—as he was wont to be called—delivered his "Second Reply to Hayne," a speech that would become famous across the nation. He attacked Hayne for treating the states as if they were separate countries, with no interest in each others' welfare. Webster rejected this view: "We look upon the States, not as separated, but as united." If a railroad in South Carolina had national importance, it deserved support from Webster as much as anyone else. (This was a subtle barb. Webster had introduced such a bill a short time before as a courtesy to Hayne, who wanted the railroad for his home state but was embarrassed to exhibit support for an "internal improvement" project, having branded such projects unconstitutional.) Nor was the federal government a creature of the states. "It is, Sir, the people's Constitution, the people's government, made for the people, made by the people, and answerable to the people." Webster based his nationalism on the supremacy clause and on the clause vesting the federal courts with the power to decide all cases arising under the Constitution. The latter was the keystone of the arch, making the Supreme Court the ultimate arbiter of constitutional law. Nor did states have any right to interpose their own interpretations of federal law. Resisting the law by force, Webster said, is treason. "Can the courts of the United States take notice of the indulgence of a State to commit treason? Talk about it as we will, these doctrines go to the length of revolution." He closed with a rousing call for "Liberty *and* Union, now and forever, one and inseparable."[34]

The next, and much more important confrontation, would also involve South Carolina. That state was unusual in several respects that made it especially sensitive to federalism issues. Because the climate was undesirable, and blacks were more resistant to malaria than whites, the lowlands were over 80 percent black. The lowland planter elite was thus even more obsessed than other Southerners with the need to maintain stringent control. State politics were dominated by elites, who fancied themselves as the true successors to the old English gentry, with majority rule being considered something of a formality. House seats were apportioned half on the basis of taxes paid (which included taxes on slaves) and half on white population, so the lowland "black belt" had disproportionate representation. The legislature selected the governor, all judges, and presidential electors. The tariff was a particularly sensitive issue for the upland cotton farmers, who believed that the tariff on imported cotton goods translated directly into a reduced price for their raw cotton. Altogether, South Carolinians took a dim view of federal intrusions into their concerns.[35]

In 1828, at Calhoun's prompting, the South Carolina legislature issued a formal protest against the recently enacted tariff statute. The protest argued that the protective tariff was not only unfair but unconstitutional. Admittedly, Congress did have the power to impose tariffs as a form of taxation. In effect, however, this particular tariff was a subsidy for domestic manufacture, which was not a legitimate subject of federal concern. This use of the tax power was "a breach of a well-defined trust, and a perversion of the high powers vested in the Federal Government for federal purposes only." Nor did the commerce power authorize federal encouragement of local industry. If this were a legitimate aim of the commerce power, it would imply "an absolute control over all the interests, resources, and pursuits of a people, and is inconsistent with the idea of any other than a simple, consolidated government." Citing the *Federalist*—but "only because the Supreme Court has recognized its authority"—the South Carolina protest contended that the commerce power was "only incidentally connected with the encouragement of agriculture and manufactures," while tariff authority "was not understood to justify in any case, a prohibition of foreign commodities" except as a lever to induce reciprocity by other nations or "for some other bona fide commercial purpose."[36]

The constitutional challenge to the tariff was strained. The taxing and commerce clauses did not contain any limitation on the purpose of the measure. Indeed, prior to the American Revolution, the British use of the protective tariff had been considered more legitimate than a revenue tariff, given the need for some centralized control of trade. There is no evidence of a change of mind at the time of the Constitution. As early as 1789, Madison had secured the passage of a tariff for "the encouragement and protection of manufacturers." Many southerners like Henry Clay (not to mention Madison) never took the constitutional argument against the tariff seriously. Nevertheless, South Carolina did not back down from its constitutional challenge to the tariff.[37]

Events between 1830 and 1832 led to a dangerous confrontation with national authority. In December 1831, President Jackson called for tariff reform in the hope of defusing the situation. The 1832 tariff did contain major overall reductions, but it continued a high tariff on woolens, cottons, and iron—all important to Northern industry. This was unacceptable to South Carolina. By October 1832, nullification advocates had sufficient support to obtain a two-thirds legislative majority for a state convention. A special session of the legislature called the convention, which issued a nullification proclamation three weeks later.[38]

Talk of nullification had been in the air. Calhoun had previously been a nationalist, but that had become a politically untenable position in his home state. This led to a transformation in his view of the constitutional system. As one historian explains, "Calhoun was never at a loss for principle. When everything else failed, some high principle or theory became his refuge of order and virtue."[39] For the remainder of his career, that principle would be nullification.

In 1831, Calhoun had given a major address defending nullification. "The great and leading principle is, that the General Government emanated from the people of the several States, forming distinct political communities, and acting in their separate and sovereign capacity," so that the Constitution is a compact between the states. Relying on Madison's Virginia Resolutions, he proclaimed the right of each state "in the last resort" to interpose itself against abuses of federal power. Because the Constitution divided power between the federal government and the states, the problem was to preserve "this sacred distribution as originally settled." The time-tested answer, in England and elsewhere, was to give "each co-estate the right to judge of its powers, with a negative or veto on the acts of the others." In the event of such a conflict, the federal government would then be forced to submit the question to three-quarters of the states, which could exercise the amending power and "whose decrees are the Constitution itself, and whose voice can silence all discontent."[40]

South Carolina's Ordinance of Nullification was a concrete implementation of Calhoun's theory. It declared the tariff statutes "utterly null and void" in South Carolina, and directed the legislature to pass statutes preventing the implementation of these statutes in South Carolina after February 1. All military and civil officers of the state except legislators had to take an oath to support nullification, on pain of being removed from office. (The timing of this requirement was left a little unclear, except as to newly elected officials who were required to take the oath immediately.) The same oath was also required of jurors hearing any cases arising under the ordinance. The ordinance also prohibited any appeals to the U.S.

Supreme Court relating to the ordinance. And if the federal government had the temerity to respond forcibly, secession would be the result: "[T]he people of this state will thenceforth hold themselves absolved from all further obligation to maintain or preserve their political connection with the people of the other states, and will forthwith proceed to organize a separate government, and do all other acts and things which sovereign and independent states may of right do."[41]

Andrew Jackson, who was already at odds with Calhoun for other reasons, was enraged. He was said to have told one congressman that South Carolina could adopt resolutions to its heart's content, but "if one drop of blood be shed there in defiance of the laws of the United States, I will hang the first man of them I can get my hands on to the first tree I can find." That story may be apocryphal, but he clearly did tell Van Buren that Calhoun should be hanged as a traitor. How serious was he? "I don't believe he would really hang anybody do you?" Senator Hayne asked a leading Jacksonian. The reply was: "Well before he invaded Florida on his own hook, few people could have believed that he would hang Arbuthnot and shoot Ambrister [two British subjects]—also on his own authority—could they? I tell you, Hayne, when Jackson begins to talk about hanging, they can begin to look out for ropes."[42]

Jackson soon made his views explicit in a presidential proclamation. The proclamation was drafted by his secretary of state, Edward Livingston, and circumstantial evidence indicates that it was partly based on consultations with Madison, whose views we will consider later. Jackson argued that nullification was unacceptable because there was no check on its abuse. Appeal to the courts was foreclosed both as matter of the nullifiers' constitutional theory and because of the oath required by South Carolina of judges and jurors. The national repercussions could be grave. The Constitution requires tariffs to be equal across the country. Hence, if South Carolina succeeded in nullifying the tariff there, it could not be collected anywhere else either. And because the challenge to the tariff's constitutionality was based on the alleged protectionist intent of Congress, it would always be easy to make such a challenge by impugning congressional motives. The threat of secession was also illegal, Jackson insisted. However the Constitution was adopted, whether as a compact or otherwise, it established a government in which all the people were represented, and which could act directly on individuals. "[E]ach State, having expressly parted with so many powers as to constitute, jointly with the other States, a single nation, can not . . . possess any right to secede, because such secession does not break a league, but destroys the unity of a nation."[43]

In Jackson's view, he had no real choice but to intervene, because Article II of the Constitution directed him to take care that the laws be faithfully executed. Before he took action, however, he asked the people of South Carolina to reconsider, in the hope of a peaceful resolution. He also said he hoped by "moderate and firm measures" to avoid the need for force. "[I]f it be the will of Heaven that the recurrence of its primeval curse on man for the shedding of a brother's blood should fall upon our land," it would not be the result of any offensive action by the government. But in a letter a few days later, Jackson indicated that the use of force was by no means out of the question. "[W]hen a faction in a state attempt to nullify a constitutional law of Congress, or to destroy the Union, the balance of the people composing this Union have a perfect right to coerce them to obedience."[44]

A prolonged process of negotiation then ensued. Jackson remained firm in his determination to resist nullification. He asked Congress for power to remove cases involving tariff enforcement from state to federal court, to move customs operations to ships offshore, and to call upon the militia. Ultimately, Congress passed a Force Act in support of the president, but only after the crisis seemed to near an end. The nullifiers proceeded cautiously in implementing their scheme. In the meantime, after much wrangling, a compromise was worked out in Congress on the tariff issue. The overall level of tariffs never rose again to its previous level until World War I, and the tariff subsided as a serious constitutional issue. Nullification and other states' rights doctrines, however, lived on.[45]

MADISON VERSUS CALHOUN

Calhoun and Madison, two highly sophisticated political theorists, had directly clashing views on nullification. Those views are worth examining in fuller detail. We begin with Calhoun, of whom an acquaintance once said, "I hate a man who makes me think so much." Rather than trying to do full justice to his ingenious theories, we will focus on a few points that have the greatest significance for the supremacy issue.[46]

The Framers were not major influences on Calhoun's constitutional thought. He did not believe in blindly following the "original understanding" of the Framers—indeed, he thought the Constitution itself was in need of revision in order to accomplish its fundamental purposes. He said the authority of the *Federalist* deserves to be destroyed—"as celebrated as it is"—because the authors mistakenly thought that the federal government was "partly federal and partly national." Such a combination is impossible. Monarchy is no more different from popular government "than a *federal* is from a *national* government." How did Hamilton and Madison fall "into an error so radical and dangerous" as blurring this fundamental logical distinction? The answer, suggested Calhoun, is that they were closet nationalists, who failed to get their way at the constitutional convention but brought their nationalist ideas into the ratification process.[47]

Calhoun's antipathy to the *Federalist* is understandable. On the crucial question of Supreme Court jurisdiction over state courts, for example, Federalist 82 is squarely on point. It is flatly opposed to Calhoun's position. According to Hamilton, an appeal "would certainly lie" from state courts to the Supreme Court on federal questions. The Constitution gives the Supreme Court appellate jurisdiction in cases arising under federal law, Hamilton emphasized, "without a single expression to confine its operation to the inferior federal courts." Whenever a federal issue is involved in litigation, according to Hamilton, the issue can be appealed to the Supreme Court. Without such federal appellate jurisdiction, state courts could not safely have been given any authority to decide issues of federal law. They would have had to be "excluded from a concurrent jurisdiction in matters of national concern, else the judiciary authority of the Union may be eluded at the pleasure of every plaintiff or prosecutor." Even more offensively from the Calhounian perspective, Hamilton maintained that the "national and State systems are to be regarded as ONE WHOLE," making the state courts "natural auxiliaries to the execution of the laws of the Union." The Supreme Court was the ideal overseer for the state courts, being "destined to unite and assimilate the principles of national justice and the rules of national decisions." Indeed, Hamilton said, Congress could even authorize appeals to be taken from state courts to lower federal courts. These views were abhorrent to Calhoun. No wonder he was at such pains to discredit the *Federalist.*[48]

But in Calhoun's view, the problem ran deeper than the suspect nationalist leanings of Madison and Hamilton. More fundamentally, they and the other Framers had failed to anticipate how their scheme would be undermined by the rise of political parties. For instance, the party system had resulted in most presidential elections being decided in the Electoral College, rather than in the House, where each state would have had an equal vote. The party system also allowed federal authorities to ally themselves with state politicians, subverting the independent role of the states in the system. It was hardly the fault of the Framers, however, that they failed to predict "what would be the working of political elements, wholly untried; and which made so great an innovation in governments of the class to which ours belonged." They had, Calhoun said, understandably but mistakenly relied on the states to act *collectively* as a check on the national government. In reality, because of the sectional nature of the party system, one section containing a majority of the states will often be aligned with the federal government against a minority based in the other section. The Constitution contained no explicit method for protecting minority rights. Hence, any effective check must be found in the implicit powers left untouched by the Constitution and reserved to the states.[49]

Like Marshall, Calhoun believed constitutional analysis should begin with the nature of the Union. His vision, however, was much different from the chief justice's. Since the federal government was created by the Constitution, which in turn was "ordained and established" by the states, Calhoun gave the states a more fundamental part in the constitutional scheme than the national government. For Calhoun, the United States is a "compact" between the states, and not a nation or a "single community . . . the American people." The Preamble of the Constitution spoke of the "people of the United States" only because of uncertainty as to which nine states would ratify. (Recall from the previous chapter that four justices on the current Supreme Court, led by Justice Thomas, endorse this view of the Constitution.) Thus, the "States, in ratifying the constitution, did not lose the confederated character which they possessed when they ratified it . . . but, on the contrary, still retained it to the full."[50]

Almost immediately after ratification, however, things began to go wrong, as the scheme was perverted from a federal to a national one. In the First Congress, Calhoun said, the political system "received an impulse in that direction, from which it has never yet recovered." The Judiciary Act "in effect, destroyed the relation of coequals and co-ordinates between the federal government and the governments of the individual States; without which, it is impossible to preserve its federal character." By providing for appeals from state courts to the Supreme Court, the Judiciary Act emasculated the state courts. They were subordinated to the federal government and "cease to stand . . . in the relation of coequal and co-ordinate departments with the federal judiciary." Along with state judges, state governors and legislators were also subordinated to the federal government. They, too, could no longer implement their independent understandings of the Constitution. "The reason," Calhoun said, "is obvious." Laws can reach people individually only through the courts; thus, when state courts became subordinate to the federal courts, so did the other branches of state government.[51]

Calhoun admitted that the acts of the First Congress, which passed the Judiciary Act, are often given greater weight because so many of the Framers sat there. But "it is a great error to suppose that they could better understand the system they had constructed, and the dangers incident to its operation, than those who came after them." Indeed, any contemporary politician, "who has had much experience of the working of the system, and does not more clearly perceive where the danger lies, than the ablest and most sagacious member of the convention, must be a dull observer." Unfortunately, he said, many of the decisions of the First Congress "evince a strong predilection for a national government," as opposed to a "federal" one.[52]

If the Judiciary Act is unconstitutional, so no appeal can be taken from the constitutional rulings of a state court, how are disagreements about constitutional issues to be resolved? Not by the exercise of federal court jurisdiction over state officials, according to Calhoun. Nothing in Article III of the Constitution, establishing the judiciary, vests any authority to enforce decisions against a state, and nothing makes states amenable to process. For no government can be made a defendant without its consent. True, the Supreme Court could decide issues of constitutional law in ordinary litigation, but its rulings were binding only on the private parties before the Court, and not "as between the United States and the several States."[53]

Instead, like the tribunes of ancient Rome, the states have the power to negate the execution of federal law. "As parties to the constitutional compact, they retain the right, unrestricted . . . to judge as to the extent of the obligation imposed by the agreement or compact." Hence, the states have the power "of interposing for the purpose of arresting, within their respective limits, an act of the federal government in violation of the constitution; and thereby of preventing the delegated from encroaching on the reserved powers." This nullification power would not be unduly disruptive. Its use would be legitimate only to deflect invasions of a state's reserved powers. Calhoun predicted that, for political reasons (particularly due to the national party system), nullification would probably be invoked only sparingly.[54]

In case of any possible abuse by individual states, however, the amending power would provide a check on nullification. The amending power allowed the other states to countermand the nullification, while giving a minority of states sufficient power, in turn, to block abusive amendments. When a state engaged in nullification, the federal government was obligated to take the initiative to invoke the amendment power. If the amendment is "consistent with the character of the constitution, the ends for which it was established, and the nature of our system of government— or, more briefly, if it comes fairly within the scope of the amending power, the State is bound to acquiesce, by the solemn obligation which it contracted, in ratifying the constitution." But if the amendment is inconsistent with the spirit of the existing Constitution, the state must then decide "whether it will, or whether it will not secede from the Union." If it stays, it must repeal the act of nullification. Nevertheless, the power to secede instead of acquiescing is inherent in the nature of the compact.[55]

Still, Calhoun was doubtful that this elaborate mechanism of nullification would be enough to save the states. He proposed a series of other legal changes, including repeal of the Supreme Court's appellate jurisdiction over state courts, various limits on the president (a particular source of danger since he represented the national majority), and even the creation of two co-presidents, one from the North and one from the South. These proposals make it clear that Calhoun's vision was sharply at odds with the general course of legal development since 1789 and would have required a major rethinking of constitutional law to be implemented. Calhoun was right that the legal order had strayed far from his own understanding of the Constitution.[56]

The most cogent response to Calhoun came from Madison. Although he viewed Webster as too nationalistic, he was more intent on combating the nullifiers. He was appalled by the nullification movement, which he linked with the rise of an ambitious, unscrupulous new generation of politicians. Heedless of history, these politicians might expose the nation to the very risk of chaos and disintegration that had been averted by the adoption of the Constitution. Madison was particularly upset with what he regarded as an effort to pervert the Kentucky and Virginia Resolutions into a pretext for disunion. During the final six years of his life, we are told, "Madison could not get the nullifiers out of his mind," with his anxiety on the subject sometimes leading to physical collapse. If the nullifiers did not yield to reason, he thought, "the explanation will lie between an impenetrable stupidity and an incurable prejudice."[57]

Madison developed his arguments in a series of widely publicized letters. The tight reasoning showed that the old man had not lost any of his analytical powers. Like Calhoun's, his analysis began with an understanding of the nature of the Constitution. Madison agreed that the Constitution was formed by "the people in each of the States, acting in their highest sovereign capacity." Being a compact among the states "constituting the people thereof one people for certain purposes," however, it could not be annulled at the will of any individual state, unlike a state constitution.[58]

Within the sphere of its powers, Madison contended, the federal government was no less fully a true government than those of the states, within the sphere of their own powers. "[L]ike them, it has at command a physical force for executing the powers committed to it." To have left questions of interpretation to each of the states "must altogether distract the Govt. of the Union & speedily put an end to the Union itself." Moreover, uniformity of the laws is "itself a vital principle," and some laws such as tariffs could not be effectively enforced at all without this uniformity. If state and federal decisions had equal weight, "[s]cenes could not be avoided" in which federal and state officers "would have rencounters in executing conflicting decrees, the result of which would depend on the comparative force of the local posse." Although negotiation might sometimes forestall conflict, an "unaccommodating spirit" in some states might well prevent compromise.[59]

Madison pointedly rejected Calhoun's effort to make the Constitution fit the mold of a classic confederation. "What can be more preposterous," he asked, "than to say that the States as united, are in no respect or degree, a Nation, which implies sovereignty; altho' acknowledged to be such by all other Nations & Sovereigns, and maintaining with them, all the international relations, of war & peace, treaties, commerce, &c." Such a position was particularly absurd because the same people claimed "that the States separately are compleatly nations & sovereigns; although they can separately neither speak nor harken to any other nation, nor maintain with it any of the international relations whatever and would be disowned as Nations if presenting themselves in that character." Rather than fitting the abstract logic of confederation or that of consolidation, "Our political system is admitted to be a new Creation—a real nondescript." Consequently, its character "must be sought within itself; not in precedents, because there are none; not in writers whose comments are guided by precedents."[60]

This understanding of the constitutional scheme, Madison said, was confirmed by both text and history. National power was secured by the supremacy clause and the extension of the judicial power to all cases arising under federal law. The checks against abuse of federal power are structural: the responsibility of members of Congress to their home state legislatures and electorates, and the impeachment power vested in Congress. In an extreme case of usurpation, revolution would remain as an "extra & ultra constitutional right." But within the constitutional scheme, the federal judicial power must be paramount: "Those who have denied or doubted the supremacy of the judicial power of the U.S. & denounce at the same time nullifying power in a State, seem not to have sufficiently adverted to the utter inefficiency of a supremacy in a law of the land, without a supremacy in the exposition & execution of the law."[61]

Nullification also upsets the balance of power between any given state, the federal government, and its fellow states. According to Madison, advocates of nullification had overlooked "the destruction of all equipoise between the Federal Govt. and the State governments," because of an asymmetry between the two levels of government. "[W]hilst the functionaries of the Fedl. Govt. are directly or indirectly elected by and responsible to the States," the "functionaries of the States are in their appointments & responsibility wholly independent of the U.S." Thus, a dangerous imbalance would exist if "no constitutional control of any sort belonged to the U.S. over the States." Turning Calhoun's reliance on the amendment procedure on its head, Madison observed that nullification would allow a single state to immunize itself from constitutional restrictions, thereby making at least a temporary de facto amendment in the Constitution without the consent of any other state, far less the three-fourths required by the amendment procedure.[62]

Madison also sought to repel efforts to claim Jefferson's support for nullification. Jefferson's statements had to be interpreted in the light of their context, including what Madison called the campaign of a semimonarchical faction (the Federalists) to control the government. In addition, "Allowances also ought to be made for a habit in Mr. Jefferson as in others of great genius of expressing in strong and round terms, impressions of the moment." Full publication of anyone's correspondence would undoubtedly "not fail to involve delicate personalities and apparent if not real inconsistencies."[63]

Madison was at particular pains to head off any reliance on his own Virginia Resolutions. The published debates on the resolutions, he said, disclose "no reference whatever to a constitutional right in an individual State to arrest by force the operation of a law of the U.S." Instead, the resolutions called for concurrent action by all the states to secure a change in federal law. Madison emphasized that to guard against misunderstanding, the words "not law, but utterly null, void, and of no force or effect" were struck out. Moreover, the state legislatures that criticized the resolutions would surely have said so, he argued, if they had understood the resolutions to authorize forcible resistance to the federal government.[64]

Ultimately, of course, Madison's view of the Constitution proved less appealing to the South than Calhoun's. Even Calhoun, as it turned out, did not go far enough. He was at heart still a bit of a nationalist, who wanted a secure place for the South within the Union. Thus, both he and Madison sought in very different ways to uphold some conception of Union. But neither was successful.

In the end, Madison was full of foreboding. He expressed his fears in a letter written a few years before his death. The threat to the Union, he wrote, was especially tragic because the Constitution had "been so fruitful of blessings" and the Union was "admitted to be the only guardian of the peace, liberty and happiness of the people of the States comprizing it." That such a Constitution "should be broken up and scattered to the winds . . . is more painful than words can express." But he had not completely given up hope. It was impossible, he still believed, that this dismembering could "ever be the deliberate act of the people, if the value of the Union be calculated by the consequences of disunion." Unfortunately, history would confirm Madison's fears rather than his lingering hopes.[65]

CHAPTER 4   *The Union Forever?*

Our study of federalism has taken us to the brink of secession. In this chapter, we continue the story through Fort Sumter. The key players vigorously disputed the constitutionality of secession. Secession obviously brought the debate over states' rights to a feverish level. In many respects, these arguments were replays of the debates over interposition and nullification.

But in some respects, secession is actually a tougher legal issue than nullification. Nullification requires state judges to follow the mandates of their state legislatures on constitutional issues, notwithstanding their own contrary views or those of the Supreme Court, thereby blocking the normal process of judicial review. This directly contradicts the supremacy clause's mandate that state judges follow the Constitution regardless of state law. Nullification is also at odds with the federal courts' authority under Article III to decide cases arising under federal law. Secessionist theory, however, is not inconsistent with a qualified form of federal supremacy. Under this view, a state must fully comply with federal law so long as it remains in the Union, just as a citizen must comply with federal law or emigrate elsewhere. Thus, secessionism can give federal supremacy its full scope with respect to whatever states happen to be part of the Union at any given time. Compared with nullification, secession requires less distortion of the constitutional structure—it merely adds an exit option. And unlike national supremacy, secession did not receive much attention from the Framers, so both the constitutional text and the historical record speak less clearly and directly to the issue.

Advocates made two very different kinds of arguments for secession. First, they claimed it was a valid state prerogative under the Constitution itself. Such an argument could be based on the compact theory that Calhoun and others had long espoused. It could also be based on a simple reversal of the act of ratification by which states became bound by the Constitution. Second, advocates defended secession as an extraconstitutional act. Like the Declaration of Independence, secession could be viewed as a justified act of revolution or as an exercise of the inherent right of self-determination. This chapter will focus on the question of whether the Constitution authorized secession, postponing to the next chapter the validity of secession as an extraconstitutional act. As a prelude to both discussions, we will begin with a closer reexamination of the events leading immediately up to secession.

THE PATH TO SECESSION

A decade before the Civil War, the Compromise of 1850 seemed to have brought peace to the sectional dispute. But when Douglas introduced his bill to organize the Kansas and Nebraska territories, he gave way to Southern pressure for more favorable treatment of the slavery question. Setting aside the Missouri Compromise, which would have barred slavery from these areas, he left the status of slavery in the new territories open. Douglas's goal was not to bring slavery into these Western territories. Rather, he considered the issue of little practical importance, doubting that slavery had any chance to take root there anyway. In repealing the Missouri Compromise, Douglas himself was merely accommodating strong Southern opposition to any territorial bill formally excluding slavery from the territories. He was much more intent on clearing the way for construction of a transcontinental railroad. But this turned out to be a terrible strategic error. It aroused a crescendo of protest in the North, and more than anything else, led to the creation of the Republican party.[1]

The Kansas-Nebraska Bill energized men like Lincoln and pushed them toward the formation of a new "anti-Nebraska" party. Although the bill purported to be indifferent to the spread of slavery, Lincoln said that in reality it shifted the balance toward slavery. He angrily rejected this favorable treatment of slavery "because of the monstrous injustice of slavery itself" and because it "deprives our republican example of its just influence in the world." He acknowledged that eliminating the institution where it already existed would pose great difficulties for the South, with which he sympathized. But the difficulty of abolition furnished no more of an excuse for extending slavery than it would for reviving the African slave trade. In the Framers' time, slavery was a necessary evil, which they prohibited in the Northwest territory where it had not yet taken hold. "But NOW," slavery was "to be transformed into a 'sacred right.'" "Near[ly] eighty years ago," Lincoln observed, "we began by declaring that all men are created equal; but now from that beginning we have run down to the other declaration, that for SOME men to enslave OTHERS is a 'sacred right of self-government.'" "These principles," he added, "can not stand together." He called on his audience to return slavery "to the position our fathers gave it," as a sad necessity where it already existed, "and there let it rest in peace."[2]

The Republican platform included provisions on the federal budget, naturalization, a Pacific railroad, and other issues. Undoubtedly, these issues were more important to some supporters than slavery. But it was the slavery issue that defined the party. Republicans opposed slavery for a variety of reasons, moral, economic, and political. Lincoln spoke for many Republicans in calling slavery a betrayal of the American creed that "all men are created equal." Economically, slavery was considered to be a barrier to economic development and a handicap to white farmers and workers. Antislavery writers compared Northern economic dynamism to the sleepy Southern agrarian economy. They also denounced the unfairness of requiring whites to compete against slave labor. Finally, Republicans feared that the country was coming under the grip of the Slavocracy, a powerful elite whose members were morally corrupted by their absolute power over slaves. Through its control of the Democratic party, its representation in the Senate, and its overrepresentation in the House under the three-fifths rule, the slave power had supposedly seized control of the country. In the Lincoln-Douglas debates, Lincoln portrayed his opponent as a supporter of a Southern conspiracy to extend slavery nationwide. Although no organized conspiracy actually existed, Southern slaveholders did have a formidable influence on the national government.[3]

Republicans focused much of their attention on slavery in the territories. This seems odd from our present-day perspective. It is hard to imagine cotton plantations in Kansas or Nebraska. Why did the antislavery Republicans focus their energy on the seemingly peripheral question of slavery in the territories? One reason is that they saw expansion as a serious possibility. Slavery had taken hold in Missouri and might do so elsewhere in the Great Plains or on the West Coast. If that happened, not only might these areas be ruined economically, but immigrants from Northern states might be excluded by the economic and social pressures of a slave society. Moreover, prominent Southerners avidly favored expansion into Latin America and Cuba, where the plantation system was well suited to slavery. Republicans also thought that if slavery was confined, it would eventually die. Declining political clout in the national arena would loosen the slaveholders' grip on the federal government. The U.S. mail would be opened to anti-slavery literature that would enlighten nonslaveholding Southern whites about their exploitation. With no new territories to provide a market for excess slaves, the growing slave population would drive down prices and make slave ownership increasingly unprofitable. Thus, as Lincoln said, confining slavery would cause its eventual extinction. Or, as Senator Charles Sumner said, slavery would die "as a poisoned rat dies of rage in its hole."[4]

Conversely, the issue of slavery in the territories was also vital to Southerners. Having been the dominant political force for so long, they feared the loss of national political power that would result from the admission of more free states. Like the Republicans, they foresaw that a hostile national government could undermine slavery by strengthening antislavery forces within the South and by making slavery increasingly unprofitable. They also feared the effects of an ever-increasing black population, with no outlet elsewhere. Without allies in the West, the South could not pursue plans to acquire Cuba and other new slave territories. Most alarmingly, once the South was opened to antislavery agitation, the burgeoning black population might be encouraged to revolt. After the Haitian revolution, slave rebellions had become something of an obsession in the South.[5]

But even more than these fears, the South resented restrictions on slavery as a slight to its honor. In Jefferson's time, Southerners had considered slavery a necessary evil, imposed on them by history. Jefferson and others predicted its ultimate extinction. But by the 1850s, leading Southerners proclaimed slavery to be a positive good. For whites, they said, it provided the basis of a distinctive civilization, for blacks, paternalistic and much needed guidance from a superior race. Excluding slavery from the territories sent the message that slavery, the whole basis of the Southern way of life, was immoral and degrading. This was an affront to Southern pride.[6]

The South became more demanding of Northern support for slavery. At the time of the Missouri Compromise, the South was willing to accept the exclusion of slavery from some territories. By the time of the Kansas-Nebraska bill, the South was demanding popular sovereignty, which would leave all the territories potentially open to slaveholders. Later, even this was not enough. Fearing that hostile territorial legislatures would either outlaw slavery or fail to give it legal protection, Southerners wanted affirmative congressional legislation protecting slavery in the territories.[7]

The quarrel over slavery in the territories came to a head, fittingly enough, in Charleston. Although Charleston's connection with secession is best known because the Civil War broke out there, another event in that city a year or so earlier was equally critical: the breakup of the Democratic party's presidential convention. The delegates arrived in late April, almost exactly a year before Sumter. Douglas entered the convention with a clear majority but less than the two-thirds required under party rules. The critical battle involved the platform. Douglas was the leading advocate of popular sovereignty, under which the people of each territory would decide the slavery issue. But this position was unacceptable to many Democrats in the South, who demanded a congressional slave code. Douglas had sworn to refuse the nomination if the platform endorsed such a slave code, while Alabama and others threatened to withdraw from the convention unless the slave code was endorsed. After the slave code provision failed, Alabama, Arkansas, Florida, Georgia, Louisiana, Mississippi, South Carolina, and Texas walked out. In June, the convention met again in Baltimore, with even worse results. California, North Carolina, Oregon, Tennessee, and Virginia also bolted, along with most of the Arkansas, Kentucky, and Missouri delegations. The bolters held their own convention, which adopted a platform endorsing the slave code and nominated Breckinridge for the presidency. The walkout shattered the party, destroying the last remaining nonsectional political coalition, and paved the way for Lincoln's election.[8]

A small but important group of Southerners welcomed, and had even planned for, this development. Southern fire-eaters had long favored secession and had sought unsuccessfully to goad their compatriots into action. They foresaw that insistence on a slave code would fracture the Democratic party and lead to a Republican victory, which would be intolerable to many Southerners. With luck, the result would be Southern independence.[9]

As the election approached, speeches and articles throughout the South warned of secession. When Lincoln's election became certain, the Deep South, particularly South Carolina, went into a frenzy. The South Carolina legislature, which had been in session to choose presidential electors, authorized the governor to spend one hundred thousand dollars for arms. It set December 6 as the date to elect representatives for a special convention on December 17. Mass rallies in Georgia, Alabama, and Mississippi called for immediate secession. By the end of November, Mississippi, Alabama, and Georgia had also made arrangements for state secession conventions.[10]

Secessionists warned that the Republicans would soon control both houses of Congress, as well as the presidency. They would ban slavery wherever the federal government had jurisdiction and would continue admitting free states until they had enough of a majority to amend the Constitution and abolish slavery nationally. Even limiting slavery geographically would be a disaster. As the black population continued to grow, a race war would break out, and either blacks would be wiped out or whites would be forced to leave. Secessionists also recalled other grievances such as the tariff. In contrast to the South's current woes, secession promised a new era of prosperity and expansion. Secessionists looked forward to the day when Southern civilization would extend "across [the American] continent to the Pacific, and down through Mexico to the other side of the great gulf, and over the isles of the sea."[11]

Whatever may be said of these dreams of glory, modern historians do not view the South's fear of a Republican presidency as wholly ungrounded. Because of the "monolithic, closed system of social and intellectual arrangements upon which the South relied for the perpetuation of slavery," the Republicans could disrupt the South without new legislation, simply by using federal patronage and control of the mails to foster the growth of white opposition. Moreover, as one historian explains, Southerners felt that the North's election of Lincoln "grossly insulted the South and proclaimed its determination to make vassals—slaves—of Southern whites."[12]

The Buchanan administration responded hesitantly to the secession movement. On November 20, Attorney General Black issued a formal opinion about secession. Black viewed the president as having little power to block secession. He did advise Buchanan that he could defend and even retake federal property. (As an example of the government's power to retake property, he pointed to Harpers Ferry, where U.S. troops under the control of Robert E. Lee had retaken the federal armory after it was seized by John Brown.) But that, he said, was the limit of the government's coercive power. The president could call out the militia to assist federal judges and revenue collectors in enforcing the law, but if these individuals all resigned (as seemed likely in the event of secession), there would be no legal enforcement actions for the militia to assist. If troops are to be "sent to aid the courts and marshals, there must be courts and marshals to be aided." Thus, the president could do little about secession except to denounce it. On the one hand, he could not acknowledge any state as independent. On the other hand, neither he nor Congress could "make war" against any of the states, so as to coerce it into rejoining the Union.[13]

The attorney general's opinion became the basis for President Buchanan's major statement about secession on December 3. Buchanan blamed the North for the crisis. The South had been patient during repeated Northern assaults on its rights, but Southerners could tolerate no more abuse when their families' safety was threatened. "The immediate peril" to the South, Buchanan said, arose "from the fact that the incessant and violent agitation of the slavery question throughout the North for the last quarter of a century has at length produced its malign influence on the slaves, and inspired them with vague notions of freedom." As a result, "Many a matron throughout the South retires at night in dread of what may befall herself and her children before the morning." Yet secession was the wrong remedy. Although the South's grievances were legitimate and should be met with constitutional amendments providing greater security for slavery, secession was unlawful. The president was entitled to maintain possession of U.S. property, which had been purchased at a fair price. But this was strictly a defensive power. The Constitution did not empower the federal government "to make war against a State." Buchanan's goal was to conciliate the South, simultaneously arguing against secession and maintaining the government's rights over its own property. Buchanan's speech has been called a "confession of national impotence" and "the last major act of the federal government truly serving the slaveholder interest."[14]

By Christmas, South Carolina had seceded. Its "Declaration of the Causes of Secession" argued that the Northern states had breached their constitutional obligations. The North had "denounced as sinful the institution of Slavery," had "permitted the open establishment among them" of antislavery societies, and had "encouraged and assisted thousands of our slaves to leave their homes; and those who remain have been incited by emissaries, books, and pictures, to servile insurrection." With a sectional party about to seize control of the federal government, the South Carolina declaration proclaimed, the South was in grave peril. For that party's nefarious program was to exclude the South "from the common territory," make over the Supreme Court, and ultimately eliminate slavery. "We, therefore, the people of South Carolina, by our delegates in Convention assembled," have declared the Union dissolved.[15]

Within a few weeks, the gulf states had followed South Carolina out of the Union. By February the Confederate States of America had adopted a provisional constitution and had elected Jefferson Davis as president. But the slaveholding states of the upper South balked, though they did vow to resist federal coercion of the seceding states. The newly born Confederacy was highly vulnerable without the support of Virginia and the rest of the upper South. Secessionist stalwarts urged an attack on Fort Sumter to rally the South in support of secession.[16]

On April 12, 1861, Confederate forces opened fire on Fort Sumter. The rest, as they say, is history.

THE CONSTITUTIONAL DEBATE

Jefferson Davis defended the constitutionality of secession in a speech shortly after Sumter. Like Calhoun, he relied on the compact theory of the Constitution. During the Revolution, he said, the British threat led the states to a "close alliance" and to the formation of a confederation under which each state expressly reserved its rights of sovereignty. The war was won under this "contract of alliance." In 1787, the "several States" appointed delegates to the Constitutional Convention, and the Constitution was then ratified by the "several States." The fact that the Constitution became effective only between those states that ratified showed its "true character—that of a *compact between* independent States." But "some alarm was felt in the States" because the sovereignty guarantees of the Articles had been omitted. The states did not rest until amendments placed "beyond any pretense of doubt the reservation by the States of all their sovereign rights and powers not expressly delegated to the United States by the Constitution."[17]

Alas, Davis said, "all these carefully worded clauses proved unavailing" against the rise of a Northern heresy, which held that the Constitution did not create a compact of states but rather "in effect a national government." Indeed, "so utterly have the principles of the Constitution been corrupted in the Northern mind" that Lincoln had asserted "as an axiom" that the Constitution was based on majority rule. In the meantime, the North was not honoring its side of the constitutional bargain. Although the Constitution had contained several clauses endorsing slavery, the North had turned against the South. In a "display of a spirit of ultra fanaticism," Northern representatives attacked the vital interests of the South. Finally, a new party had gained power "with the avowed object of using its power for the total exclusion of the slave States from all participation in the benefits of the public domain acquired by all the States in common, whether by conquest or purchase; of surrounding them entirely by States in which slavery should be prohibited; of thus rendering the property in slaves so insecure as to be comparatively worthless, and thereby annihilating in effect property worth thousands of millions of dollars."[18]

Southern legislatures, Davis continued, had then invited the sovereign people to select delegates for state conventions to determine the proper response. In this, Davis insisted, they were following a long-established tradition. "From a period as early as 1798," the majority party nationally (the Democrats) had adopted the "creed that each State was, in the last resort, the sole judge as well of its wrongs as of the mode and measure of redress." Indeed, Davis said, "it is obvious that under the law of nations this principle is an axiom as applied to the relations of independent sovereign States, such as those which had united themselves under the constitutional compact." (Here, he relied on the Kentucky and Virginia Resolutions and on Madison's response to criticism from other state legislatures.) Exercising this power, the Southern state conventions had decided on secession.[19]

After the Civil War, Jefferson Davis's vice president, Alexander H. Stephens, presented a far more elaborate version of Davis's arguments, which became the postwar Southern orthodoxy. Although much more detailed and heavily documented, the heart of Stephens's argument was the same. He maintained that "absolute right of local Self Government, or State Sovereignty, was the primal and leading idea throughout" the formation of the Union. The Union was only an "artificial or conventional Nation" created for certain limited purposes such as foreign relations. "Can any proposition within the domain of reason be clearer," he asked, "than that the Sovereignty of the States, that great Paramount authority which can rightfully make and unmake Constitutions, resides still with the States?" As to secession, it is "the inherent right of Nations" to "disregard the obligations of Compacts of all sorts, by declaring themselves no longer bound in any way by them." Disowning a compact is proper whenever "there has been a breach of the Compact by the other party or parties." The refusal of Northern states to comply with their obligation to return fugitive slaves was itself a sufficient breach of the compact to justify secession. By way of Stephens's later exegesis, the same arguments made by Davis in 1861 became an article of faith among many Southerners long afterward.[20]

The Northern view was much different. Lincoln had presented his view of secession in his own inaugural address, partly in response to an earlier speech by Davis. He began with the proposition that "[p]erpetuity is implied, if not expressed, in the fundamental law of all national governments." Even if the "United States be not a government proper, but an association of States in the nature of contract merely," a contract cannot be rescinded without the consent of all of the parties.[21]

"Descending from these general principles," Lincoln contended that the history of the Union confirmed its perpetuity. "The Union is much older than the Constitution." "It was formed in fact" in 1774 by the Articles of Association, "matured and continued" by the Declaration of Independence, and further matured by the Articles of Confederation, in which the states "expressly plighted and engaged that it should be perpetual." Finally, the Constitution was ordained "to form a more perfect union." But, Lincoln continued, if the Union could be destroyed by one or more states, "the Union is *less* perfect than before the Constitution, having lost the vital element of perpetuity."[22]

True, Lincoln admitted, if a majority deprived a minority "of any clearly written constitutional right, it might, in a moral point of view, justify revolution—certainly would, if such right were a vital one." But no such claim could be made by the South. At most, there was a reasonable difference in opinion about constitutional issues. If minorities seceded over every dispute about the meaning of the Constitution, democracy would be impossible. "Plainly," he said, "the central idea of secession, is the essence of anarchy." The "only true sovereign of a free people" is a majority "held in restraint by constitutional checks, and limitations, and always changing easily, with deliberate changes of popular opinions and sentiments."[23]

History is written by the victors, and the idea of secession has been dead since Appomattox. But Jefferson Davis's view of the Constitution was not a frivolous one. Compact theory had been an important current in American constitutional thought since at least 1798. We have already seen that the evolution of sovereignty in the United States was complex and ambiguous; Davis's view of that evolution was not completely lacking in historical support.[24]

Indeed, even today, traces of this constitutional vision survive. Recall that in the *Term Limits* case, Justice Thomas and three other conservative justices endorsed the compact theory. In their view, "The ultimate source of the Constitution's authority is the consent of the people of each individual State, not the consent of the undifferentiated people of the Nation as a whole." Thomas's reading of the Tenth Amendment also bears some

similarities to Jefferson Davis's. According to Thomas, in reserving authority to the "states respectively, or the people," the Tenth Amendment must
have meant the people of each individual state. "[I]t would make no sense
to speak of powers as being reserved to the undifferentiated people of the
Nation as a whole, because the Constitution does not contemplate that
those people will either exercise power or delegate it." After all, federal
elections are held state by state. Thus, "the notion of popular sovereignty
that undergirds the Constitution does not erase state boundaries, but rather
tracks them."[25]

Consequently, Thomas maintained, the presumption is against any alleged limitation on a state's powers. In his view, this presumption applies
not only to those powers that the states held before the Constitution was
ratified, but also to powers (such as setting term limits for federal representatives) that could exist only in relation to the federal government. Thus, to
invalidate *any* action of a state's people, "we must point to something in the
Federal Constitution that deprives the people of [the state] of the power to
enact such measures."[26]

Presumably, no member of the Supreme Court today would endorse
the idea of secession. But Davis could have found comfort in some of the
language of Thomas's opinion—though not enough comfort to overcome the horror of finding a black justice on the Supreme Court! If the
sole source of the Constitution's authority is the consent of the sovereign
people of each individual state, why cannot that consent be withdrawn by
those same sovereign people? And if the Tenth Amendment applies, not
only to preexisting powers of state legislatures but also to state laws concerning the state-federal relationship, why shouldn't secession be considered a reserved right of the people of each state? Thus, if Davis were alive
today, he would argue (using Thomas's language in *Term Limits*) that to invalidate the right of the people of a state to secede, "we must point to
something in the Federal Constitution that deprives [them] of the power to
enact such measures."

The parallelism between the arguments made by conservative justices
today on behalf of states' rights, and those made earlier by Calhoun and
Davis, is not hard to understand. The reason is probably not any secret
sympathy by today's justices for the Lost Cause of the Confederacy.
Rather, it derives from the nature of American constitutional discourse.
Apart from the Supreme Court's own precedents, the main ingredients of
constitutional debate are the text and original understanding of the Con-

stitution. Putting aside the Reconstruction Amendments, which are generally viewed as relating only to civil rights and civil liberties, we have essentially the same text and historical records that were available to debaters before the Civil War. This limits the potential arguments available in federalism debates.

The balance of power between the states and federal governments has changed drastically over time. But at any given moment, whatever the current balance may be, some will argue for shifting the existing balance toward greater national power and others for greater state power. Those arguing for greater state power turn instinctively to the same elements of text and history, whether they are arguing for secession like Jefferson Davis or for decentralization like today's conservative justices. The fact that these arguments can be deployed even today and can win the assent of four justices, proves their durability and continuing allure. Consequently, they deserve our careful consideration.

To be fair in assessing the constitutional arguments, we must also put aside our revulsion against the Confederacy's proslavery aims. Whether the Constitution provides states with an exit option does not depend on the state's motivations. If Jefferson Davis had won the U.S. presidency on a proslavery platform and New England had attempted to secede, no doubt our attitude toward secession would be more favorable. Yet the legal issues would be the same.[27]

In the end, however, making all these allowances for Davis's argument, the constitutional case for secession is ultimately unpersuasive. In the interest of clarity, we can distinguish two basic secessionist arguments. The first grounds secession in the very nature of the Union as a compact between several states. The second focuses more narrowly on the act of ratification, arguing that a state could revoke its ratification of the Constitution. Neither argument holds up under scrutiny.

SECESSION AND THE COMPACT THEORY

The weakest part of Davis's argument is his view of the nature of the Union—that the Union was purely a compact of independent sovereigns rather than "in effect a national government." The first part of this view, that the Union is based on a compact, is not indefensible, but the second part, denigrating the status of the federal government, is clearly wrong.

As a text, the Constitution looks much more like an organic document such as the earlier state constitutions than it looks like a treaty. The histori-

cal evidence fails to overcome the most natural reading of the document itself. It is conceivable that something might be understood to be a treaty,
even though its text does not appear to be one. But the presumption is to
the contrary.

Davis's argument was essentially extratextual. Except for his invocation
of the Tenth Amendment as confirmatory evidence, Davis and other secessionists had little to say about the text of the Constitution. A textualist
might be inclined to dismiss Davis's theory out of hand. An analogy to
contract law, however, shows why this response would be too hasty. Normally, a party to a written contract is not allowed to introduce evidence that
contradicts the terms of the writing. In many situations, even evidence
supplementing those terms is inadmissible. But there is an exception when
the nature of the writing itself is at issue. Thus, evidence is admissible to
show that what appears to be a valid written contract was instead intended
as a sham or a joke, or that the parties understood the effectiveness of the
contract to be conditioned on some later event. Just as what appears to be
a real contract can turn out to be something quite different, so too, the
Constitution's text cannot conclusively establish whether it was created as a
treaty between sovereign states or a new social compact among the American people. Thus, Davis's theory of the Constitution should escape textualist condemnation.[28]

Nevertheless, Davis's theory is ultimately unpersuasive. He staked everything on the "federation versus nation" issue. As a conception of American sovereignty, compact theory has a respectable pedigree and some basis
in the historical record. But as we have already seen, the historical record is
complex and ambiguous. The Articles of Confederation proclaimed that
the states were sovereign and independent. But, especially before and during the Revolutionary War, Congress did not merely function as the agent
for a league of independent states. Rather, Congress and the state governments had coevolved.

Because of its virtually metaphysical nature, it is hard to answer the theoretical question of whether the state peoples wholly retained their separate identity, or whether adoption of the Constitution signified the
existence of a unified "People of the United States." To the extent that the
Framers had any shared understanding on this point, which is itself somewhat dubious, they probably leaned toward the view that ratification signified the emergence of a national People. On the whole, however, the best
conclusion seems to be Madison's—that the United States was unique and

could not be considered either a consolidated nation or a compact of sovereign states.

As to whether the Constitution created a national government or merely a league, the answer is clearer. Here we can turn to none other than James Buchanan. In his response to secession, Buchanan maintained that the perpetuity of the Union was inherent in the "nature and extent of the powers conferred by the Constitution on the Federal Government." He continued: "These powers embrace the very highest attributes of national sovereignty. They place both the sword and the purse under its control." Buchanan then referred to the war power, the treaty power, and the commerce power. "[T]he Constitution has not only conferred these high powers upon Congress, but it has adopted effectual means to restrain the States from interfering with their exercise." And "[i]n order to carry into effect these powers, the Constitution has established a perfect Government in all its forms, legislative, executive, and judicial; and this Government, to the extent of its powers, acts directly upon the individual citizens of every State, and executes its own decrees by the agency of its own officers." Or, as Madison had put it almost thirty years earlier, "What can be more preposterous than to say that the States as united, are in no respect or degree, a Nation, which implies sovereignty."[29]

Nationhood and territorial integrity are linked concepts. On this point, a discussion of territorial integrity by the Framers is illuminating. The issue came up during a debate over the treaty power. Some feared that the federal government might enter into a treaty giving up American rights over the Mississippi. Since only two-thirds of a quorum of the Senate would be needed to approve a treaty, the votes of only ten senators (or five states) would be required, and the president might arrange to submit the treaty when Southern senators were absent. This was a somewhat far-fetched hypothetical, but one that was seriously debated. Madison and other Federalists responded that such a treaty would not be valid under the law of nations. According to Madison, the law of nations invalidated treaties dismembering a nation. Indeed, he said, even the king of Great Britain "has no power of dismembering the empire, or alienating any part of it. Nay, the king of France has no right of alienating part of his dominions to any power whatsoever." To be sure, this language does not speak directly to the issue of secession, but it does suggest a presumption in favor of national territorial integrity.[30]

Nor can secession be justified, as Davis appeared to argue, as a corollary of a state's purported authority, as a party to the compact, to interpret the federal Constitution. Congress had vested the federal courts with the authority to review state court decisions and to prevent state officers from interfering with the operation of federal law. Despite the contrary claims of Calhoun, the law on this point was well settled by 1860. For example, the Taney Court had no hesitancy about reversing the Wisconsin Supreme Court when that court attempted to grant habeas to a federal prisoner. As we've seen, this view of federal supremacy had the cogent backing of James Madison in his arguments against nullification. Thus, the constitutional regime did not assign the states any independent interpretative role that could provide a foundation for secession.[31]

As a precedent for secession, Davis could have cited the creation of the Constitution itself. To go into effect, the Constitution needed only the approval of nine states, and it was not certain that the others would follow. In theory, then, by ratifying the Constitution these nine states were "seceding" from the Articles of Confederation and forming a new government. This is not, however, a good precedent for Southern secession. To begin with, the Constitutional Convention had been called by Congress, and Congress, without endorsing the Constitution, also approved its transmission to the states for consideration. Thus, as Madison argued in Federalist 40, the convention had some colorable claim to be operating under the authority of the existing government. Secession, on the other hand, was a wholly unilateral action by individual states. Moreover, at the convention itself, Madison had pointed to the ratification process as a method of making the Union more solid than it had been under the Articles. Because they were more treatylike, the Articles of Confederation were more easily broken. So far as the Articles "were to be considered as a Treaty only of a particular sort, among the Governments of Independent States, the doctrine might be set up that a breach of any one article, by any of the parties, absolved the other parties from the whole obligation." Hence, Madison said, it was "indispensable that the new Constitution should be ratified in the most unexceptionable form, and by the supreme authority of the people themselves." Thus, the Framers would have regarded secession under the Constitution as raising much different issues than under the Articles.[32]

The Tenth Amendment really adds nothing to Davis's argument. To the extent that the states had the power to secede prior to 1789, it was not because such a power was granted by the Articles of Confederation. On the contrary, the Articles purported to be perpetual and irrevocable. Rather, any such power existed only because, under international law, nations have the power to repudiate their treaties. That power is relevant only if the Constitution was a treaty between sovereign nations, as the compact theory insists. So the Tenth Amendment argument is really only a restatement of the compact argument, rather than a source of additional support.[33]

In basing his argument on compact theory, Davis built on a weak foundation. The evolution of American concepts of sovereignty was too complex and confused to support confident conclusions about the right to secede. Davis focused on one aspect of the record, ignoring a great deal of evidence with more nationalist implications. For the argument to work, not only did states have to retain some residual sovereignty after ratification, but they had to be the exclusive receptacles of sovereignty. Neither the text of the Constitution nor the weight of the historical record can support such a strong version of state sovereignty.

CAN RATIFICATION BE RESCINDED?

Davis's efforts to ground secession in a grand theory of the Constitution are ultimately unavailing. But this does not dispose of the issue. Putting aside all general talk about the nature of the Union and sovereignty, secession still remains a logical possibility. The Constitution became effective with respect to each state because of its voluntary ratification. It is certainly possible that this act was understood to be revocable. Similarly, it is logically possible that the act of admitting a new state when it applies for entry into the Union might be revocable by Congress or by that state. Indeed, as Madison pointed out, one could argue that the power to secede implies a parallel power to expel, since all the remaining states can simply "secede" en masse, leaving a single state on its own.[34]

We should be careful not to jump to conclusions. When the law requires voluntary consent to an agreement, it does not always allow voluntary withdrawal. Rather, it is at least as plausible to argue as Madison did, that this "fallacy" stems from "confounding a *single* party, with the *parties* to the Constitutional compact of the United States." "The latter having made the compact may do what they will with it." In contrast, the "former as one only of the parties, owes fidelity to it, till released by consent, or absolved by an intolerable abuse of the power created." (Although we will consider the question in more detail in the next chapter, for now we can set to the side Davis's insistence that the South, which had been a dominant political force ever since at least 1800, had suffered "intolerable abuse" from the federal government.) So there is nothing inherent in the nature of the voluntary act of ratification that implies an exit right. Just as either party can prevent the formation of a contract but only both together can rescind it, so the consent of all the states might be needed to rescind the Constitution, even though each individual state could have unilaterally decided not to make itself subject to the Constitution in the first place.[35]

But again, this does not dispose of the question—contracts in general cannot be unilaterally terminated, but it is certainly possible to create such a "contract at will." For example, the typical employment contract is at will. The employee can quit or the employer can fire her at any time, without having to provide a justification. Was the Constitution an at-will contract?

The principle of self-determination might support the idea of an at-will constitutional contract. But, the Constitution does not recognize any general right of a dissatisfied local group to secede and form its own government. Instead, it expressly rejects the right of self-determination for localities. Article IV, section 3 provides that "no new State shall be formed or erected within the Jurisdiction of any other States [or any parts of states merged] without the Consent of the Legislatures of the States concerned as well as of the Congress." Thus, a dissatisfied region within a state might be trapped under the thumb of an unwanted state government indefinitely, with no constitutional recourse. In short, under the Constitution, localities lack any constitutional right of self-determination, and even the state as a whole lacks power to subdivide without congressional approval. Thus, the Constitution does not endorse any general view of governments as at-will associations. The constitutional argument for secession must rely instead on the specific relationship between states and the federal government rather than on some more general constitutional principle of self-determination.

We can therefore focus on the narrow question of whether the act of ratification by an individual state is revocable. The text of the Constitution does not speak explicitly to this point. Lincoln relied on the language of the Preamble establishing a "more perfect Union." When it considered the legality of secession after the Civil War, the Supreme Court also relied on this language. The Articles of Confederation claimed "to be perpetual," and a more temporary union could hardly be considered more perfect than a permanent one. This argument does have some support in ordinary usage. We would not be likely to say that a new welding method created a "more perfect Union" between two pieces of pipe if it was less permanent than the existing method. Furthermore, the "perfect Union" phrase can be traced back to the 1707 union between England and Scotland, which was clearly viewed as permanent.[36]

Admittedly, this is hardly an ironclad argument. Several possible counterarguments exist: the Preamble is merely introductory, the question of what makes a union more perfect is subject to debate, and the supposedly permanent Articles had, after all, been torn to pieces by the Framers themselves. Still, the "more perfect Union" clause does provide at least some support for the irrevocability of ratification.

As a further textual argument, one could also point to the supremacy clause, making the Constitution the supreme law of the land, notwithstanding any contrary provision of a state's laws. True, the supremacy clause could be read as having an unspoken proviso: "except an ordinance of secession." Still, on its face, the supremacy clause provides no room for a state government or its people to nullify all or part of this "supreme law" within its own territory. Another possible textualist argument would rely on the document's description of itself as a constitution. As Justice Joseph Story suggested, the word *constitution* itself implies binding legal status rather than a mere voluntary association. None of this language seems really conclusive. Yet, to the extent that the Constitution does contain any relevant language, that language seems to disfavor any state exit option.[37]

What about the original understanding? The debates contain scattered statements about the permanence or impermanence of the Union. The occasional references to the possible impermanency of the Constitution are hard to interpret. They might have referred to a legal right to revoke ratification. But they could equally have referred to an extraconstitutional right of revolution, or to the possibility that a new national convention would rewrite the Constitution, or simply to the factual possibility that the national government might break down. Similarly, references to the permanency of the Union could have referred to the practical unlikelihood of withdrawal rather than to any lack of legal power. The public debates seemingly do not speak specifically to whether ratification under Article VII was revocable.[38]

In short, in determining the original understanding of the permanence of ratification, we are largely condemned to interpreting the meaning of silence. Buchanan made a persuasive case against interpreting silence to reflect an understanding in favor of revocability. Speaking of the adoption of the Constitution, he said that "[i]n that mighty struggle between the first intellects of this or any other country, it never occurred to any individual, either among its opponents or advocates, to assert, or even to intimate, that their efforts were all vain labor, because the moment that any State felt herself aggrieved she might secede from the Union." If the Constitution had been generally understood as a contract at will, the existence of a right to rescind ratification would have been a powerful argument for trying the experiment, offering the equivalent of a "money back guarantee" to anyone with doubts about the wisdom of ratifying. As Buchanan said, "What a crushing argument would this have proved against those who dreaded that the rights of the States would be endangered by the Constitution!"[39]

The permanence of ratification is supported by at least one significant piece of direct evidence. In a letter to Hamilton during the ratification process, Madison expressed his view that ratification must be permanent. He was concerned about proposals to reserve an express right to withdraw. Madison maintained that "a reservation of a right to withdraw if amendments be not decided on under the form of the Constitution within a certain time, is a *conditional* ratification . . . it does not make N. York a member of the New Union, and consequently . . . she could not be received on that plan." He based this on the principle that contracts must be reciprocal, so New York's commitment must match that of the other states. "The Constitution," he continued, "requires an adoption *in toto,* and *for ever.*" Completing the logic, he added: "It has been so adopted by the other States." Ratification for a limited time would be as ineffective as ratification of some but not all of the articles. "In short," he said, "any *condition* whatever must viciate the ratification." The whole idea of "reserving [a] right to withdraw," he said, "was started at Richmd. & considered as a conditional ratification which was itself considered as worse than a rejection."[40]

Moreover, strong structural arguments exist against secession, supporting Madison's view that ratification must be irrevocable. Recognizing an exit option would seriously compromise the general purposes of the Constitution. According to Federalist 40, the Convention's mandate was "to establish in these States *a firm national government*" which would be "*adequate to the exigencies of government* and *the preservation of the Union.*" The availability of an exit option would weaken the federal government's ability to take decisive action, particularly in a crisis, when some states might object strongly to drastic measures. The federal government would be in somewhat the same position as a general whose troops have the legal right to desert on the eve of battle. Buchanan spoke too strongly when he said that if the

Union were a "mere voluntary association of States," the Constitution would be a "rope of sand, to be penetrated and dissolved by the first adverse wave of public opinion in any of the States." Genuine incentives would still exist for remaining in the Union. Still, an exit right would undermine national unity, complicating relations with foreign powers who might either fear or encourage separation. Although not specifically addressed to secession, various remarks by Framers such as Madison and Hamilton indicate that they saw an overbearing national government as less of a risk than the centrifugal force of state autonomy. The Constitution itself contains several indications of this fear of centrifugal tendencies such as the supremacy clause and the commerce clause.[41]

Secession would also have some of the same flaws as nullification. Recognizing a right of exit would encourage settling disputes through multistate negotiation, undermining the decisional processes provided by the Constitution. As Madison said, a "political system that does not provide for a peaceable & authoritative termination of occurring controversies, would not be more than the shadow of a Govt.; the object & end of a real Govt. being the substitution of law & order for uncertainty confusion, and violence." "To have trusted to negotiation, for adjusting disputes between the Govt. of the U.S. and the State Govts. as between independent & separate sovereignties, would have lost sight altogether of a Constitution & Govt. for the Union; and opened a direct road from a failure of that resort, to the ultima ratio between nations wholly independent of and alien to each other."[42]

If the states could not manage to coexist within the framework of the Constitution, Madison asked, what would the prospect be if they were independent? Conflicts about commercial matters and fugitive slaves, he feared, "would of themselves quickly kindle the passions which are the forerunners of war." The whole purpose of the Constitution was to replace this regime of anarchy and potential war with one of law.[43]

Recognizing a secession option would undermine another key structural feature of the Constitution. Under the Articles of Confederation, any one state could veto critical federal initiatives. In arguing against requiring unanimous consent before the new Constitution went into effect, Madison emphasized the dangers of giving a single state such veto power. He rejected "the absurdity of subjecting the fate of twelve States to the perverseness or corruption of a thirteenth." Federalist 22 also argues that a minority veto power "gives greater scope to foreign corruption, as well as to domestic faction, than that which permits the sense of the majority to decide."[44]

Except with respect to changes in its own boundaries or Senate representation, the Constitution does not give any such veto power to an individual state. Instead, the states are bound by the actions of differently constituted interstate majorities—a majority of states in the Senate, a majority of the population in the electoral college or in the House of Representatives, or a supermajority of states in the amendment process. Secession threats might well give individual states like South Carolina an effective veto over unwanted legislation, in effect replacing majority rule with unanimous consensus as a rule of decision for the most controversial issues.

Of course, a unilateral secession option could conceivably help head off oppression of individual states by national majorities, just as no-fault divorce laws can help empower an oppressed spouse. But the Constitution explicitly protects states with a host of other safeguards for geographic minorities. In terms of population, they are highly overrepresented in the Senate. The supermajority requirements of the Constitution for important actions like amendments and treaties also give them protection. And of course, like other minorities, they are protected by the division of legislative authority between two houses, which are further checked by the president and by power of the federal courts to invalidate congressional enactments. Geographic minorities were also protected from discrimination by constitutional requirements that bankruptcy laws, immigration laws, and tariffs be nationally uniform. Given the careful protections for geographic minorities embodied in the Constitution, the case for implying such a drastic additional remedy as secession appears weak.

As with most legal issues, the question of secession does not lend itself to complete certainty. But neither the text nor the ratification debates provide any foothold for an exit option. On the contrary, such evidence as exists seems to lean in the other direction. Recognizing an exit option would also make the Constitution an at-will contract rather than the "law of the land," undermining the Framers' desire to provide an orderly legal framework for the country. In short, perhaps not surprisingly, Madison's view of the constitutionality of secession is ultimately more persuasive than that of John Calhoun and Jefferson Davis.

The basic flaw in the secession argument is its failure to recognize a key aspiration of the Constitution: to replace a regime of multilateral negotiation with the democratic rule of law. Rather than allowing states to use the threat of exit as a bargaining chip, the Constitution made federal legislation "the supreme law of the land." Instead of multilateral negotiation by sovereign states, the Constitution called for nationwide democratic institutions and authoritative dispute resolution by the federal courts. It was this fundamental aspect of constitutional law that the South refused to recognize.

CHAPTER 5   *The Legitimacy of Coercion*

Even James Buchanan agreed that secession was unconstitutional. But Buchanan did not believe that the federal government could do much about secession beyond defending its own property. He offered two arguments against "coercion" of the seceding states. First, he said, coercion would be unconstitutional. "[T]he power to make war against a State," Buchanan argued, "is at variance with the whole spirit and intent of the Constitution." Indeed, Buchanan maintained, the Framers had deliberately withheld from Congress the power to use military force against the states. Second, Buchanan argued that coercion would be wrong even if it were constitutional. "The fact is," he said, "that our Union rests upon public opinion, and can never be cemented by the blood of its citizens shed in civil war. If it cannot live in the affections of the people, it must one day perish." In the meantime, such a war would be a calamity. "[W]ho can foretell what would be the sufferings and privations of the people during its existence?" When the war began, no one knew just how prophetic Buchanan's forebodings would be.[1]

Whether the use of force to halt secession was justified is a serious question. The Civil War was by far the bloodiest conflict in our history, with a death toll of six hundred thousand men. This nearly equals the total from all other wars combined. The statistics are appalling. One out of fifty Americans died in the Civil War, including a quarter of Southern white males of military age. There were four times as many casualties at Antietam as they were on D-Day. Even the figures for individual attacks were fearsome. Of the fourteen thousand Confederates who charged with George Pickett at Gettysburg, only half returned. At Shiloh, Grant later recalled, casualties covered the field so thickly that "it would have been possible to walk across the clearing in any direction stepping on dead bodies without a foot touching the ground." At Cold Harbor, realizing that the attack was doomed, Union soldiers pinned their names onto their uniforms so that their corpses could be identified. They suffered seven thousand casualties, most in the first few minutes. By the time the bodies could be safely retrieved, the stench had become unbearable, as the bodies covered more than five acres "as thickly as they could be laid." At the "Bloody Angle" at Spotsylvania, bodies were piled four layers deep, and the wounded and dying were trapped beneath layers of decaying corpses.[2]

Statistics cannot communicate the reality of the war. The surviving photographs do more to bring the true cost of war home to us today. Even so, the mind is soon numbed by pictures of dead men laid out in lines in a farmer's field or along a road. Perhaps we have all seen too many war movies. But films do not feature scores of dead horses left rotting in the yard of a big house, or a battleground like the Wilderness littered with bones and skulls from the battle fought in the same location the previous year. And Hollywood would never show even dead soldiers in such pathetically ill-fitting uniforms. Perhaps most chilling is the catalogue of photographs of war wounds assembled by one hospital director, clinically depicting the various forms of amputation and mutilation produced by the war. Sherman was only reporting facts when he said that war is hell.[3]

We must take seriously the claim that even if secession was unconstitutional, the North should have acquiesced. The human price of coercion was too great to take the answer for granted. Although the war was a long time ago, the extent of the human sacrifice—and the critical importance of the war in our history—still make the legitimacy of the Union cause a gripping issue today.

We will begin by examining Buchanan's constitutional qualms about using force against the South. These qualms were not, as is often believed, completely groundless, but on balance they were mistaken. Even if coercion was constitutional, however, it may have been morally unjustified. If the South had a moral right to go its own way, even if not a legal right, then coercion was unjust. We will consider two arguments based on American political thought for the morality, if not the legality, of secession: that it was a legitimate revolutionary act and that it was an exercise of the inherent right of self-determination. In short, we will ask, was secession justified by the same principles as the American Revolution? Finally, putting aside such theoretical questions, we will wrestle with the nearly unanswerable question of whether Lincoln's actions were, in the end, for the best. Regardless of the legal or theoretical niceties, would it have been better in the long run simply to have let the South go in peace?

THE CONSTITUTIONALITY OF COERCION

Buchanan argued that making war against a state "is not among the specific and enumerated powers granted to Congress; and it is equally apparent that its exercise is not 'necessary and proper for carrying into execution' any one of these powers." Indeed, he said, the Constitutional Convention had specifically considered a clause "authorizing an exertion of the force of the whole against a delinquent State." Madison had said in the debate on this proposal that the "use of force against a State would look more like a declaration of war than an infliction of punishment; and would probably be considered by the party attacked as a dissolution of all previous compacts by which it might be bound." The proposed clause was stricken on his motion. About a week later, Buchanan reported, Madison spoke again of the impracticability of using force against a state and said any constitutional scheme requiring recourse to force would "prove as visionary and fallacious" as the Articles of Confederation.[4]

Part of Buchanan's argument rests on the notion that coercion would place the federal government in the position of being at war with the states. The Constitution does not seem to contemplate the possibility of a declaration of war against a legitimate state government. But this seems irrelevant. It is one thing for a legal state of war to exist between the various entities recognized by the Constitution. Congress cannot declare war on the state of Minnesota; nor, for that matter, could Wisconsin do so. But if the individuals who occupy state offices in Minnesota mobilized the state militia to invade Wisconsin, the president could clearly defend Wisconsin by force against the intruders. This might look very much like a war—indeed, it might even be a war for some purposes of international law, such as protection of prisoners of war. In terms of constitutional theory, however, we would not say that the United States was at war with the state of Minnesota. Rather, we would say that certain individuals who happened to occupy state offices in Minnesota were engaged in an unlawful attack on a neighboring state. Thus, it was not enough for Buchanan to decry the notion of a formal state of war between states and the nation. Rather, he had to show that if state officers with local support used force or the threat of force to block federal authority, Congress could not authorize the use of military force against the individuals in question. Specifically, Buchanan had to show that Congress's powers to put down insurrections, rebellions, and invasions did not apply.

The question of congressional power was considered in more detail in a formal opinion by Buchanan's attorney general. He concluded that none of Congress's delegated powers authorized the use of force against a state. He focused on two congressional powers. The war power authorizes Congress "to declare war," but Attorney General Black said this "certainly means nothing more than the power to commence and carry on hostilities against the foreign enemies of the nation." Another clause grants Congress the power "to provide for calling forth the militia." But this power, Black said, could be used only for three designated purposes: (1) to "execute the laws of the Union; that is, to aid the federal officers in the performance of their regular duties"; (2) to "suppress insurrections against the State; but this is confined by article 4, section 4 to cases in which the State herself shall apply for assistance against her own people"; and (3) to "repel the invasion of a State by enemies who come from abroad to assail her in her own territory." None of these applied to the current situation: there were no federal officers performing their duties in the seceded states and therefore none to assist; the seceding states had not applied for assistance to suppress an insurrection; and the seceding states had not been invaded by foreign enemies.[5]

Like the Tenth Amendment argument for secession considered in the last chapter, the anticoercion argument has some resonance with some recent opinions by Supreme Court justices. These views are worth considering, if only to show that Buchanan's position was not utterly frivolous. In the end, however, we will see that they fail to provide much support for Buchanan.

Admittedly, there are some similarities. The general principle that Congress may not directly coerce the states was endorsed in Justice O'Connor's opinion for the Court in *New York v. United States*.[6] Like Buchanan, she stressed the decision of the Framers to abandon the scheme of the Articles of Confederation, under which the state governments were subject to federal mandates, in favor of a system relying on direct federal legislation over individual citizens.[7]

O'Connor attached much significance to the rejection of the New Jersey plan at the Constitutional Convention. The version of the supremacy clause in the New Jersey plan provided that "if any State, or any body of men in any State shall oppose or prevent ye. carrying into execution such acts or treaties, the federal Executive shall be authorized to call forth ye. power of the Confederated States, or so much thereof as may be necessary to enforce and compel an obedience to such Acts, or an observance of such Treaties." Thus, the New Jersey plan shared the vice of the Articles of Confederation by requiring enforcement actions against states. "One frequently expressed objection to the New Jersey Plan," according to Justice O'Connor, "was that it might require the Federal Government to coerce the States into implementing legislation." This was unacceptable to the Framers, who considered coercion "impracticable, expensive, cruel to individuals." Madison, O'Connor observed, had taken the same view, saying that the "practicability of making laws, with coercive sanctions, for the States as political bodies, had been exploded on all hands." Hence, the Framers opted for "a Constitution that confers upon Congress the power to regulate individuals, not States."[8]

A more recent opinion by Justice Scalia extended this holding. *Printz v. United States*[9] involved a federal requirement that local police conduct background checks on gun buyers. Like the federal statute in *New York v. United States,* this was struck down as an unacceptable coercion of state government. Again, the Court quoted Madison on the impracticability of "making laws, with coercive sanctions, for the States as political bodies." Thus, the Framers "rejected the concept of a central government that would act upon and through the States."[10]

These recent decisions seem, at first blush, to support the idea that the states are immune from federal coercion. But the Court conceptualized these federal statutes as imposing affirmative duties on state officials, rather than merely forbidding them to act in violation of federal law. Beginning in John Marshall's time, the Supreme Court has rejected any power of state officials to actively interfere with the implementation of federal law. Although the Court in *Printz* and *New York* invoked some of the same history as Buchanan, the Court's basic argument had nothing to do with whether states could be "coerced" into allowing the execution of federal law. Active cooperation, rather than passive compliance, was the federal demand in these cases. But secession amounted to a refusal to obey federal law.[11]

Hamilton drew a similar distinction in Federalist 16. The main argument in Federalist 16 is that the Articles required active cooperation from the states, which would often be available only through federal coercion. By allowing the federal government to operate directly on individuals, the Constitution would obviate the need to coerce states. But what if a state interfered with the enforcement of federal law? Arguably, this would create the same difficulty: "[I]f any state should be disaffected to the authority of the Union it could at any time obstruct the execution of its laws, and bring the matter to the same issue of force" as would be required under the Articles to obtain state cooperation. Thus, it could be claimed that allowing the federal government to operate directly on individuals would do nothing to obviate the need for coercion of states. But Hamilton objected that this claim overlooked the much lesser need for coercion because of "the essential difference between a mere NONCOMPLIANCE and a DIRECT and ACTIVE RESISTANCE." Active resistance, unlike noncooperation, is overt and unmistakable. State officials would be "obliged to act, and in such a manner as would leave no doubt that they had encroached on the national rights." This would normally bring into play the state judges, who had a duty to enforce federal law, as well as alerting the public, which would presumably still be loyal. Thus, "Attempts of this kind would not often be made with levity or rashness, because they could seldom be made without danger to the authors." And the government would possess ample means to repress limited rebellions. "As to those partial commotions and insurrections which sometimes disquiet society from the intrigues of an inconsiderable faction, or from sudden or occasional ill humors that do not infect the great body of the community," the government would possess greater resources than the states to suppress such disturbances.[12]

Federalist 16 ends on an ominous note. Hamilton turned to the worst-case scenario: "those mortal feuds which in certain conjunctures spread a conflagration through a whole nation, or through a very large proportion of it, proceeding either from weighty causes of discontent . . . or from the contagion of some violent popular paroxysm." Such catastrophes "do not fall within any ordinary rules of calculation" and "commonly amount to revolutions and dismemberments of empire." No system could completely guard against this possibility. "No form of government can always either avoid or control them. It is in vain to hope to guard against events too mighty for human foresight or precaution, and it would be idle to object to a government because it could not perform impossibilities." Serious as such a situation would be, Hamilton only seemed to fear that the federal government might lack the practical power to defend itself. He did not suggest that it would lack the legal authority to do so.[13]

As to the practical problem, Hamilton was notoriously concerned with ensuring that the federal government have sufficient resources to defend its authority. In Federalist 25, he pointed to Shays's Rebellion as showing "in its application to the United States, how little the rights of a feeble government are likely to be respected, even by its own constituents." Near the end of the ratification debates, Hamilton summarized his view: "Sir, when you have . . . rendered your system as perfect as human forms can be—you must place confidence; you must give power." Everyone knows, he said, that the federal government's purposes were "numerous, extensive, and important," so everyone also "must acknowledge the necessity of giving powers, in all respects, and in every degree, equal to those objects." Inasmuch as a constitution "cannot set bounds to a nation's wants; it ought not therefore to set bounds on its resources." Above all, Hamilton continued, "Unexpected invasions, long and ruinous wars, may demand all the possible abilities of the country." "[T]he contingencies of society are not reducible to calculations. They cannot be fixed or bounded, even in imagination." It is hard to imagine a view more at odds with Buchanan's supine confession of federal impotence in the face of secession.[14]

In reality, the Constitution clearly empowers the government to suppress state interference with its operations. The obvious source of federal authority to resist secession is clause 16 in the list of federal powers granted in section 8 of Article I. It empowers Congress to "provide for calling forth the Militia to execute the Laws of the Union, suppress Insurrections and repel Invasions." Attorney General Black's counterargument was based on a different provision of the Constitution. Article IV, section 4 provides that the United States shall "guarantee to every State in this Union a Republican Form of government, and shall protect each of them against Invasion; and on Application of the Legislature, or of the Executive (when the Legislature cannot be convened) against domestic Violence." Black argued that the reference to suppressing insurrections in Article I referred to the domestic violence mentioned in Article IV, and hence required a request from some organ of state government before the militia could be mobilized. Obviously, the seceding states were not about to make such a request.

This is hardly an inevitable interpretation of the text. The linkage between Article I and Article IV is not obvious. Black's argument assumes that "insurrection" in Article I means the same thing as "domestic violence" in Article IV. But the more natural interpretation is that the use of different words was deliberate. The record supports this more natural interpretation. At the Constitutional Convention, a motion to use the word *insurrection* in Article IV, which would have required state consent to the use of the militia to suppress insurrections, was defeated.[15]

Indeed, Attorney General Black is also wrong in thinking that an "invasion" must proceed from a foreign source. In Federalist 43, Madison discussed the possibility that one state might invade another. The term *invasion,* he indicated, "seems to secure each State not only against foreign hostility, but against ambitious or vindictive enterprises of its more powerful neighbors." He added that the history of other confederacies "proves that the weaker members of the Union ought not to be insensible" to the advantages of this protection. Madison also observed that "illicit combinations, for purposes of violence" may be formed not only by a minority but "as well by a majority of a State."[16]

Black's interpretation of the "execute the laws" clause also seems implausibly narrow. He suggests that the militia can only be used to enforce specific orders of judges or government officers, and hence has no role if there are no judges or officers in place. By this reasoning, rebels could constitutionally paralyze federal intervention through terrorism. Simply by killing all federal officials in the state and frightening off any potential replacements, they would prevent the use of the "execute the laws" power under Article I. As John Marshall probably would have said, this is a conclusion too ridiculous to be countenanced.

But it is unnecessary to descend into the minutiae of the militia clauses. In the famous case of *McCulloch v. Maryland,*[17] Marshall held that the necessary and proper clause authorized any federal actions, not otherwise impermissible, which are conducive to the execution of the government's powers. If the state government refuses to allow the enforcement of federal law in its territory, all of the federal government's powers are equally frustrated within its domain. By Marshall's light, using force is certainly "necessary" if the state fails to cooperate voluntarily, and we have already dealt with the objection that using force against rebellious state officials is not constitutionally "proper."

In the end, Buchanan's view is simply untenable—less defensible, even, than secessionism. If a seceding state proved obdurate, Buchanan's view would leave the federal government in an absurd position. Since the state would still be part of the Union, the federal government could not treat it as a foreign power. It could not enter into treaties to settle disputes or regulate relations with the state after secession. But since the government lacked any power to enforce its laws there, the state would be a member of the Union in little more than name. Other states could find themselves in an untenable position as well, forced by Article IV to honor the seceding state's court decrees, return its fugitives, and provide nondiscriminatory treatment to its citizens, with no guarantee of similar treatment in return. Presumably this bizarre state of affairs would go on forever.

Other absurdities could be added. If more than a quarter of the states purported to secede, the remainder would be unable ever to amend the Constitution. Citizens of the seceding states could still invoke the diversity jurisdiction of the federal courts in other states, but could not be subjected to that jurisdiction in their own state. All of this merely confirms the obvious: the Constitution makes no provision for "ghost states" that are dead in terms of federal authority but allowed to haunt the rest of the Union. Recognition of such a ghost status would have all the defects of secession and nullification, combined with serious flaws of its own.

Thus, contrary to Buchanan's theory, it seems clear that the federal government must have power to use force against state officials who interfere with the execution of federal law. As a fallback, Buchanan might reply that the federal government can use force against state officials, but may not initiate a genuine war. It is true that a war between the Union and one of its components seems not only horrible but paradoxical. The alternative, however, is to allow a state to block federal law simply by making a sufficiently large show of force. But this too seems absurd. If the government is entitled to coerce the state, the state cannot acquire some form of constitutional immunity by increasing the violence of its resistance. If it insists on resisting to the point where war with the federal government results, the state rather than the federal government is responsible for the consequences.

Indeed, widespread armed resistance to the federal government invokes another federal power: the treason clause. For state officials to make war against the United States is treason. Article I authorizes Congress to declare the punishment for treason. Under Article III, section 3, "treason against the United States" consists of "levying War against them, or in adhering to their Enemies, giving them Aid and Comfort." The drafters specifically contemplated the possibility that a person might be faced with the choice of committing treason against the United States or treason against his own state. The Convention considered prohibiting states from punishing treason against themselves for this reason, but ultimately rejected such a prohibition as unnecessary. Although allowing states to define treason against themselves posed this possible conflict, it could pose "no danger to the general authority" as "the laws of the United States are to be paramount." State officers or residents who escalated the level of their resistance to the level of war, thus, would be guilty of treason.[18]

In short, once again, Madison was right. He relied on Jefferson for the proposition that "it was not necessary to find a right to coerce in the Federal Articles, that being inherent in the nature of a compact." "It is high time," he continued in an 1832 letter, "that the claim to secede at will should be put down by the public opinion."[19] When public opinion failed to do so, the government had the clear constitutional authority to resort to force.

SECESSION AS REVOLUTION

To say that something is constitutional is not necessarily to say that it is just. If the South was within its moral rights to secede—if it was exercising inherent human rights of revolution against oppression or of self-determination—coercion would have been unjust. And Southerners did make such claims on behalf of secession.

Particularly, the South sought to connect secession with the American Revolution. South Carolina's "Declaration of the Causes of Secession" recounted the origins of the American Union, beginning with the Declaration of Independence. After the English "undertook to make laws" governing the colonies, a "struggle for the right of self-government ensued," resulting in the Declaration of Independence's proclamation that the colonies "are, and of right ought to be, FREE AND INDEPENDENT STATES." The South Carolina declaration itself ends with a similar proclamation that South Carolina was a "separate and independent State," with all the powers attending that status. Similarly, in his inaugural address, Jefferson Davis said that the South had "merely asserted the right which the Declaration of Independence of July 4, 1776, defined to be 'inalienable.'"[20]

Southerners who were skeptical of the constitutionality of secession frequently invoked the right of revolution instead. Senator Iverson of Georgia said that "each State has the right of revolution" and that secession "is an act of revolution." Some even sang "The Southern Marseillaise." Virginia's ex-governor Henry Wise enjoyed having a reputation as the "Danton" of secession. But the American Revolution was more frequently the model than the French. " 'Were not the men of 1776 . . . Secessionists?' " asked one ardent Southerner.[21]

According to a recent historian, the "identification of the Confederate cause with that of the earlier cause of Independence was propagated endlessly." The *New Orleans Picayune* said, for instance, that the Confederacy was "acting over again the history of the American Revolution of 1776." Officials also tried to reinforce this connection. Jefferson Davis's inauguration was held on Washington's birthday, on a platform next to a statue of Washington. He called on Southerners to prove themselves worthy of the legacy "bequeathed to us by the patriots of the Revolution."[22]

Indeed, even today, the Declaration of Independence is sometimes invoked as support for secession. According to one recent writer, "[T]he Declaration announces a lawful *secession* by the colonies from Great Britain based on the right of the people to alter or abolish their form of government." It is "thus apparent that the Declaration of Independence establishes that the right of secession is among the *inalienable* rights of men."[23]

In invoking the Declaration of Independence, Southerners were appealing to a shared assumption of Americans on both sides. In his First Inaugural, for example, Lincoln explicitly reaffirmed the right to revolution proclaimed by the Declaration. If a majority deprived a minority of "any clearly written constitutional right, it might, in a moral point of view, justify revolution—certainly would, if such right were a vital one." But, Lincoln continued, "such is not our case." Later in the speech, he added that "[t]his country, with its institutions, belongs to the people who inhabit it. Whenever they shall grow weary of the existing government, they can exercise their *constitutional* right of amending it, or their *revolutionary* right to dismember, or overthrow it."[24]

What were the Southern grievances that might justify a right to revolution? The tariff, of course, had been a long-standing irritant. Some secessionist leaders reemphasized this old complaint. But by 1860, it was hard to take this seriously as a justification for secession. As Alexander Stephens admitted, the existing tariff was just what the South's "own Senators and members of Congress made it." The trend for the past twenty years had been toward lower tariffs, and Stephens was right that the tariff in effect in 1860 was "largely Southern-made," as a leading historian puts it.[25]

The remaining justifications related to slavery. The official statements accompanying secession stressed this point. Texas charged the Republicans with "proclaiming the debasing doctrine of the equality of all men, irrespective of race and color—a doctrine at war with nature, in opposition to the experience of mankind, and in violation of the plainest revelations of Divine Law." Having gained power, Republicans would be sure to pursue "the abolition of negro slavery" and "political equality between the white and negro races." South Carolina charged that the North had "encouraged and assisted thousands of our slaves to leave their homes; and those who remain, have been incited by emissaries, books, and pictures to servile insurrection." After the Republicans took office, the South Carolina manifesto complained, the South would be excluded from the "common territory" and a war would be "waged against slavery until it shall cease throughout the United States." Mississippi's proclamation listed hostile acts against slavery from the Northwest Ordinance onward. It concluded that Southerners "must either submit to degradation and to the loss of property worth four billions of money, or we must secede from the Union." The Confederacy's vice president, Alexander Stephens, exclaimed that the original Framers had erroneously believed in human equality. "Our new Government," he said, "is founded upon exactly the opposite idea; its foundations are laid, its cornerstone rests, upon the great truth that the negro is not equal to the white man; that slavery, subordination to the superior race, is his natural and moral condition."[26]

The centrality of slavery to secession is demonstrated by the appeals made by South Carolina and the gulf states to the remainder of the South. In order to foment secession elsewhere, these states appointed commissioners to advocate the great cause. The commissioners emphasized the Northern threat to slavery. Andrew Calhoun, son of the Great Nullifier, was South Carolina's commissioner to Alabama. He said the Republicans would institute "a depraved government" and "seduce the poor, ignorant and stupid nature of the negro." The Haitian blacks, Calhoun said, had been stirred by the slogans of the French revolution to massacre whites, a massacre that the Republican "white fiends would delight to see re-enacted now with us." South Carolina's commissioner to Florida was a leading advocate of reinstating the African slave trade. He told Floridians that South Carolina's secession had "erected at least one nationality under the authority of which the powers of slavery may stand in that fearful contest for existence which at some time or other was bound to come."[27]

According to a recent study, the commissioners had three main themes in their efforts to persuade other states to secede. The first was the threat of racial equality that would attend Republican control of the government.

For instance, Alabama's commissioners to North Carolina predicted that the children of Southern whites would either have to flee or "submit to the degradation of being reduced to an equality with them [the slaves], and all its attendant horrors." The second theme was the risk of race war. Alabama's commissioner to Missouri predicted that the "scenes of San Domingo and Hayti, with all their attendant horrors, would be enacted in the slaveholding States." Third, the ultimate outcome would be racial amalgamation. After black emancipation, " 'our women' would suffer 'horrors . . . we cannot contemplate in imagination.' "[28]

This study of the commissioners merely confirms the consensus among historians today about the centrality of slavery to secession. "What were these rights and liberties for which Confederates contended?" asks one historian. He answers, "The right to own slaves; the liberty to take this property into the territories; freedom from the coercive powers of a centralized government." To Southerners, said another leading historian, Lincoln's election meant that abolitionism "would soon place its stamp of possession upon the federal government, its gloss of interpretation upon the Constitution." Thus, the election "became the signal for pursuing the logic of states-rights constitutionalism to its ultimate conclusion." Perhaps most notable is the verdict of an eminent historian a half-century ago—a historian who, unlike those more recent writers, expressed sympathy for the South's racial problems. Even so, he concluded that the war was about one fundamental issue: "Was the Negro to be allowed, as a result of the shift of power signalized by Lincoln's election, to take the first step toward an ultimate position of general economic, political, and social equality with the white man? Or was he to be held immobile in a degraded, servile position, unchanging for the next hundred years as it had remained essentially unchanged for the hundred years past?"[29]

The centrality of the slavery issue is sometimes misunderstood because of Lincoln's repeated insistence early in the war that abolition was not a war aim. The sole aim of the war, he proclaimed, was restoration of the Union. To this end, he was willing to accommodate Southern demands to a great extent. He was willing to agree to a constitutional amendment permanently barring the federal government from interfering with slavery within the states. He thought this amendment merely entrenched the existing meaning of the Constitution anyway. He was willing to enforce the Fugitive Slave Law. But he was not willing to compromise on the Republican program of confining slavery to its current territory in order to gradually extinguish it. Southerners correctly perceived that the ultimate future of slavery was at stake, and this was no incidental part of the secession movement. Recall that it was the Southern demand for a congressional slave code that split the Democratic party and paved the way for the Republican victory. As Lincoln said in his First Inaugural, "One section of our country believes slavery is *right,* and ought to be extended, while the other believes it is *wrong,* and ought not to be extended. This is the only substantial dispute."[30]

Protecting slavery was not the sole motive for secession, but it was an essential ingredient. Of course, there had always been a certain irony in the demands of slave owners for liberty. Even in 1776, slavery had been an embarrassment to the American cause. As one Pennsylvanian wrote, "It is astonishing that men who feel the value and importance of liberty" should keep "such numbers of the human species in a state of so absolute vassalage." Every argument "in favor of our own liberties will certainly operate with equal force in favor of that of the Negroes; nor can we with any propriety contend for the one while we withhold the other."[31]

But 1776 was not 1861. In 1776, rebel states that happened to have slavery contended for their inalienable human rights. This was an irony. In 1861, rebel states invoked their inalienable human rights in defense of their very ownership of slaves. That was not an irony but a self-contradiction. Although both rebellions were tainted by association with slavery, in one case the connection was reluctant, in the other it was embraced. Thus, the American Revolution was no moral precedent for secession.

Secession simply cannot be justified as an effort to shake off an oppressive government. The federal government had, as yet, done nothing to harm the South, and had been dominated by the South much of the time. In terms of the future, the great fear was that the government would move, directly or indirectly, against slavery. But unless we are to take the position that, among the "inalienable rights" with which men are "endowed by their Creator," is the right to own other human beings, no violation of the right to own slaves could count as a justification for revolution. Thus, in coercing the South, the North cannot be accused of violating any moral right to revolution. Southerners of the time, who did not share our understanding of the injustice of slavery, understandably took a different view, but theirs is a perspective that we cannot regard as legitimate today.

SECESSION AS SELF-DETERMINATION

But perhaps the South did not need to show any violation of its rights, past or future. Perhaps it was enough for the South simply to say, "We prefer to govern ourselves." Such a right of self-determination certainly has an honorable pedigree.

While serving as a congressman from Illinois, Lincoln himself endorsed this right during the Mexican War. In determining whether the war had begun on Mexican territory, he said, it was necessary to determine the allegiance of the inhabitants. In his famous (and ill-received) Spot Resolution, he demanded that the president inform Congress "[w]hether the *People* of that settlement, or a *majority* of them, had ever, previous to the bloodshed . . . submitted themselves to the government or laws of Texas, or of the United States, by *consent,* or by *compulsion,*" such as by accepting office or paying taxes. Lincoln's demand was based on the concept of self-determination.[32]

In his speech defending the resolution, Lincoln said that ownership of the disputed territory depended on whether Texas had actually "carried her revolution" into the region "by obtaining the *actual,* willing or unwilling, submission of the people." Ultimately, Texas's claim was based on the right of revolution, a right that Lincoln described in some detail. "Any people anywhere," according to Lincoln, "being inclined and having the power, have the *right* to rise up, and shake off the existing government, and form a new one that suits them better." He called this "a most valuable,—a most sacred right—a right, which we hope and believe, is to liberate the world." Nor did exercise of this right require the support of all of the subjects of the existing government. Rather, "Any portion of such people that *can, may* revolutionize, and make their *own,* of so much of the territory as they inhabit." Realistically, of course, such a movement would not have unanimous support in any given region. But unanimous support was not needed: a "*majority* of any portion of such people may revolutionize, putting down a *minority,* intermingled with, or near about them, who may oppose their movement." As Lincoln explained, "Such minority, was precisely the case, of the tories of our own revolution."[33]

Lincoln's argument for the Spot Resolution seems tailor-made for the secessionists. If every people has the "most sacred right" to "rise up and shake off the existing government, and form a new one that suits them better," then why not the South? And if any portion of a people can "revolutionize, and make their own" as "much of the territory as they inhabit," why not the Southern portion of the American people? Lincoln seems to be hoist with his own petard.

Based on similar arguments, some recent writers have argued that "on any reasonable interpretation of the Declaration of Independence and the Constitution, the South was right!" On this view, Jefferson Davis correctly believed "his cause was the same as those who originally formed the Union: to create and preserve an ideal of government by consent of the governed, an ideal he accused the North of having systematically violated." The premise of the argument is that "government by consent of the governed includes the right to secede, and to form a new government."[34]

Lincoln would have disagreed that the facts presented this issue. He firmly believed at the beginning of the war that a silent Southern majority favored the Union. In his message to Congress on July 4, 1861, he said that it "may well be questioned whether there is, to-day, a majority of the legally qualified voters of any State, except perhaps South Carolina, in favor of disunion." He found "much reason to believe that the Union men are the majority in many, if not in every other one, of the so-called seceded States." His belief was reasonable, given the irregularity of the secession process, but he was most likely wrong. For present purposes, however, let us put aside the question of whether secession did enjoy majority support among Southern whites, not to mention the question of whether such a majority should be regarded as legitimate given the exclusion of blacks. What follows?[35]

Secession poses a difficult problem for democratic theorists. The arguments in favor of secession are that any group has a right to self-government, that the majority within a territory has the right to govern it, and that minority rights should be respected (including the right of a minority to withdraw). The values invoked by these arguments, however, can be invoked just as easily against secession.

As to the right of self-government, the larger group presumably also has such a right. If Americans constitute a group, self-government requires that the American people as a whole make the laws for the United States as a whole, despite the objections of dissenters. Unless self-government means anarchy, it must at some point include the right to coerce those who disagree with the government's decisions. Otherwise, the "government" part of self-government becomes meaningless. Indeed, the secessionists themselves claimed the right to coerce an unwilling minority, their local opponents who wished to stay in the Union. But if a regional group has the right to demand compliance from dissidents, the group defined by the larger nationality would seem to have the same right.

Majority rule also cuts both ways. There are two relevant majorities. One majority lives in the disputed territory and seeks to secede. The other majority covers the whole country and opposes secession. The norm of majority rule cannot tell us which majority should prevail. Majority rule means that the majority in any given group is normally entitled to control at the expense of the minority. But secession raises the problem of defining the relevant domain for calculating this majority. This requires some standard beyond the notion that in any election, the side with the larger number of votes wins. When the issue is secession, what we need to know is the identity of the relevant electorate, not the required margin of victory. Embracing the right of a majority to rule does not answer the question, "which majority?"

Asking whether majority rule implies a right to secede is ultimately question-begging. Majority rule takes as given political units defined in terms of currently existing boundaries. The concept of majority rule provides no traction on the question of the proper scope of political units, because majoritarianism itself takes political units as given. It does not tell us whether the thirteen colonies should have united in 1789, and for the same reason it does not tell us whether they should have divided in 1861. It merely tells us that, in whatever political units may exist at any specific time, decisions should be made by a majority of the population of those units.

Equally little guidance is provided by the notion of protecting minority interests. The supporters of secession are one minority, and they seek to protect their interests by withdrawing from the larger government. But the local opponents of secession are another minority. Secession leaves them with only two choices: to abandon their right to remain citizens of the home country, or to abandon their homes and emigrate to the remaining portion of the country. Either way, they suffer a severe loss. Thus, allowing secession protects one minority but by the same token coerces another.

In fact, Lincoln himself made such arguments in opposition to secession. In his first inaugural, he said that "the central idea of secession, is the essence of anarchy." Minorities must acquiesce in majority decisions, for "[u]nanimity is impossible; the rule of a minority, as a permanent arrangement, is wholly inadmissable; so that, rejecting the majority principle, anarchy, or despotism in some form, is all that is left." If, in case of disagreement, a minority "will secede rather than acquiesce, they make a precedent which, in turn, will divide and ruin them; for a minority of their own will secede from them, whenever a majority refuses to be controlled by such minority."[36]

Thus, as important as those concepts are, merely invoking majority rule, self-governance, or minority rights cannot resolve the issue of secession. A more careful analysis is needed of the relationship between democratic values and secession. One way to frame the question is to ask whether a democratic constitution ideally should provide for an unlimited right of secession. If such a provision would be inappropriate, the implication is that democratic liberty does not require a right to secede.

There are several reasons for rejecting such a provision. Leaving open the option of secession undermines democratic governance. To begin with, the existence of a secession option invites strategic threats. The South threatened secession on a number of occasions to extract legislative concessions like the Compromise of 1850. In some ways, the threat of secession has more serious effects than its implementation. When a state secedes, the result can be two majoritarian regimes, whereas the threat of secession undermines the majoritarian nature of the existing regime.[37]

If a secession option does have any justification, it is as a protection of minority rights. But providing this option is at best a clumsy way of protecting minorities. A secession option rather arbitrarily protects only minorities that happen to be concentrated in discrete geographic regions; it does nothing for more diffuse minorities for whom secession is not a practical possibility. Furthermore, a secession option makes no distinction between fundamental minority interests such as individual liberty and mere pocketbook disputes. It also opens the door, as in the South, for a group that is a minority on the national scene to secede in order to augment its power to oppress a local minority. Thus, secession is not in general a promising method to protect minority rights.

Societies may have other good reasons to commit themselves in advance against secession. The very possibility of secession weakens the country as a whole in its foreign relations, encouraging outsiders to seek separate deals with subgroups. Moreover, in times of crisis, it may be important to take action which is beneficial to society as a whole but sacrifices the interests of a sub-group. In advance, it may be to the advantage of each subgroup to empower the national government to make such decisions, taking the risk that when the actual situation arises, they will be the disfavored group rather than part of the benefited national majority. As an economist would say, an antisecession clause may be a rational choice for all parties *ex ante,* though *ex post* some will regret their decision and seek to secede. There may be good reason to precommit to a perpetual Union, just as it may be advantageous to enter into a binding legal contract, even though such contracts do not always turn out to be beneficial in the end.[38]

Thus, from the point of view of democratic theory, "secession on demand" is not a particularly attractive concept. Yet, rejecting the possibility of secession completely may seem too facile. For some region to be perpetually governed against its will by an unsympathetic national government also seems at odds with our idea of democracy. True, the residents may be able to vote. But as blacks in some parts of the modern South discovered, the right to vote means little if you are a minority and the majority is determined to freeze you out of power. If "secession on demand" is unacceptable, "perpetual union at all costs" is also a troublesome idea. In pondering the possibility of secession, we are presented with a democratic dilemma that has no easy answer.

The Canadian Supreme Court recently grappled with this issue in the context of Quebec's possible bid for independence. The ruling suggests a possible accommodation of the conflicting claims regarding secession. The court ruled that no unilateral right of secession existed under either Canadian or international law. Yet, it said, "the continued existence and operation of the Canadian constitutional order could not be indifferent to a clear expression of a clear majority of Quebeccers that they no longer wish to remain in Canada." Given such unmistakable evidence of popular will, Quebec would then have the right to "pursue secession" so long as "in doing so, Quebec respects the rights of others." Negotiations would take place after such a vote, addressing "the potential act of secession as well as its possible terms should in fact secession proceed." These negotiations would need to address the interests of other provinces and of the federal government, as well as "the rights of all Canadians both within and outside Quebec, and specifically the rights of minorities."[39]

In terms of international law, the Canadian court said that self-determination generally refers to governance over internal affairs and is limited by the territorial integrity of existing states. International law recognizes circumstances in which territorial integrity may be broken. Colonial territories under foreign occupation may have a right to secede, as do peoples "subject to alien subjugation, domination or exploitation outside a colonial context." More controversially, some commentators contend that "when a people is blocked from the meaningful exercise of its right to self-determination internally, it is entitled, as a last resort, to exercise it by secession." But none of these exceptions applied to Quebec, the court said: "Quebeccers occupy prominent positions within the government of Canada," and "freely make political choices and pursue economic, social and cultural development within Quebec, across Canada, and throughout the world."[40]

Whether the Canadian Supreme Court was right in its assessment of Canadian constitutional law or international law or in its appraisal of the situation of Quebec is obviously beyond the scope of this book. The court's opinion is, however, a thoughtful effort to reconcile the conflicting claims of nationalist and secessionist groups in a democracy. How would the South fare under such an analysis?

Not well. In terms of international law's concept of self-determination, the South could not reasonably claim to be a colony of the North or an oppressed people. Losing an election, even a key election, is not the same as vassalage. Moreover, although a popular majority in favor of secession probably did exist in the Deep South, it could hardly be said that a "clear expression of majority will" existed. The process for electing representatives to the secession conventions and the proceedings of those conventions left genuine doubt on this score. And even if such a clear sentiment did exist, the South would have been entitled only to good faith negotiations with the North about the possibility of secession rather than being authorized to take unilateral action. Finally, and most importantly, the Canadian Supreme Court stressed that a seceding region must respect the rights of others, whereas a major purpose of Southern secession was to ensure that white Southerners could freely deprive blacks of their fundamental human rights.

Lincoln's position seems consistent with this tempered view of secession. He was adamant in opposing unilateral secession, but he did not insist that the South remain in the Union. In his First Inaugural, he said that he recognized the "rightful authority of the people over the whole subject" to be exercised through the amendment power. He suggested that a constitutional convention would be an appropriate method of resolving the difficulties between the sections. He called on all sides to submit their positions to the people: "If the Almighty Ruler of nations, with his eternal truth and justice, be on your side of the North, or on yours of the South, that truth, and that justice, will surely prevail, by the judgment of this great tribunal, the American people." In the meantime, however, he said that it was his duty as chief magistrate to administer the Constitution as it currently existed.[41]

If Southern secession was to be justified, it could not be on the basis of any history of oppression by the federal government, or even on the basis of any prospect of such oppression, unless the possible decline of slavery could be considered a violation of Southern rights. Nor could it be justified, along the lines sketched by the Canadian Supreme Court, as the outcome of a deliberative process of negotiation between the affected parties. The secessionists went to great efforts to stampede the South into secession rather than allowing full deliberation. Instead, the birth of the Confederacy could only be justified on the basis of an unlimited, unilateral right of secession. But neither as a matter of democratic theory, nor international legal norms, nor of American constitutional law, does such a legal right to "secession on demand" exist. Rather, secession was a lawless act, to which the government was legally and morally entitled to respond with force.[42]

THE PRICE OF UNION

And yet . . . all talk of legality and political theory aside, if the Southern states wanted to leave, was it really worth waging a brutal war to force them to stay?

Of course, we cannot know how history would have turned out if secession had been peaceful. Possibly, only the seven cotton states would have seceded, since the upper South left only in response to Northern "coercion" of the Confederacy. But perhaps the world would not have been much the worse even if, as Lincoln feared, secession by the Deep South set a precedent for other regions. Would the world be a worse place if we had two or three or four American republics instead of one?

This question is impossible to answer, even if we assume that the various republics peacefully coexisted and cooperated with each other on economic issues. The international implications are impenetrable. How would the great powers of Europe have responded? Would they have entered into conflicting alliances with different American republics, with the end result that the European wars of the twentieth century would also have been fought out on American soil by their allies? Or would the fragmentation of American power have created more complex webs of alliances and helped stabilize the balance of power?

The domestic consequences are equally unfathomable. Would the South have voluntarily ended slavery and ultimately achieved harmonious race relations without the lasting embitterment caused by the Civil War? Or would the South have become even more entrenched into white supremacy, allying with South Africa as a fortress of apartheid? Would the South and the North eventually have peacefully reunited? We will never know.[43]

But it is far from clear that, even if secession itself had been peaceful, the two sections would have remained at peace. Perhaps, like Canada and the United States, the United States and the Confederacy would have lived amicably side by side. Yet this seems far from inevitable. Madison had pointed out many years earlier that if two regions could not reconcile their differences within a shared constitutional regime, they would be likely to do no better as autonomous nations. Slaves would still escape to the North, which would not have agreed to a treaty requiring their return. The existing territories would have either become a bone of contention or remained with the Union, where the Republican majority would never have allowed slavery to take root. The South would have been able to pursue a free trade policy with Europe, but it might have had difficulty establishing free trade with the North. And additional causes of conflict could easily have arisen, such as the North's right of free navigation on the Mississippi. War might also have resulted if the South had carried through on talk of expansion southward to Latin America, if the North got drawn into the dispute. Whatever the nature of the underlying conflict, war would have been all the more likely because of Southern willingness to resort to violence in defense of honor.

Asking whether it was worth six hundred thousand deaths to stop secession is really the wrong question to ask. No one on either side anticipated the extent of the carnage. The war might have ended earlier, at smaller cost, if events had gone differently. Moreover, if Lincoln is to be blamed for the unanticipated extent of the bloodshed, he should also get credit for the equally unanticipated constitutional amendments that banned slavery, barred state violations of equal protection and due process, and gave blacks the legal right to vote.

Asking whether Lincoln was wrong to begin the Civil War also overestimates his responsibility for the outbreak of war. He had made a number of conciliatory gestures toward the South, including support for a constitutional amendment to guard against federal interference with Southern slavery. His First Inaugural can hardly be called confrontational. He said he would not appoint outsiders as federal officers where local residents were unwilling to serve, and even said that the federal government would only continue to deliver the mails "unless repelled." He closed with a famous plea for reconciliation—expressing the hope that the "mystic chords of memory, stretching from every battle-field, and patriot grave, to every living heart and hearthstone, all over this broad land, will yet swell the chorus of the Union, when again touched, as surely they will be, by the better angels of our nature."[44]

True, Lincoln did insist on holding the remaining federal forts, but he could hardly be expected to have given those away, when even the spineless Buchanan had insisted on the right to use force in defense of federal property. Even if secession had been constitutional, South Carolina's claim to immediate possession of the forts was hardly unimpeachable. In the end, one fact is crucial. It was the Confederacy that fired the first shot. After that happened, war was inevitable, just as it would have been if the French or Russian military had sacked a U.S. fort.

Buchanan was wrong about coercion, but he was right that civil war would create constitutional conundrums. Once war came, it led to a series of legal anomalies. The requirements of civil war did not fit easily within the constitutional structure. Instead, the war brought two different sets of legal rules into collision. Generally, the federal government was limited in its authority within the United States. In normal times, Congress had defined legislative powers, which were not construed nearly as broadly as they are today, and the president's main duty was to enforce federal legislation. In so doing, he was bound by elaborate legal procedures, including the requirements of the Bill of Rights. But in a foreign war, the situation was much different. There, the commander in chief was entitled to take any action required by military circumstances, without the need for specific legislative authorization and without regard to the normal legal rights of the inhabitants under domestic law. We might think of one regime as governing a typical federal law enforcement effort such as an FBI raid, the other regime as governing the army after D-Day in Europe. Normally, we deal with the inconsistency of these legal regimes through geographic and demographic separation: one regime applies abroad, the other on American soil; one regime applies to foreigners, the other to American citizens. In a civil war, however, these distinctions threatened to evaporate.

In the secession crisis, Lincoln insisted that the rule of law, rather than negotiation or unilateral action, governed even fundamental disputes about national policy. But after secession, as we will see, the exigencies of war put the rule of law under increasing stress.

CHAPTER 6 *Presidential Power*

Unlike Buchanan, Lincoln did not believe the federal government was powerless to resist secession. But a further question remained: who in the government was authorized to act? Arguably, only Congress could make the critical policy decisions required by the crisis. Or, if the president had any authority to act before Congress reconvened, perhaps that authority could only derive from some earlier congressional mandate.

Lincoln, as we will see, did take decisive action. Apart from calling up the militia, most of his acts were not explicitly authorized by any specific statute. Indeed, a few of his actions were apparently contrary to express statutory language or appeared to violate explicit constitutional commands. Yet charges of a presidential dictatorship were overblown. Lincoln remained very much a democratic leader throughout the war. But he was a democratic leader who often operated without explicit legal sanction. Part of our notion of the rule of law is that officials are guided by legal standards, not merely by their own judgment. Thus, even apart from their impact on specific individual rights, Lincoln's actions challenged the usual concept of legality.[1]

Was Lincoln acting above—or outside—the law? Lincoln claimed to find a constitutional basis for his wartime actions in his role as chief executive. This chapter will focus on whether Lincoln usurped congressional power in playing this independent role. But separation of powers was far from the only constitutional issue raised by Lincoln's actions. He also claimed that his powers, under the laws of war, allowed him to negate such individual rights as habeas corpus, jury trial, free speech, and private property. The next chapter will consider that aspect of Lincoln's conduct. Finally, Lincoln seemingly claimed the power to ignore at least some judicial rulings, and even the right to violate statutes or the Constitution when necessary. This stark challenge to the normal operation of the rule of law is the subject of the final chapter.

In assessing the legitimacy of Lincoln's actions, we will look backward toward the framing of the Constitution and forward toward the present. As it turns out, the Framers had only a rough notion of the scope of executive power, leaving it to the future to fill in the outlines. By Lincoln's time, only limited progress had been made in mapping the perimeters of presidential power, partly because many of his predecessors had been so timid in exercising their authority. If we want to know whether Lincoln exceeded the acceptable bounds of executive power in our constitutional scheme, we must consider not only the views of his own time but the verdict of history. Our purpose is not just the legal historian's, which is to understand Lincoln in the legal context of his own time. In addition, we will try to understand how his actions fit within our understanding today of American democracy.

LINCOLN AND PRESIDENTIAL POWER

Although the secession crisis was described in the first chapter, a brief reprise is helpful just to see how much Lincoln did on the basis of uncertain legal authority. On April 4, 1861, Lincoln approved the expedition to Fort Sumter. Unless attacked, the task force was only supposed to carry supplies to the fort. If the supply boats were attacked, however, the ships would return fire and attempt to land additional troops at Sumter. Thus, Lincoln sent troops into a possible combat situation without prior congressional approval. On April 6, he sent a messenger to inform the South Carolina governor that an "attempt will be made to supply Fort-Sumter with provisions only; and that, if such attempt be not resisted, no effort to throw in men, arms, or ammunition, will be made, without further notice," unless the fort was attacked. Apart from outright surrender, this was the least confrontational course open to Lincoln, but he could not have been surprised at the violent Southern reaction. After consulting with his cabinet, Jefferson Davis ordered the fort's capture before the relief expedition arrived. Major Anderson surrendered after a day and a half of heavy bombardment on April 14.[2]

Northerners reacted with fury. Stephen A. Douglas joined the popular outcry: "Every man must be for the United States or against it. There can be no neutrals in this war, *only patriots—or traitors.*" While the popular mood was strong, the position of the government was not. Most of the sixteen-thousand-man army was busy guarding the frontier. The army lacked even accurate maps of the South, and the available arms consisted mostly of muskets rather than rifles. Fewer than a dozen warships were available for immediate use in coastal waters.[3]

Nevertheless, Lincoln took prompt steps to rally the nation. On April 15, the day after the flag was lowered at Sumter, Lincoln issued a proclamation calling out the militia. According to the proclamation, "[T]he laws of the United States have been for some time past, and now are opposed, and the execution thereof obstructed" in the seceding states "by combinations too powerful to be suppressed by the ordinary course of judicial proceedings, or by the powers vested in the Marshals by law." Calling for seventy-five thousand troops, Lincoln said that his first step "will probably be to re-possess the forts, places, and property which have been seized from the Union." On April 19, he proclaimed a blockade of Southern ports; two days earlier, Jefferson Davis had invited privateers to attack American shipping. In addition to these measures, Lincoln convened Congress into session on the Fourth of July, a date that was undoubtedly not chosen by accident. Apart from its symbolic implications, delaying the special session until July also had a practical significance. By statute, the militia would remain active until thirty days after Congress convened. Convening Congress earlier would have interfered with effective mobilization. Of course, this also gave Lincoln more time to control war policy before Congress could intervene.[4]

The intervening weeks were not spent idly. The proclamation was applauded throughout the North, with the main criticism being that Lincoln had not called for enough men. But the reaction in the upper South was different. Virginia, Tennessee, North Carolina, and Arkansas promptly seceded in defense of their Southern brethren. Kentucky, Missouri, and Delaware declined to send troops, but the reaction in Maryland was more critical because it controlled access to the capital. On April 19, a regiment from Massachusetts was attacked by an angry Baltimore mob. Four soldiers and a dozen civilians died, and thirty-one were wounded. The railroad bridges and telegraph lines connecting Baltimore to the North were cut. Believing that Washington itself was in jeopardy, General Winfield Scott made a contingency plan to post troops in Lafayette Square and use the Treasury building as a fortress, hiding the president and cabinet in the basement. Lincoln then suspended habeas corpus on the route between Washington and Philadelphia.[5]

Lincoln took other bold actions. He expanded the regular army by ten regiments and ordered the enlistment of eighteen thousand additional sailors. According to his proclamation, "The call for volunteers hereby made, and the direction for the increase of the regular army, and for the enlistment of seamen hereby given, together with the plan of organization adopted for the volunteer and for the regular forces hereby authorized, will be submitted to Congress as soon as assembled." (Oddly enough, this proclamation was the brainchild of Treasury secretary Chase, not Cameron from the War Department.) Lincoln also directed the Navy to purchase and arm fifteen steamboats. He closed the mails to disloyal publications. Finally, he authorized the Treasury to advance two million dollars to a New York group (John Dix, George Opdyke, and Richard Blatchford), who were instructed to make such payments "as should be directly consequent upon the military and naval measures necessary for the defence and support of the government." Lincoln bypassed normal government channels and used private citizens for these payments because he feared that much of the bureaucracy was disloyal, Washington being much more of a Southern town than it is today.[6]

When Congress convened, Lincoln presented an elaborate defense of his actions in a special July 4 message. He began with a defense of his attempt to resupply Sumter. He claimed that the attack on Sumter "was, in no sense, a matter of self defence on the part of the assailants," who knew that the Fort could not possibly attack them. The attackers "knew—they were expressly notified—that the giving of bread to the few brave and hungry men of the garrison, was all which would on that occasion be attempted." They attacked Sumter, then, not in self-defense but "to drive out the visible authority of the Federal Union, and thus force it to immediate dissolution."[7]

In response to the attack, Lincoln recounted, he had called up the militia and closed Southern ports. "So far," he said, "all was believed to be strictly legal." Other steps, such as calling for volunteers to serve three years and expanding the regular military, were admittedly more dubious. "These measures, whether strictly legal or not, were ventured upon, under what appeared to be a popular demand, and a public necessity; trusting, then as now, that Congress would readily ratify them." "It is believed," he continued, "that nothing has been done beyond the constitutional competency of Congress."[8]

This vigorous use of executive power was something of a shock. With few exceptions, the presidents between Jackson and Lincoln had been weak and ineffective. The customary scope of presidential activity is indicated by the fact that Congress did not appropriate any funds for White

House staff until 1857. It was not until Grant's administration that the size of the White House staff reached six. Other parts of the executive branch were equally understaffed. The attorney general did not become a full-time government employee until 1855. Nor had most recent presidents taken leadership in making policy. As a leading historian of the presidency says, with the exception of Lincoln, "the nineteenth-century presidents continued to be little more than chief clerks of personnel."[9]

Lincoln's use of executive power was particularly noteworthy because of his past views about the presidency. Lincoln's roots were in the Whig party, which had formed largely in opposition to Jackson's aggressive use of presidential power. The Whigs viewed strong executives like "King Andrew the First" as a threat to democracy. When Jackson withdrew the government's deposits from the Bank of the United States, Whigs denounced him as a tyrant. Lincoln himself had endorsed such views more than once.[10]

Oddly, the most vehement critic of Lincoln's use of executive power was that old Jacksonian, Chief Justice Taney. In his *Merryman* opinion, besides discussing the specific issue of habeas suspension, he minimized the general extent of executive power. According to Taney, the short term of office and "narrow limits to which his power is confined" demonstrate the Framers' "jealousy and apprehension" about the presidency. So too, did the care with which they withheld many of the powers of the English monarch that were considered dangerous to liberty. Taney painted a portrait of a relatively weak chief executive. For example, he pointed out, the president is commander in chief, but the two-year limit on military appropriations ensures that the House can disband the army "if, in their judgment, the president used, or designed to use it for improper purposes." Similarly, the states appoint the militia's officers "as a security against the use of the military power for purposes dangerous to the liberties of the people, or the rights of the states." In terms of the "life, liberty, or property" of ordinary citizens, the only presidential power is to "take care that the laws shall be faithfully executed." But, said Taney, the president "is not authorized to execute them himself, or through agents or officers, civil or military, appointed by himself." Rather, it is merely the president's duty "to come in aid of the judicial authority, if it shall be resisted by a force too strong to overcome without the assistance of the executive arm; but in exercising this power he acts in subordination to judicial authority, assisting it to execute its process and enforce its judgments."[11]

Taney's cramped view of presidential power was extreme, but even on the modern Supreme Court, not everyone has taken as elastic a view of executive power as Lincoln did. A notable example of the more formalistic view is Justice Black's opinion for the Court in the *Steel Seizure Case*. Faced with a possible steel strike that might disrupt essential production for the Korean War, President Truman had assumed federal control over the steel mills. Justice Black argued that the president's power must be based either on statute—an express authorization or a statute "from which such a power can fairly be implied"—or else directly from the Constitution. Finding no source of statutory authorization, Justice Black turned to the president's authority under Article II. The seizure could not, he argued, be defended "as an exercise of the president's military power as Commander in Chief." The government had cited cases "upholding broad powers in military commanders engaged in day-to-day fighting in a theater of war." Those cases "need not concern us here," for they could not encompass the power "to take possession of private property in order to keep labor disputes from stopping production." That "is a job for the Nation's lawmakers, not for its military authorities." Nor could the seizure be sustained under the provisions that grant executive power to the president. "In the framework of our Constitution, the President's power to see that the laws are faithfully executed refutes the idea that he is to be a lawmaker." To fall within the executive power, apparently, the seizure order would have had to "direct that a congressional policy be executed in a manner prescribed by Congress." In short, Black said, the Founders "entrusted the law making power to the Congress alone in both good and bad times."[12]

Justice Black's opinion seemingly would have left little room for many of Lincoln's early decisions. Apart from calling up the militia, very little of what Lincoln did can be characterized as directing "that a congressional policy be executed in a manner prescribed by Congress." Rather, key actions were akin to lawmaking—banning the use of Southern ports without any statutory authority, appropriating funds without any legislative authorization, temporarily abolishing the legal writ of habeas corpus, and so forth. At least some of these actions were clearly within fields of express congressional authority, such as the power to raise armies. Even the Emancipation Proclamation, which we will discuss in the next chapter, would seem to be unconstitutional under Justice Black's view (at least unless the entire South was considered to be the theater of war). But Black's *Steel Seizure* opinion is not the final word on executive power; it was not necessarily even the final word on that case itself. To assess the legality of Lincoln's action, we need to take a closer look at the bases of presidential power.

THE ARTICLE II PUZZLE

The starting point in evaluating Lincoln's actions must be the language of Article II of the Constitution, which establishes the presidency. Article II opens with the statement: "The executive Power shall be vested in a President of the United States of America." After this "vesting" clause, almost half of Article II is dedicated to describing the election procedure, qualifications for office, salary arrangements, and the like. The first section of Article II then closes with the oath clause, requiring the president to swear that he will "faithfully execute the Office of President of the United States, and will to the best of [his] Ability, preserve, protect and defend the Constitution of the United States." The next two sections are about half as long, combined, as section 1. They list some specific presidential duties. For present purposes, two of these duties are crucial. First, the president is "Commander in Chief of the Army and Navy of the United States, and of the Militia of the several States, when called into the actual Service of the United States." Second, the president "shall take Care that the Laws be faithfully executed." Article II also contains a hodgepodge of less relevant powers of varying degrees of significance—to make treaties and appoint key officials with Senate consent, to issue pardons, to give the State of the Union Address, to receive ambassadors, and to demand the opinions of cabinet officers in writing. Article II closes on a stern note with a section establishing the procedures for impeaching the president and all other civil officers.[13]

The language of Article II does not convey any clear impression about the stature of the office. On the one hand, the office is vested with "the executive power," which sounds weighty, not to mention the power to command the armed forces. On the other hand, one might question whether the president was such a momentous figure after all, since the drafters thought it necessary to include express sanction for him even to get written opinions from the cabinet or to recommend legislation to Congress.

The Framers might have devoted more care to explaining the powers of the office if they had not had to devote so much time to more basic questions about its structure. The Virginia Plan, which provided the basic framework for discussion at the Constitutional Convention, called for a national executive but left unspecified the term of office or even the number of individuals who would compose the executive. The delegates then spent most of the summer going around in circles, as they debated whether the president would be elected by Congress or otherwise, whether there would be one chief executive or several, and other basic attributes of the office. As of the end of July, they had decided on election by Congress and ineligibility for reelection, and they assigned the president almost all the powers that would ultimately be found in Article II, except the treaty and appointment powers. In late August, when they took up the subject again, the confusion continued. On August 31, they threw up their hands and referred the matter to a special Committee of Eleven, which reported back on September 4 with the essentials of the current Article II.[14]

One source of the Framers' difficulty was the shortage of good models. The English colonial governors had been widely reviled. In reaction, the post-Revolution state constitutions truncated executive power. Most state executives were chosen by the legislature; only New York originally provided for a popularly elected executive. Terms of office were as short as one year, and governors shared their authority in many states with a council. Executives were given few specific powers, and even these were often subject to legislative interference or oversight. Just to be on the safe side, Virginia warned its governor that he should not, "under any pretence, exercise any power or prerogative, by virtue of any law, statute or custom of England." In contrast, New York's popularly elected governor had a three-year term and turned out to be a more powerful figure. The New York constitution directed him "to transact all necessary business with the officers of government, civil and military; to take care that the laws are faithfully executed, to the best of his ability; and to expedite all such measures as may be resolved upon by the legislature." He was also commander in chief of the militia. The later state constitutions, like Massachusetts in 1780 and New Hampshire in 1784, moved in the direction of the New York model. No clear understanding apparently existed about the scope of executive power. As Madison said, the boundaries of executive, legislative, and judicial power, though clear in theory, "consist in many instances of mere shades of difference." Little wonder that one historian remarked about early conceptions of executive power, "What strikes anyone who examines the era in any depth, especially those historians who have devoted years to the exercise, is its complexity, contradictions, and, at times, confusion."[15]

Whatever else may be said about the meaning of Article II, it has not suffered from a lack of vigorous debate. The relatively sparse language of

Article II has been scrutinized with microscopic care. One key question has been the significance of the clause vesting the executive power in the president. Is this vesting clause merely descriptive, or is it an independent source of presidential authority—and if so, of how much?

Strictly speaking, there are three logically independent issues here. First, is the vesting clause merely a description of the office of the presidency, or is it an actual grant of power? Second, if it is a grant of power, can Congress subdivide this power and transfer portions of it to officials independent of the president? Third, is this a broad grant of power, which places many presidential actions outside the realm of congressional control? Although these questions are independent in theory, in practice today the answers all seem to go together. Advocates of the "unitary executive" believe that the vesting clause is a source of power (indeed, the primary source of presidential power), that independent administrative agencies and special prosecutors are unconstitutional efforts to remove parts of that power from the president, and that the president has sweeping authority independent of Congress.

Advocates of broad presidential power argue that the vesting clause is the key to Article II. Like the clause vesting the judicial power in the federal courts, they contend, it infuses the relevant officials with general powers. In contrast, the similar clause in Article I merely vests Congress with "[a]ll legislative Powers herein granted," leaving the actual granting of the powers until later sections. With so much emphasis placed on the introductory vesting clause, the question obviously arises of what to make of the rest of Article II. If the president's primary source of power is the vesting clause, what function is left for sections 2 and 3? Advocates of the unitary executive have offered several responses. To the extent sections 2 and 3 are not merely redundant reminders of some specific executive powers, they argue, the more specific clauses merely "help to limit and give content to the otherwise potentially vast grant of power that the Vesting Clause of Article II confers on the President." Apart from the vesting clause, according to advocates of the "unitary" executive, what appear to be grants of power are actually limitations—the treaty clause, for example, limits the president's power to make treaties by requiring him to get Senate approval. In short, its more enthusiastic advocates conclude, "the textual case" for their theory "is as free of ambiguity as the textual case that the President must be at least thirty-five years old."[16]

Their argument has not gone unchallenged. Critics retort that there was no well-understood bundle of executive powers that could simply be conveyed by the vesting clause. They also insist that the subtle differences of phrasing between the vesting clauses for the various branches simply escaped any notice at the time. What the term "executive power" actually meant was unclear. What the evidence does not allow, says one critic, "is an assertion that the cryptic phrase 'executive power' refers to a clear, eighteenth-century baseline that just happens to dovetail with the modern formalist conception of that same term." Other critics of the unitary executive theory rely on other subtle differences in constitutional language. The appointments clause allows certain officers to be selected by the "Heads of Departments," while the opinions clause speaks of the "principal Officer" of "each of the executive Departments." Does this suggest that some "departments" have heads, but are not "executive Departments" with "principal Officers"? If so, perhaps the government has officers who are not "executive" and therefore not part of the "executive power" or subject to presidential control. In turn, advocates of the unitary executive argue that this difference in terminology (unlike the different phrasing of the various vesting clauses) is entirely meaningless.[17]

This minute dissection of the constitutional text makes little sense. The main argument for reliance on the original understanding is based on popular consent: We the People gave life to the Constitution through ratification, and therefore its meaning must correspond to the understanding of a reasonable person of the time. Whether this is actually a sufficient argument for some form of originalism, it does suggest some limits on textual analysis. There is a limit to the amount of weight that can be placed on the idea of the reasonable reader. Is the reasonable reader supposed to be someone with microscopic powers of linguistic analysis, a complete knowledge of English and American legal history, and an unlimited amount of time to ponder the logical implications of subtle structural features? If so, perhaps this so-called reasonable reader would have finally settled on the unitarian interpretation (or on its opposite). But such a "reasonable reader" never existed and had no connection with the limited human abilities of the people who in fact had to vote on the Constitution.

If the legitimacy of the Constitution rests on the consent of real human beings rather than imagined ideal interpreters, its meaning ought to be tied to what they had some reasonable chance of understanding, not to the possible deductions of some entirely hypothetical reader with unlimited expertise, time, and intelligence. And if we ask what an intelligent eighteenth-century reader, who made a reasonable effort to understand the text, would actually have understood about Article II, the answer can only be that such a reader would have been unsure about the exact parameters of executive authority. To bind the ratifiers to esoteric deductions made long after the fact would make the Constitution an exercise in bait-and-switch, not in the consent of the governed.

As Justice Robert Jackson said in a famous opinion on presidential power, "Just what our forefathers did envision, or would have envisioned had they foreseen modern conditions, must be divined from materials almost as enigmatic as the dreams Joseph was called upon to interpret for Pharaoh." He added that a "century and a half"—now two centuries—"of partisan debate and scholarly speculation yields no net result but only supplies more or less apt quotations from respected sources on each side of any question." It is an exaggeration to say that the historical records teach us nothing, but they clearly fail to provide precise guidance about the boundaries of presidential power. Thus, the most accurate originalist answer is that the original understanding of the text was ambiguous. For the nonoriginalist, of course, there is even less reason to obsess over eighteenth-century linguistics in an effort to decode Article II.[18]

This is not to say that presidential power was a complete cipher. The specific grants of power to the president, as well as related grants of power to Congress in military and foreign affairs, give some guidance. The Framers built on a history of disputes about executive power. We know that they considered the post-Revolutionary governors too weak. We also know that they considered the pre-Revolutionary governors and the English monarch too strong. Like Goldilocks, they wanted something that was not too strong and not too weak, but "just right." They wanted as much executive energy and initiative as possible without upsetting the proper balance of republican government. But these principles were too general to resolve hard cases. Thus, when specific questions about executive power arise, text and original understanding can provide only limited guidance.[19]

It is not merely speculation to say that reasonable readers would have found the meaning of Article II to be unclear. We know that, in fact, quite a number of very intelligent, careful readers did find it obscure. No sooner was the Constitution ratified than the very men who had drafted and enacted it found themselves divided and confused about the scope of executive power. In a Congress full of members of the Constitutional

Convention and participants in the ratification debate, no consensus existed even on the basic question of whether the president had the power to fire his subordinates. After considerable debate, Madison seems to have persuaded a majority of his colleagues in the House that the president did have this power—though the sequence of votes and coalitions makes this a little uncertain. Half the senators disagreed. Since Senate approval was required to appoint cabinet members, many senators thought it should also be required for their removal. And even Madison seems to have been confused about the issue: shortly thereafter, he suggested that Congress did have some control over the tenure of certain officials. Later in Washington's administration, Madison and Hamilton battled over whether the president could constitutionally issue a proclamation of neutrality without congressional approval. Hamilton posited broad presidential control over foreign affairs. Madison insisted that the president's function was only to execute congressional decisions and to serve as an organ of communication with foreign governments. As a recent historian remarks, "[L]eading framers thought about the executive in notably divergent ways." It was "precisely because their views diverged so sharply that disagreements over the power of the presidency emerged as a potent source of constitutional controversy in the 1790s."[20]

Even earlier, Madison had commented on the difficulty of defining the separate powers of the three branches. In Federalist 37, he said that "[e]xperience has instructed us that no skill in the science of government has yet been able to discriminate and define, with sufficient certainty, its three great provinces—the legislative, executive, and judiciary; or even the privileges and powers of the different legislative branches." He observed that questions arise on a daily basis "which prove the obscurity which reigns in these subjects, and which puzzle the greatest adepts in political science." After all, he said, "When the Almighty himself condescends to address mankind in their own language, his meaning, luminous as it must be, is rendered dim and doubtful by the cloudy medium through which it is communicated." He sagely added that "[a]ll new laws, though penned with the greatest technical skill and passed on the fullest and most mature deliberation, are considered as more or less obscure and equivocal, until their meaning be liquidated and ascertained by a series of particular discussions and adjudications." In the remainder of this chapter, we will examine how the "more or less obscure and equivocal" language of Article II has been "liquidated and ascertained" over the years.[21]

THEORIES OF CRISIS AUTHORITY

Whatever may be said about the legalities, the reality is that presidents generally have not hesitated to do whatever, in their view, needed to be done. From the first days of the Republic, presidents have not waited for statutory authority to take necessary actions, either domestic or international. Washington, D.C., itself stands as a physical memorial to this presidential willingness to take independent action. The site chosen by Washington was outside the area designated by Congress, and he had to obtain after-the-fact legislation to protect himself from legal liability. More significantly, he acted without congressional authorization when he proclaimed American neutrality between France and England. Similarly, Jefferson refused to spend money that Congress had voted for fifteen gunboats that he considered no longer necessary. Without approval by Congress, he decided to protect American shipping in the Mediterranean by dispatching a squadron that promptly attacked and nearly destroyed an enemy vessel.[22]

Today, as one constitutional scholar has said, "Most Americans expect modern Presidents to provide solutions for every significant political, military, social, and economic problem. In the face of such demands, various organizational and legal categories possess little meaning for the President." But that does not mean that the "expansive and perhaps ill-formed views of 'inherent' presidential power" have been unquestioningly accepted. Instead, the proper scope of presidential power remains vigorously debated by Congress and the president, as well as scholars and the public.[23]

As we have seen, the text and history of Article II fail to offer decisive guidance regarding presidential power (even for those inclined to take it). The result has been a long debate through the course of our history about presidential authority during a crisis. At one extreme, Woodrow Wilson wrote (as a professor, not as president) that the Framers "seem to have thought of the President as what the stricter Whig theorists wished the king to be: only the legal executive, the presiding and guiding authority in the application of law and the execution of policy." At the other extreme, Richard Nixon claimed that the president had unlimited power to take actions on grounds of national security or a "threat to internal peace and order of significant magnitude." Although perhaps an unfortunate spokesman for this view, he did not speak merely for himself. In surveying these debates, scholars have distinguished five main arguments for inherent executive authority. Each has both appealing features and significant shortcomings.[24]

The first argument for extensive crisis authority posits the existence of extraconstitutional powers, vested in the president not by the Constitution but by the very nature of his position as chief executive of a nation. If there are essential powers that go with nationhood and cannot be effectively exercised by other organs of government, then the mere act of creating a nation might be thought to convey these powers, without the need for any specific constitutional language. Locke is often cited as support for this doctrine because he argued that the executive had inherent power to take steps to preserve society. This approach seems to be in tension with the whole idea of a written Constitution, at least as applied to domestic matters rather than foreign policy. It also begs the question of just what specific executive prerogatives are inherent in the nature of things. Yet when the nation is faced with disaster, the public often does expect the president to take decisive action, with or without specific legal authority.[25]

A second argument, akin to the unitary executive theories discussed above, suggests that the source of emergency power is to be found in the vesting clause of Article II. In this view, the president may take whatever action is required under the circumstances, so long as it is not solely within the jurisdiction of another branch or prohibited by the Constitution. We have already explored the arguments for and against reading the vesting clause as an independent grant of power to the president. Even if it is read as such a source of power, the language of the clause gives us little guidance about just which powers it provides the president. Positing inherent executive power is one thing; mapping its boundaries is another.

The other arguments rely on Article II's more specific provisions regarding the presidency. The third argument stresses the oath clause as investing the president with authority to protect and defend the Constitution. The oath clause does seem to place the president in a special position of responsibility regarding the Constitution. No other official is required to swear that he or she "will to the best of my Ability, preserve, protect and defend the Constitution of the United States." But this language does not purport to grant any additional powers. Rather, it is an injunction to use whatever powers the president does have as needed to achieve certain ends. The "take care" clause, the focus of the fourth argument, has similar problems. It is phrased as a duty rather than a grant of power, and requires the president to act only to the best of his abilities, which presumably means acting within the confines of the law. The "take care" clause presumably does give the president some discretion in implementing the laws. But it arguably undermines inherent executive power by stressing the president's subordinate role with respect to the lawgivers. A final approach relies on the commander-in-chief clause, which is undoubtedly a source of some independent power, but clearly cannot convey the right to use troops whenever and for whatever purpose the president chooses.

In the end, the concept of inherent executive power—whether extraconstitutional or via the vesting clause or the oath clause—is largely irrelevant to the question of what specific presidential actions are legally authorized. If the president *does* have inherent power, we are still left with the very difficult task of determining its scope. Presumably, we must understand that scope within the overall constitutional scheme of democratic government. If the president does *not* have inherent powers, Article II still clearly gives him primary responsibility for seeing that the laws are executed and some degree of control over the use of force. The vesting clause, the oath clause, and the "take care" clause all suggest that the specific grants of power should be given a generous reading. Thus, although the question of inherent power seems important in theory, it may have little real concrete significance for disputes over presidential authority.

Champions and opponents of inherent executive power have more in common than they suspect. One approach begins with an indefinite expanse of executive power and contracts it in order to preserve the overall constitutional scheme. The other begins with narrower executive powers and expands them to meet the needs of the nation. Most likely, both end up in about the same place, coming from opposing directions. Thus, however we read the specific clauses, we are left with the problem of accommodating the need for an energetic executive and the need to maintain balanced democratic government.

We have not yet found a magical formula for drawing a precise line between bold, energetic leadership and incipient autocracy. Nor has the Supreme Court attempted to provide such a formula. Instead, in line with Madison's advice of looking to experience in order to "liquidate and ascertain" constitutional meaning, the Court has proceeded cautiously and with great attention to the history of previous presidential actions and of Congress's responses. This approach is most clearly articulated in two modern opinions.

The first opinion was issued in the *Steel Seizure Case*. I have already mentioned the relatively formalist approach taken by Justice Black in his majority opinion. But the more influential opinion has turned out to be Justice Jackson's concurrence, with its judicious analysis of executive power. Jackson began with the observation that a "judge, like an executive adviser, may be surprised at the poverty of really useful and unambiguous authority applicable to concrete problems of executive power as they actually present themselves." In disputes over the separation of powers, he said, courts cannot look merely to "isolated clauses or even single Articles torn from context." For just as it diffuses power "the better to secure liberty," the Constitution also "contemplates that practice will integrate the dispersed powers into a workable government." Consequently, presidential powers "are not fixed but fluctuate, depending upon their disjunction or conjunction with those of Congress."[26]

Jackson proposed a three-part taxonomy of presidential actions. In the first category are presidential acts "pursuant to an express or implied authorization of Congress." Here, the president's power "is at its maximum, for it includes all that he possess in his own right plus all that Congress can delegate." Hence, such a presidential act "would be supported by the strongest of presumptions and the widest latitude of judicial interpretation, and the burden of persuasion would rest heavily upon any who might attack it." In the second category, where Congress is silent, the president "can only rely upon his own independent powers, but there is a zone of twilight in which he and Congress may have concurrent authority, or in which its distribution is uncertain." Thus, congressional inertia or acquiescence "may sometimes, at least as a practical matter, enable, if not invite, measures on independent presidential responsibility." In the third category—including the *Steel Seizure Case* in Jackson's view—the president flouts congressional directives. Any "claim to a power at once so conclusive and preclusive [of congressional action] must be scrutinized with caution, for what is at stake is the equilibrium established by our constitutional system."[27]

With respect to the third category, Justice Jackson rejected broad claims of presidential power. In his view, the president enjoys only delegated powers, though these should be given "the scope and elasticity" required by practical needs "instead of the rigidity dictated by a doctrinaire textualism." Nor did Justice Jackson accept the government's assertion that the vesting clause "constitutes a grant of all the executive powers of which the Government is capable." "If that be true," he tartly observed, "it is difficult to see why the forefathers bothered to add several specific items, including some trifling ones." George III was hardly likely to be the model for such a sweeping vision of executive power. And "if we seek instruction from our own times, we can match it only from the executive powers in those governments we disparagingly describe as totalitarian." Nor did Justice Jackson accept the government's sweeping interpretation of the commander-in-chief clause. Being commander in chief of the army and navy did not mean also being "commander in chief of the country, its industries and its inhabitants." As to the "take care" clause, it had to be viewed in conjunction with the Fifth Amendment's guarantee of due process: "One gives a governmental authority that reaches so far as there is law, the other gives a private right that authority shall go no farther. These signify about all there is of the principle that ours is a government of laws, not of men, and that we submit ourselves to rulers only if under rules."[28]

Jackson's was only a concurring opinion, but it became the basis for the opinion of the full Court three decades later in *Dames & Moore v. Regan*.[29] *Dames & Moore*—which was written by Jackson's former law clerk, William Rehnquist—involved the aftermath of the Iranian hostage crisis. Negotiations between the United States and the Iranians to secure the release of the hostages resulted in an agreement to terminate all litigation in American courts against Iran and transfer the cases to a special Iran–United States Claims Tribunal. According to Rehnquist, the case exemplified the "never-ending tension between the President exercising the executive authority in a world that presents each day some new challenge" and a Constitution "which no one disputes embodies some sort of system of checks and balances." He agreed, however, that Jackson's concurrence "brings together as much combination of analysis and common sense as there is in this area."[30]

Rehnquist began his legal analysis with a recital of Jackson's three-part test. He added an admonition that although the test is "analytically useful," such categories were necessarily somewhat artificial. Rehnquist found that some other aspects of the president's actions fell within the first category of actions authorized by Congress. The president's suspension of all claims against Iran in American courts, however, lacked such statutory authorization. Nevertheless, the fact that Congress had authorized some presidential action invited "measures on independent presidential responsibility" (quoting Jackson), at least absent any "contrary indication of legislative intent." Rehnquist also stressed the significance of a "history of congressional acquiescence in conduct of the sort engaged in by the President." He argued that such a past practice of congressional acceptance did exist regarding presidential handling of citizens' claims against foreign sovereigns. Furthermore, he emphasized, Congress had expressed nothing but approval of the president's resolution of the hostage crisis. "We are thus clearly not confronted with a situation in which Congress has in some way resisted the exercise of Presidential authority."[31]

Thus, the Court's approach to issues of presidential power has been sensitive to context, particularly to the multiple possible relationships between an executive act and past or present congressional action. It has also recognized the tension between practical needs for executive initiative and the system of checks and balances, seeking to deal with those tensions on a case-by-case basis. Jackson's three-part test provides a framework for this flexible analysis of presidential power. Although this framework was articulated much later, it provides the most useful available method for analyzing executive power, even for earlier executive actions. With this framework in mind, we are finally in a position to assess the legality of Lincoln's actions.

LINCOLN'S USE OF FORCE TO EXECUTE THE LAWS

For the moment, we can put aside two difficult questions: the legality of the blockade (dealt with in the next section) and the suspension of habeas (discussed in the next chapter). That leaves us with a laundry list of actions whereby Lincoln used force to execute the laws, protect federal property and personnel, and put down the rebellion. Lincoln had of course ordered Major Anderson to defend his position if attacked and had sent armed ships to resupply him. He called up the militia, the action that provoked secession in the upper South. Similarly, he expanded the army and navy, both in manpower and supplies. Finally, he authorized disbursement of funds through private parties in aid of these activities. Along the lines of Justice Jackson's analysis, we can divide these activities into three categories.

The first, and easiest category to defend, includes presidential actions authorized by Congress. In this category falls perhaps the most important of Lincoln's actions, the call for seventy-five thousand militiamen. Here, Lincoln was acting on the basis of statutes dating back to the early years of the Republic. His actions were constitutional if the federal government, taken as a whole, had the power to use the militia to suppress the rebellion. Despite Buchanan's misgivings, we saw in the previous chapter that no real doubt exists about this federal power. Indeed, even Chief Justice Taney had previously endorsed the inherent right of every government to "use its military power to put down an armed insurrection, too strong to be controlled by the civil authority." This power, he had remarked, "is essential to the existence of every government" and "essential to the preservation of order and free institutions."[32]

The second category consists of the "twilight zone," where Congress has not spoken and the president claims some independent authority. Lincoln's actions regarding Sumter may have fallen into this category, along with his assignment of troops to defend the capital and other federal property. To what extent does the president have the power, without congressional authorization, to use the forces of the federal government to protect its property, personnel, and operations (including law enforcement)? Does the president have what has sometimes been called the "protective power" to defend the federal government?[33]

The answer seems to be yes, judging from later precedents. A trilogy of cases from around the turn of the last century clearly endorsed aspects of the protective power. These cases are an implicit endorsement, in calmer times, of Lincoln's view of crisis authority.

The earliest of these cases was *Cunningham v. Neagle*.[34] Neagle was a deputy U.S. marshal who had been assigned to protect Justice Field from an individual who had threatened his life. The underlying quarrel was colorful enough to make a good movie script but would be an unnecessary digression here. In any event, after the suspect physically assaulted Justice Field on a train, Neagle killed him in the belief that he was about to draw a gun. Neagle sought federal habeas corpus to avoid trial for murder in state court. No specific statute authorized the use of marshals to protect judges outside of court. Nevertheless the Court upheld his actions in sweeping terms.

Justice Miller's majority opinion emphasized the inherent power of the government to protect itself and execute its laws. He quoted extensively from earlier cases—one of which proclaimed the "incontrovertible principle that the government of the United States may, by means of physical force, exercised through its official agents, execute on every foot of American soil the powers and functions that belong to it, "emphasizing that the United States "must execute its powers, or it is no government." Miller then considered the scope of presidential power. If the president is advised that the U.S. mail ("possibly carrying treasure") is likely to be robbed, "who can doubt the authority of the president to make an order for the protection of the mail, and of the persons and lives of its carriers?" Similarly, with respect to national forests, "Has the president no authority to place guards upon the public territory to protect its timber? No authority to seize the timber when cut and found upon the ground? Has he no power to take any measures to protect this vast domain?" Here, Miller cited precedents under the public lands laws in favor of broad presidential authority. "We cannot doubt," Justice Miller concluded, "the power of the president to take measures for the protection of a judge of one of the courts of the United States who, while in the discharge of the duties of his office, is threatened with a personal attack which may probably result in his death."[35]

Five years later, the Court reemphasized the protective power of the president in a case with much broader national significance. *In re Debs*[36] arose out of a nationwide rail strike sparked by a labor dispute with the Pullman Company. The strikers had allegedly destroyed railroad switches and signals, ruined track and derailed trains, and assaulted switchmen. The United States sued in federal court for an injunction against the strike, on the ground that the strikers had conspired to destroy interstate commerce and thereby (among other things) prevent the delivery of the U.S. mail. Although the lower court had relied on a federal statute as the basis for the injunction, the Supreme Court held that no statutory basis was required.

The Court held not only that the injunction was proper, but that it would have been equally proper for the government simply to halt the strike by force, in aid of various federal statutes regulating commerce and establishing the mail service. The government did not have to rely on the criminal law to control the strikers. The use of an injunction or direct force, rather than the criminal law, might be a practical necessity. After all, the Court said, if a large number of inhabitants of a state combined to block commerce or halt the mails, criminal trials of the perpetrators might be useless because of resistance by local juries. If the federal government could rely only on the criminal laws, "the whole interests of the nation in these respects would be at the absolute mercy of a portion of the inhabitants of that single state." Fortunately, the Court said, "there is no such impotency in the national government." Rather, the "entire strength of the nation may be used to enforce in any part of the land the full and free exercise of all national powers and the security of all rights intrusted by the constitution to its care." Thus, "If the emergency arises, the army of the nation, and all its militia, are at the service of the nation, to compel obedience to its laws." From the right of the president to use force, his right to take the more moderate route of seeking an injunction followed naturally.[37]

The final case in the trilogy may have gone even farther in endorsing executive power, because the presidential action seemed inconsistent with statutory language. *Midwest Oil* involved the rapid exhaustion of California oil fields owned by the government. Under the public lands statutes (which were a relic of the gold rush period), these lands could be claimed and "patented" by private parties. The process was proceeding so rapidly that within a few months, the oil might all be in private hands, and the navy might have to buy back the oil that the government had just given away. President Taft issued an emergency order to preserve the oil. "In aid of proposed legislation," the lands in questions were "hereby temporarily withdrawn" and made unavailable for public use or acquisition. Challenging the executive order, the oil companies argued that "it appears on its face to be a mere attempt to suspend a statute—supposed to be unwise—in order to allow Congress to pass another more in accordance with what the Executive thought to be in the public interest." In upholding the withdrawal order, the Court relied on the "long-continued practice" of such presidential orders. Despite the apparently clear statutory language, there had been a long series of earlier presidential withdrawal orders of various kinds (none of them exactly like this one). That was enough support for the president's action. The counterargument, as the Court said, was "that while these facts and rulings prove a usage, they do not establish its validity." But, the Court said, "government is a practical affair, intended for practical men." Officials, legislators, and citizens "naturally adjust themselves to any long-continued action of the Executive Department, on the presumption that unauthorized acts would not have been allowed to be so often repeated as to crystallize into a regular practice."[38]

Taken together, these three cases seem to provide ample endorsement for Lincoln's efforts to protect federal property (including both Sumter and the District of Columbia) and personnel (including troops). The cases may, indeed, go farther in supporting the idea of presidential emergency power, but at least they seem to stand for this much, and this rationale has not been questioned by the modern Supreme Court. Of course, these cases came decades after Lincoln's actions. But they are nonetheless significant. They show that presidential power to defend the government's operations from direct threats has stood the test of time. Experience thus has shown that the "executive power" can be extended at least this far without threatening democratic government.[39]

We ought to be reluctant to construe the Constitution so as to exclude any implicit power of the president to deal with true emergencies. As Madison said in Federalist 41, the "means of security can only be regulated by the means and the danger of attack." Indeed, he said, "They will, in fact, be ever determined by these rules and by no others," for it is "in vain to oppose constitutional barriers to the impulse of self-preservation." ("[W]orse than in vain," he continued, because it would make unavoidable "usurpations of power, every precedent of which is a germ of unnecessary and multiplied repetitions.") Similarly, in Federalist 23, Hamilton had argued that, once the decision was made to entrust the government with responsibility for the common defense, it ought "to be clothed with all the powers requisite to complete execution of its trust." Since threats to the public safety could be unexpected and unprecedented, "it must be admitted as a necessary consequence that there can be no limitation of that authority which is to provide for the defense and protection of the community in any matter essential to its efficacy—that is, in any matter essential to the *formation, direction,* or *support* of the NATIONAL FORCES."[40]

Although these observations were not directed to the issue of presidential authority, they show that the Framers were well aware of the possibility of unforeseen threats to the nation's security and the difficulty of planning for all contingencies. As the Court has consistently recognized, unlimited presidential power to respond to perceived emergencies regardless of Congress would be too dangerous. Yet, a limited ability to take the initiative without prior statutory authorization is probably unavoidable. Thus, when Lincoln acted to protect the federal government within Jackson's second category—the "twilight zone" in which the president has some authority where Congress has been silent—he was on solid ground.

This brings us to the third category, presidential actions contrary to the expressed will of Congress. Lincoln's unilateral call for volunteers to join the regular military (as opposed to state militias) is not easy to defend constitutionally. Article I gives Congress, not the president, the power to raise armies. That authority, like the power to declare war, was a royal power that the Constitution deliberately gave to the legislature rather than the executive. It is hard to think of a check more important than that the commander in chief of the army lacks the power to decide how large the army should be. Lincoln's unauthorized uses of federal funds are even harder to defend constitutionally. He did not claim that any existing appropriations law could be read to justify his diversion of federal funds into private hands in aid of the war effort. With the possible exception of *Midwest Oil,* where the Court found implicit authorization in a long history of prior congressional acquiescence, the Supreme Court has never upheld a presidential claim to take emergency action in violation of statute. At the very least, any such claim of presidential authority must be scrutinized with great caution. We might be a little more inclined to accept the claim because no rights of private individuals were threatened by these financial decisions and because Congress obviously had not anticipated the problem.

On balance, Lincoln's transfers of federal funds are probably best regarded as unconstitutional. Although not completely unprecedented, they lack the support of substantial prior (or even later) presidential practice, of the kind that was present in *Midwest Oil.* Thus, the general judgment of history is that this power is not required for an effective executive branch. Last—but certainly not least—Lincoln's actions on their face violated explicit constitutional language. Article I, section 9 provides that "No Money shall be drawn from the Treasury, but in Consequence of Appropriations made by Law." There may be times for implying qualifications to seemingly absolute constitutional language, but this is not one of them. By disabling Congress's control of the purse, recognizing a broad presidential power to reappropriate funds would remove a key check on presidential authority, thus upsetting the fundamental balance of power among the branches.[41]

Indeed, Lincoln made no real effort to defend the legality of these actions. Although he argued that calling up the militia and imposing the blockade were "strictly legal," he did not make the same claim in support of his call for additional volunteers and his expansion of the regular army and navy. Rather, these actions were "ventured upon, under what appeared to be a popular demand, and a public necessity; trusting, then as now, that Congress would readily ratify them." Saying nothing about whether they were within the scope of Article II, Lincoln said only that "[i]t is believed that nothing has been done beyond the constitutional competency of Congress."[42]

Thus, while most of the other actions considered in this section survive constitutional scrutiny, Lincoln's diversion of appropriated funds does not. Although not quite as clear a case, the same is probably true of his expansion of the regular military. Given the Framers' fear of standing armies, they hardly would have been likely to authorize the president to expand the military on his own. It is Congress, not the president, which is given the power to "raise and support Armies" and to "provide and maintain a Navy." The constitutional requirement that army appropriations be limited to two years at a time confirms the need for ongoing congressional involvement.

And yet, it is difficult to condemn these actions too harshly. Neither later historians nor Lincoln's contemporaries seem to have questioned the urgent need to expand the military. Moreover, Congress did ultimately endorse these actions. On August 5, it almost unanimously passed a bill declaring that "all the acts, proclamations and orders of the President" taken after Lincoln took office "respecting the army and navy of the United States, and calling out or relating to the militia or volunteers from the States, are hereby approved and in all respects legalized and made valid . . . as if they had been issued and done under the previous express authority and direction of the Congress of the United States." (The only negative votes came from five Democrats.) And, as noted earlier, no private rights were violated along the way. Thus, this is as sympathetic a case as we could ever expect to see for the claim that the president is sometimes justified in violating the law in the name of necessity. We will return to this question in chapter 8, after we have finished examining the constitutionality of Lincoln's other key actions.[43]

GOING TO WAR: THE *Prize Cases*

On April 19, 1861, Lincoln proclaimed a blockade of ports in the Deep South "in pursuance of the laws of the United States, and of the law of Nations." The blockade was to last "until Congress shall have assembled and deliberated on the said unlawful proceedings [of secession], or until the same shall have ceased." (Somewhat inconsistently with the theory of a blockade, which is that a state of war exists, the proclamation also called for treating Confederate privateers and naval officers as pirates rather than combatants. Fortunately, this idea was never actually implemented.) Just over a week later, Lincoln extended the blockade to the seceding states of the upper South. The grounds were that "public property of the United States has been seized, the collection of the revenue obstructed, and duly commissioned officers of the United States while engaged in executing the orders of their superiors have been arrested . . . by persons claiming to act under authorities of the States of Virginia and North Carolina."[44]

Blockades are now something of a historical curiosity, due to changes in technology and methods of warfare. During the nineteenth century, however, they were the subject of an elaborate set of rules under international law. According to these rules, a violation of a blockade had occurred when three elements were present: [1] the presence of blockading ships near enough to the port to control access, [2] the blockade runner's entering or leaving the blockaded port, [3] and notice to the alleged violator. A ship violating the blockade could not only be seized in the act but could be captured at any point during the return voyage. The blockading party also had the right to stop and search neutral vessels at sea to determine whether they had broken the blockade or were carrying contraband or enemy-owned cargo. This was apt to be an unpleasant process. As an authority on international law explained, a "search at sea is exceedingly annoying, not only because it may affect an innocent party, and may cause expensive delays, but also because those who are concerned in it are often insolent and violent."[45]

These rules could be harsh, as shown by the facts of the *Prize Cases,* which involved several ships seized under the blockade of Southern ports.[46] In examining the application of the blockade, the Court stressed that all residents of enemy territory are "enemies" for purposes of prize law, regardless of their personal actions or loyalties. "The produce of the soil of the hostile territory, as well as other property engaged in the commerce of the hostile power, . . . are always regarded as legitimate prize, without regard to the domicil of the owner, and much more so if he reside and trade within their territory." The brig *Amy Warwick* was captured on the high seas. The Court upheld the condemnation of her cargo—about five thousand bags of coffee—because the cargo was owned by residents of Richmond. The British ship *Hiawatha* was in port in Richmond when the blockade was announced, effective in fifteen days. The ship had loaded a cargo of tobacco but was unable to leave port because a stronger steam tug was needed. It finally left port on day 16 and was captured a few days later. The *Brilliante* was a Mexican vessel, owned by the American consul at Campeche. He had had permission from the blockading squadron to go to Mobile to pick up his son, but the crew refused to go there, and the mate steered the ship to New Orleans. The *Brilliante* then took on a cargo of flour and left New Orleans. The Court found this to be a sufficient basis for seizing and selling the ship and its entire cargo.

Under international law, the blockade order had immense significance. It amounted to recognition (if not creation) of a state of war between the

United States and the Confederacy, though not to recognition of the Confederacy as a legitimate state. If the blockade was legal, then Lincoln was not only engaged in a large-scale law enforcement action, he was engaged in a war. And along with this came whatever powers accrue to a military commander in dealing with hostile or contested territory and its inhabitants. Yet few issues have been as contested in American history as the president's authority to take the nation to war without prior congressional authorization. At the time, some observers feared that the Court would hold the blockade illegal, which "would end the war, and how it would leave us with neutral powers, it is fearful to contemplate!"[47]

By a slim five-to-four vote, the Supreme Court upheld Lincoln's action. True, the Court said, "Congress alone has the power to declare a national or foreign war." In contrast, the president "has no power to initiate or declare a war either against a foreign nation or a domestic State." But by statute, he is authorized to call out the militia and use American military forces to repel invasion or suppress insurrection. Then comes the critical language: "If a war be made by invasion of a foreign nation, the President is not only authorized but bound to resist force by force. He does not initiate the war, but is bound to accept the challenge without waiting for any special legislative authority." Whether the hostile force is a foreign invader or a rebellious state, "it is none the less a war." When the rebellion burst out, the president "was bound to meet it in the shape it presented itself, without waiting for Congress to baptize it with a name; and no name given to it by him or them could change the fact."[48]

The Court also clarified a key question: Did recognizing a state of war implicitly concede the legitimacy of the Confederacy? The answer was no. "It is not the less a civil war, with belligerent parties in hostile array, because it may be called an 'insurrection' by one side, and the insurgents be considered as rebels or traitors." The independence of a rebelling province does not need to be recognized in order for it to qualify as a "party belligerent in a war according to the law of nations." Such a state of war had been recognized by England and other European states that had declared themselves neutral in the Civil War. The Court roundly rejected the argument that "insurgents who have risen in rebellion against their sovereign" are "not *enemies* because they are *traitors*." As a belligerent, the United States was entitled "not only to coerce the other by direct force, but also to cripple his resources by the seizure or destruction of his property." This applied to everyone living in Confederate territory. "They have cast off their allegiance and made war on their Government, and are none the less enemies because they are traitors."[49]

The dissent agreed that if a civil war existed between the Confederacy and the United States, the blockade would be valid. They argued, however, that only an action by Congress can "change the legal status of the Government . . . from that of peace to a state of war." This did not mean, however, that the president was powerless to resist the rebellion until Congress met. Both under the Constitution and by statute, the dissenters agreed, he was entitled to call forth the militia to suppress insurrection and execute the laws. He therefore "can meet the adversary upon land and water with all the forces of the Government." But what he cannot do on his own is to invoke the laws of war, which "convert every citizen of the hostile State into a public enemy, and treat him accordingly, whatever may have been his previous conduct." For that purpose, "Congress alone can determine whether war exists or should be declared." Hence, according to the dissent, a formal state of war did not exist until July 13, when Congress passed legislation endorsing the president's activities.[50]

Thus, the Court was unanimous in holding that the president had the right to mobilize the nation to do battle after Sumter, and that an actual state of war existed by mid-July at the latest. The only disagreement was whether a state of war existed earlier. The existence of a legal state of war did not determine the government's ability to use force, but it did change the legal rights of almost everyone connected with the war. A legal state of war would limit the rights of neutral nations to conduct trade with the South, end the ability of noncombatant Southerners to invoke their normal rights as American citizens, and allow combatant Southerners to be treated as prisoners of war rather than criminals or traitors. Even Chief Justice Taney, who joined the dissent, evidently agreed that such a legal transformation had taken place by July 13.

Except for the hapless owners of the few vessels captured by one side or another between mid-April and July 13, the exact date at which the Civil War became an official war was not a matter of great practical importance. What was important was Lincoln's power, without specific approval by Congress, to engage in what was in fact a war. The Court's unanimity on this point is supported both by history and by common sense.

The Framers understood the president to have the power to make war in response to attack, though not necessarily to initiate it without authorization from Congress. Earlier drafts of the Constitution originally gave

Congress the power to "make war." On August 17, this language was amended to read "declare war." Madison and Gerry, who made the motion, argued that the change would leave "to the Executive the power to repel sudden attacks." Sherman agreed that the president should "be able to repel and not to commence war."[51]

The common sense of the matter is also clear. The president must have the power to respond to attacks and other urgent threats when advance authorization from Congress is impractical. Under Article I, section 10 of the Constitution, even the state governments have this power: "No State shall, without the Consent of Congress ... engage in War, unless actually invaded, or in such imminent Danger as will not admit of delay." Although similar language does not appear in Article II, there is no reason to believe that a different rule was meant to apply. Surely, the president of the nation should have at least as much discretion to take the country to war as is possessed by a state government.

Even under the most Congress-centered view of the war powers, the president has been accorded this power to defend the nation. The War Powers Resolution of 1973 is a powerful statement of Congress's claim to control the initiation of hostilities. Even this resolution, however, recognizes the president's authority to introduce the military into hostilities in "a national emergency created by attack upon the United States, its territories or possessions, or its armed forces." The resolution calls for consultation with the congressional leadership and gives the president up to ninety days to get congressional authorization. Naturally, Lincoln did not comply to the letter with a statute that was not passed until over a century later. But he did in effect "comply" with the substance of the statute. He did receive full authorization from Congress by July 13, within ninety days after he called up the militia. Thus, even under a highly Congress-centered view of the war power, Lincoln acted appropriately. Indeed, given current laments about the ineffectiveness of the War Powers Resolution, it is somewhat ironic that Lincoln's record of "compliance" with the resolution is better than that of the modern presidents at whom it was aimed.[52]

As to whether a formal state of war existed before Congress acted, the *Prize Cases* majority seems to have the better of the argument, given the agreement that a de facto war properly existed anyway. It would make little sense to say that, until Congress was able to act, the United States was entitled to fight but not to invoke its full rights under international law as a belligerent, while its enemy was free to do so. Nor would it make sense to say that until Congress acted, the United States was required to treat captured soldiers as criminals and captured sailors as pirates. Such actions would only have sparked reprisals against Union prisoners. In short, since even the dissent conceded that Lincoln could engage in what was in reality a war without congressional approval, the majority seems right to take the logical next step of saying that he could recognize the legal existence of a state of war when it was thrust upon him.

Thus, putting aside the issue of habeas corpus for now, the constitutional verdict on Lincoln's bold initial response to secession is almost entirely favorable. On the most important items—calling up the militia, deploying the military, and imposing a blockade—he was clearly acting within constitutional bounds. Only in two respects did he cross the line—in diverting funds to private parties to help pay for the early stages of the war and in expanding the regular military without prior congressional approval. On both points, as on the blockade, he was promptly supported by Congress after the fact. Whether he was justified in ignoring the Constitution's requirement of prior approval is a question to which we will return later. For now, it is enough to know that the Union marched to war in general compliance with the Constitution.

Except in some relatively minor respects, Lincoln's actions were faithful to the separation of powers (still leaving aside the habeas question). His major actions could not be faulted for invading the province of Congress. But there are some things that even Congress and the president acting together cannot do under a Constitution that guarantees certain individual rights. The war's impact on civil liberties is a question of graver concern than the more abstruse issues of federalism and separation of powers. This question of basic human rights is the topic of the next chapter.

CHAPTER 7 *Individual Rights*

Individual rights were undoubtedly curtailed during the Civil War. Having said that, the exact extent of the intrusions on individual rights is hard to determine. According to the best recent estimate, at least thirteen thousand civilians were held under military arrest during the course of the war. Most of these arrests involved suspected deserters or draft dodgers, citizens of the Confederacy, possible blockade runners, or individuals trading with the enemy. Some were arrested purely for disloyal speech. Some arrestees, such as the deserters and possibly the draft evaders, were properly under military jurisdiction. Others may have been wrongfully deprived of their right to a jury trial and other procedural protections. Property rights were also impaired. As the Union armies moved through the South, they destroyed or seized property such as cotton, imposed military rule, and (eventually) freed slaves. Some of these actions had precedents of one kind or another, but certainly nothing on a similar scale has ever happened in American history. It is these actions that lend credence to the accusations of dictatorship made against Lincoln.[1]

Military actions during the war give rise to a series of interlinked constitutional issues. We begin with the simplest constitutional issues, those relating to the Union army's activities in the theater of war and in conquered territory. Here, the primary constitutional issues involve martial law and the seizure or destruction of property, including the liberation of millions of slaves. (Recall that prior to the war, Lincoln had consistently maintained that the federal government had no power to interfere with slavery in the South. The Thirteenth Amendment, overturning state slave laws, became effective only after Lincoln's death.) Normally, all of these actions would be unconstitutional under a slew of constitutional provisions: the takings clause, the guarantee to the states of a republican form of government, the jury trial guarantee of the Sixth Amendment, or the due process clause. In the wake of the Union army, however, these constitutional rights seemingly evaporated.

Although these intrusions on individual rights farther south were massive, they actually are easier to justify legally than the more limited intrusions in the North. The status of the South—which was legally a part of the United States for some purposes and a belligerent power for others—was unique in American history. The legal analysis is correspondingly distinctive. The issues in the North were more akin to those in later national crises. Here, we must consider Lincoln's suspension of habeas corpus, the military trials of civilians in the North, and significant invasions of freedom of speech. After analyzing the Union army's legal authority in the field, we will turn to these more complex issues concerning civil liberties on the home front. Thus, the discussion will reverse the actual chronology of events. The Southern issues arose only after the Union army began to retake Confederate soil, whereas the Northern issues were posed almost immediately.

These various intrusions on civil liberties might appear to be signs of incipient dictatorship. We are conditioned to think that strong governments are a threat to civil liberties, whereas weak governments promote liberty. This is a notion that goes back at least to Jefferson's admiration for "that government which governs least." In the context of the Civil War, the most widespread deviation from normal legal procedures—military trials—did not result from the government's being too strong and centralized, but from its being too weak and decentralized. Military arrests and trials were required by the pathetic state of the federal government's legal apparatus. The only civilian federal law enforcement officers were a scattering of U.S. marshals. In the entire country, there were only seventy federal judges, and eighty-one federal attorneys, marshals, and other court officers. The modern Justice Department did not exist, nor did the FBI. As we saw in the last chapter, the attorney general was not even a full-time federal employee, and his staff was minimal. And if the federal government had not appeared to be such an easy target, secession might never have happened in the first place.[2]

Lincoln was in no position to act as a dictator even if he had wanted to. He had to struggle to maintain control of his cabinet and stave off challenges by his own party in Congress. Often, he was reduced to playing the role of arbitrator between cabinet members or generals. He had a minimal staff. As a result, he was forced to leave subordinates with broad discretion. Instead of systematic supervision, he had to rely on personal review of individual cases if and when they crossed his desk. His interventions helped to soften the harshness of the regime, but were hopelessly inadequate as a method of systematic control. When individual generals went off the tracks, he was sometimes able to correct the situation, as with Grant's notorious order expelling all Jews from his region of command. On other occasions, such as the Vallandigham affair discussed at the end of the chapter, Lincoln was faced with a fait accompli. Although he was able to temper Vallandigham's punishment, Lincoln was forced to defend an action that he plainly disliked but had been incapable of preventing.[3]

Thus, intrusions on civil liberties were no sign of impending dictatorship. This does not mean, however, that they were not serious for the individuals involved. Each individual was entitled to his or her constitutional rights. If those rights were violated, it is no defense that the violations were sporadic or that democracy itself was not at risk. The question remains, however, whether those rights were indeed violated. The answer is yes, though not on a massive scale.

Although the full explanation is much more elaborate, the basic point is simple. Lincoln was right that the war power authorized extraordinary actions that might otherwise have violated individual rights. He was probably wrong to the extent that he viewed this extraordinary authority as completely vested in him rather than in Congress. He was more clearly wrong if he thought it gave him unlimited discretion to decide what was necessary for the war effort. But the closer a given situation came to the heart of the war, the more likely that Lincoln's actions were supported by precedent, and also the more likely that those actions pass the tests of later times. The single most important factor is the proximity between the action and specifically military concerns. The more closely an action was related to the actual operations of the army, the more likely it was to pass constitutional muster.

MILITARY RULE IN THE THEATER OF WAR

We begin our consideration of martial law with situations where civilian government was interrupted or at least sharply curtailed, as opposed to the sporadic use of military law in areas of the North under firm Union control. These distinctions are necessary because different constitutional issues were posed in various geographic areas. A distinctive body of law applies in the vicinity of military conflict. It allows not only military arrests but wholesale military rule.

Martial law is not a term with any fixed legal meaning. It clearly contemplates, however, the replacement of the normal legal regime with military directives and enforcement. In the Civil War, military rule supplanted civilian government in three different settings.

First, in the actual arena of war, where armies were on the march, civilian government was displaced by military rule. The county sheriff in Gettysburg was obviously in no position to maintain normal law enforcement. Indeed, during Lee's march northward, some Philadelphians requested that the city be placed under martial law so as to prepare more effectively for battle. That summer, large areas of Delaware, Maryland, and Pennsylvania were placed under martial law, without complaint.[4]

Second, in the border states where sabotage or guerilla war were rampant, the military also exercised firm though not necessarily exclusive control. Missouri was the most important example. As early as May 1861, an army captain captured militiamen who appeared to threaten the St. Louis arsenal. Missouri became the scene of military operations, both regular and guerilla, for years to come. Grant authorized his subordinates to arrest civilians and take hostages if needed. When four Union soldiers were shot, Grant promptly ordered that the area in question be "cleaned out, for six miles around, and word given that all citizens making their appearance within those limits are liable to be shot." After he assumed command, Fremont ordered courts martial for "[a]ll persons who shall be taken with arms in their hands within these lines." Military trials of individuals caught burning bridges were common. After a bloody raid on Lawrence, Kansas, by Confederate guerrillas, a Union general ordered the evacuation of four counties in western Missouri where they had their supply base. Even before this famous General Order No. 11, the general had ordered the arrest of suspected guerillas and expulsion of the families of known guerillas from the area.[5]

Third, the military governed areas of the South recaptured by the Union army. New Orleans was one of the early examples. When General Butler entered New Orleans in May 1862, he found a hostile population. Butler allowed local institutions such as banks, newspapers, and courts to function. But he was severe in punishing any challenge to Union authority. Almost immediately after taking charge, Butler ordered a man who had torn down the Union flag to be tried by a military tribunal, which sentenced him to death. The man was executed despite the pleas of his family. Women frequently insulted Union troops, sometimes even spitting on them, and in one notable case, emptying a chamber pot on the head of the Union fleet's commander. In response, Butler issued his famous (or infamous) "Women's Order," directing that if "any female shall by word or gesture or movement insult or show contempt for any officer or soldier of the U.S. she shall be regarded and held liable as a woman of the town plying her avocation." When the mayor protested, Butler deposed him and replaced him with a military officer. The order was a shock to Southern gentility and earned Butler the hatred of many Southerners.[6]

We begin our analysis with the use of martial law in contested territory, whether in the border states or the South. Such use of martial law was not unprecedented. During the American revolution, the Continental Congress reacted to threatened British attacks in Pennsylvania and Delaware by authorizing a form of martial law: "[W]hereas, principles of policy and self-preservation require all persons who may be reasonably suspected of aiding or abetting the cause of the enemy may be prevented from pursuing measures injurious to the public weal," Congress authorized state governors to arrest and confine disloyal residents. Similarly, General Jackson imposed martial law on New Orleans when the city was threatened by the British during the War of 1812. He took martial law to extraordinary lengths, expelling the French consul (though France was a friendly power), arresting the author of a letter to the editor for repeating rumors that peace had arrived (which turned out to be true), and ultimately arresting a federal judge and district attorney for interfering with these actions.[7]

In a third pre–Civil War instance of martial law, the issue ultimately reached the Supreme Court. In *Luther v. Borden*,[8] the Supreme Court resoundingly upheld the use of martial law, in an opinion by none other than Chief Justice Taney. The case involved a dispute over the legitimacy of the state government in Rhode Island, a dispute that had been resolved by the president in favor of the existing government. In putting down an effort to displace this government by a rival group, the governor had declared martial law. "[U]nquestionably," Taney pronounced, "a State may use its military power to put down an armed insurrection, too strong to be controlled by the civil authority." The power to do so "is essential to the existence of every government, essential to the preservation of order and free institutions, and is as necessary to the State of this Union as to any other government." Thus, "[I]f the government of Rhode Island deemed the armed opposition so formidable, and so ramified throughout the State, as to require the use of its military force and the declaration of martial law, we see no ground upon which this court can question its authority." The case involved "a state of war; and the established government resorted to the rights and usages of war to maintain itself, and to overcome unlawful opposition." Hence, the military could arrest suspected supporters of the insurrection and could break into houses where such individuals might be hidden, all without a warrant. "Without the power to do this, martial law and the military array of the government would be mere parade, and rather encourage attack than repel it."[9]

The Court has never repudiated the view that martial law is an appropriate measure in contested or occupied territory. The basic concept has remained intact throughout our history, with some refinements and qualifications. *Luther* was later strongly reaffirmed in Justice Holmes's opinion in *Moyer v. Peabody*.[10] In response to a violent miners' strike, the governor had declared the affected county to be in a state of insurrection and called out the national guard. He arrested the union's president and held him for several months without trial. Justice Holmes saw no constitutional difficulty. "Of course," Holmes said, the "plaintiff's position is that he has been deprived of his liberty without due process of law." But due process depends on the circumstances. Under federal law, the governor was authorized to call out the national guard in response to invasion or insurrection. "That means that he shall make the ordinary use of the soldiers to that end; that he may kill persons who resist, and, of course, that he may use the milder measure of seizing the bodies of those whom he considers to stand in the way of restoring peace." Such arrests are a necessary precaution. "When it comes to a decision by the head of the state upon a matter involving its life, the ordinary rights of individuals must yield to what he deems the necessities of the moment." There was no violation of due process: "Public danger warrants the substitution of executive process for judicial process." This necessity was conceded "with regard to killing men in the actual clash of arms; and we think it obvious, although it was disputed, that the same is true of temporary detention to prevent apprehended harm."[11]

The Supreme Court has been more cautious in allowing military punishment, as opposed to preventive detention under martial law. Even here, however, the Court has been careful to distinguish the use of martial law in areas of actual combat or conquered territory. In *Duncan v. Kahanamoku,*[12] the Court rejected the use of military trials for civilian offenses in Hawaii during World War II. But the Court was careful to exclude from its ruling several other scenarios involving the possible use of martial law. It put aside cases where the military is exercising jurisdiction over enemy belligerents, prisoners of war, or individuals charged with violating the laws of war. It also put aside cases where the military is exercising its "recognized power" to try civilians as part of a temporary military government over "occupied enemy territory or territory regained from an enemy where civilian government cannot and does not function." The opinion also explicitly did not address any possible "power of the military simply to arrest and detain civilians interfering with a necessary military function at a time of turbulence and danger from insurrection or war." Finally, the Court put aside possible situations where the military enforced only orders relating to military functions, such as curfews or blackouts. Thus, the Court went to some length to avoid any wholesale rejection of martial law, and the ultimate holding was narrow. Rather than involving any of these possibly defensible uses of martial law, *Duncan* was a case where, long after Pearl Harbor, the military continued to displace the ordinary function of the civilian courts in friendly territory. The question was simply whether "loyal civilians in loyal territory should have their daily conduct governed by military orders substituted for criminal laws," with trial and punishment by military tribunals. The answer was no.[13]

As Chief Justice Stone said in his concurrence, *Duncan* was entirely consistent with *Luther v. Borden.* Although there might be "circumstances in which the public safety requires, and the Constitution permits, substitution of trials by military tribunals for trials in the civil courts," the record left no doubt that those circumstances were not in fact present. "The military authorities themselves testified and advanced no reason which has any bearing on public safety or good order for closing the civil courts to the trial of these petitioners, or for trying them in military courts."[14]

Rather than standing for the invalidity of martial law, then, *Duncan* merely indicates that the government does not have unlimited discretion in imposing it. In this, it follows *Sterling v. Constantin,*[15] in which the Court responded to abuses of martial law by state governments. The Court agreed that "there is a permitted range of honest judgment as to the measures to be taken in meeting force with force, in suppressing violence and restoring order, for, without such liberty to make immediate decisions, the power itself would be useless." Such decisions, "conceived in good faith, in the face of the emergency, and directly related to the quelling of the disorder or the prevention of its continuance, fall within the discretion of the executive in the exercise of his authority to maintain peace." But, contrary to dicta in some earlier cases, the Court held that the executive does not have the final word. Executive discretion does not mean that "every sort of action the Governor may take, no matter how unjustified by the exigency or subversive of private right and the jurisdiction of the courts, otherwise available, is conclusively supported by mere executive fiat."[16]

Thus, beginning with *Luther,* the Court's decisions seem roughly consistent. The earlier cases endorse—and the later cases are careful not to reject—martial law in areas of actual military conflict. If judicial doctrine has evolved, it has not been in terms of modifying the basic rule; it has only been in the direction of greater scrutiny of the factual basis for invoking that rule. That factual basis was relatively clear in the Civil War. The situation along the battlefront and in areas of guerilla warfare obviously fell within this rule. Hence, although the use of military trials in secure areas farther north may have been a different matter, their use in contested territory was probably constitutional.

The same rule applied in recently conquered territories where Union control was not yet secure. As the Supreme Court said in a post–Civil War case, *Dow v. Johnson,*[17] the situation was governed by the laws of war. The Civil War, "though not between independent nations, but between different portions of the same nation, was accompanied by the general incidents of an international war." Therefore, when "our armies marched into the country which acknowledged the authority of the Confederate government," they were governed only by military law. Although an invading army generally chooses to allow local laws to remain in force to regulate the relationships between private citizens, these laws continue only on sufferance, "unless suspended or superseded by the conqueror." "What is the law which governs an army invading an enemy's country?" the Court asked. "It is not the civil law of the invaded country; it is not the civil law of the conquering country: it is military law,—the law of war,—and its supremacy for the protection of the officers and soldiers of the army, when in service in the field in the enemy's country, is as essential to the efficiency of the army as the supremacy of the civil law at home, and, in time of peace, is essential to the preservation of liberty."[18]

An absolutist might argue that, notwithstanding these long-standing practices dating back to the American Revolution, martial law remains unconstitutional even in the very midst of insurrection or invasion. The true purist might be unfazed by the absurdity of expecting the county sheriff or the local judge and jury to administer the law at Gettysburg or Antietam, or during Sherman's march to the sea. But even such a staunch civil libertarian as Justice Black, a century later, admitted that "military commanders necessarily have broad power over persons on the battlefront." "From a time prior to the adoption of the Constitution," Black conceded, "the extraordinary circumstances present in an area of actual fighting have been considered sufficient to permit punishment of some civilians in that area by military courts under military rules."[19]

Still, the absolutist might insist, military rule at least must come to an end the moment that the battle ends. Such a purist might be undeterred by the danger of expecting juries composed of rebels and their sympathizers to administer the law just after the guns fall silent. For the reader who wants more than tradition and common sense as justifications, two additional arguments can be given. First, the general guarantee of due process is, as Justice Holmes said almost a century ago, a flexible one. Even today, and even outside the context of war or insurrection, due process leaves some room for preventive detention, according to the Supreme Court. Second, as to the more specific criminal procedure guarantees of the Bill of Rights, they apply only to criminal prosecutions. But that term is undefined, and may reasonably be considered to include only trials in civilian courts, rather than detention or penalties assessed by military courts where the normal operation of civil law has been impaired by insurrection or rebellion. Indeed, the habeas clause of the Constitution, which allows detention during insurrection or rebellion where required for public safety, necessarily implies that the full panoply of procedural protections does not apply in this situation.[20]

We will consider later the extension of martial law, piecemeal, into areas far removed from the war front. But the difficulty of resolving those cases should not obscure the validity of martial law in its most common exercise farther south.[21]

EMANCIPATION

The Emancipation Proclamation was a great victory for human liberty. It was also an extraordinary use of executive power. With the stroke of a pen (backed, admittedly, by Union guns), Lincoln wiped out property rights worth many millions of dollars. Normally, this assault on property rights would at the very least raise grave constitutional issues.

Emancipation was not a decision that Lincoln reached lightly. Historians have carefully traced how his views changed in response to military and political circumstances. The initial war aim was to restore the Union, not to eliminate slavery. Even if Lincoln had wanted to make abolition a war aim after Sumter, he could not have done so. He urgently needed to retain the support of slave states such as Kentucky and Maryland. (He is reputed to have said that while he hoped for God's support, his more immediate need was for Kentucky's.) After the border states were firmly secured, emancipation became a more tenable option. In the meantime, Lincoln had laid the groundwork with proposals for gradual and compensated emancipation in the border states, to be followed by colonization of the former slaves in Africa. Although these proposals were never adopted, they helped to shift the political climate. As the war became increasingly bloody, the feeling swelled that the root of the rebellion, the slave system, needed to be destroyed. Congress began to move in the direction of emancipation with two Confiscation Acts, providing a mechanism to free the slaves of active rebels on a case-by-case basis.[22]

In one sense, slavery had always been a target of the war. Lincoln had taken office on the platform of driving slavery toward gradual extinction. But attacking slavery became more urgent as the war progressed. First, slavery was obviously critical to the economy that sustained the Confederate war effort. To destroy the Confederacy, it became increasingly clear, its economic base needed to be destroyed as well. Second, the Union had with some reluctance begun to allow blacks, many escaped from the South, to serve in its military. These black soldiers and sailors became increasingly vital to the Union cause. But they could not be expected to fight a war that would merely restore the prewar status quo, returning some of them to slavery. (Indeed, the same reasoning was to push even the Confederacy itself toward a promise of emancipation for black soldiers at the very end of the war.) Third, maintaining foreign neutrality, particularly English neutrality, was critical to the Union's chances. Emancipation would harness the strong antislavery sentiment in England and France to the neutrality effort.[23]

For all these reasons, Lincoln's thinking moved toward emancipation. When he initially proposed the idea, however, the cabinet was dubious. Lincoln was persuaded that without Union success on the field, emancipation would look like a sign of desperation. Such an appearance of desperation might actually encourage European intervention on behalf of the South. After the Union victory at Antietam, qualified as it was, Lincoln felt able to move ahead. He issued the Preliminary Emancipation Proclamation on September 22, 1862. It provided that, on January 1, 1863, "all persons held as slaves within any state, or designated part of a state, the people whereof shall then be in rebellion against the United States shall be then, thenceforward, and forever free." When January 1 came, Lincoln issued the final proclamation as a "fit and necessary war measure for suppressing said rebellion." Listing the portions of the South still under Confederate control, he declared that "all persons held as slaves within said designated States, and parts of States, are, and henceforward shall be free." The Emancipation Proclamation was not up to Lincoln's usual standard of eloquence, but it said what it needed to say.[24]

Lincoln made it clear that his justification for emancipation rested solely on the war power. If he could save the Union without freeing a single slave he would do so; if saving the union meant freeing all the slaves, he would also do that. "What I do about slavery, and the colored race, I do because I believe it helps to save the Union; and what I forbear, I forbear because I do *not* believe it would help to save the Union." (He hastened to add that he was giving his "view of *official* duty; and I intend no modification of my oft-expressed *personal* wish that all men every where could be free.") He insisted that the "constitution invests its commander-in-chief, with the law of war, in time of war." "Is there—has there ever been—any question that by the law of war, property, both of enemies and friends, may be taken when needed? And is it not needed whenever taking it, helps us, or hurts the enemy?" Lincoln added that some key generals "believe the emancipation policy, and the use of colored troops, constitute the heaviest blow yet dealt to the rebellion."[25]

Lincoln was correct about the law of war. According to the leading American treatise on international law, published in 1855, a "belligerent has, strictly speaking, a right to use every means necessary to accomplish the end for which he has taken up arms." Thus, "From the moment one State is at war with another, it has, on general principles, a right to seize on all the enemy's property, of whatsoever kind and wheresoever found, and to appropriate the property thus taken to its own use, or to that of the captors." Private property on land was not normally seized (except for "military contributions levied upon the inhabitants of the hostile territory"). But this limitation arose out of "the same original principle of natural law, which authorizes us to use against an enemy such a degree of violence, and such only, as may be necessary to secure the object of hostilities." The ultimate question was necessity. "The same general rule, which determines how far it is lawful to destroy the persons of enemies, will serve as a guide in judging how far it is lawful to ravage or lay waste their country. If this be necessary, in order to accomplish the just ends of war, it may be lawfully done, but not otherwise." The lawfulness of seizing enemy property is confirmed by the U.S. Constitution, which empowers Congress to "make Rules concerning Captures on Land and Water."[26]

On these principles, the Supreme Court upheld the seizure and destruction of Confederate property in aid of the war effort. In *Miller v. United States*,[27] the Court upheld the Confiscation Act on this basis. The Court observed that confiscation "is an instrument of coercion, which, by depriving an enemy of property within reach of his power, whether within his territory or without it, impairs his ability to resist the confiscating government, while at the same time it furnishes to that government means for carrying on the war." The same was true in a civil war: "It would be absurd to hold that, while in a foreign war enemy's property may be captured and confiscated as a means of bringing the struggle to a successful completion, in a civil war of equal dimensions, requiring quite as urgently the employment of all means to weaken the belligerent in arms against the government, the right to confiscate the property that may strengthen such belligerent does not exist." But there is "no such distinction to be made." The reasons for the right to confiscation in foreign wars "exists in full force when the war is domestic or civil." Anyway, the Court said, this issue had been settled in the *Prize Cases*.[28]

On the same theory, the Court also upheld the legality of military seizure and destruction of other property by both armies in the theater of war. In *Ford v. Surget*,[29] the Court held that as a soldier for a belligerent power, a Confederate officer was not liable for destroying cotton to prevent it from falling into Union hands. The Court observed that cotton was critical to Southern efforts to finance the war, and "was therefore liable, at the time, to seizure or destruction by the Federal army, without regard to the individual sentiments of its owner, whether the purpose or effect of such seizure or destruction would have been to strengthen that army, or to decrease and cripple the power and resources of the enemy." In turn, the Confederate officer was justified in destroying the cotton before the Union army could seize it. In *New Orleans v. The Steamship Co.*,[30] the Court upheld the power of the city's military government to transfer seized real estate to third parties. The transfer remained valid even after the war was over. The

Union had "the same power and rights in territory held by conquest as if the territory had belonged to a foreign country and had been subjugated in a foreign war," including the exercise of "all the powers and functions of government." Indeed, its powers were even broader: "It may do anything necessary to strengthen itself and weaken the enemy. There is no limit to the powers that may be exerted in such cases, save those which are found in the laws and usages of war."[31]

Judged by this standard, the Emancipation Proclamation seems clearly justified as a war measure. Just like the enemy's legal interest in other property, its property interest in slaves could be extinguished if necessary to the war effort. Lincoln gave cogent reasons for thinking that emancipation was indeed needed to weaken the South and strengthen the Union army by encouraging the recruitment of black soldiers. Even if he was wrong about that—and who will ever know for sure?—he made a reasonable judgment well within his authority as a military commander.

Emancipation might be challenged on more specific constitutional grounds. One possible argument is that it violated the takings clause. But this argument should fail. Even the greatest defenders of property rights on today's Supreme Court admit that those rights are limited by background rules of state law, such as the law of nuisance. The government's power to seize enemy property when required for military purposes predates the Constitution, and must be considered an implicit condition on title to all real and personal property.[32]

Even assuming that the federal government had the power to free the slaves as a war measure, one might question whether this power could be exercised by the president without authority from Congress. After all, the Supreme Court struck down another such taking of property in the *Steel Seizure Case,* which was discussed in the last chapter. But *Steel Seizure* is distinguishable. Whereas in *Steel Seizure,* Congress had clearly refused to authorize such seizures, no such history existed in Lincoln's case. Emancipation was consistent with the general trend of congressional action against slavery, including the Confiscation Acts. Thus, while Truman's action fell into the third category of presidential actions (those contravening congressional dictates), Lincoln's fell into the more acceptable second category (congressional silence). Moreover, in *Steel Seizure,* the president had no real argument that the seizure was covered by the commander-in-chief clause. In contrast, the Emancipation Proclamation was effectively an order to military commanders in the field, directing them to liberate slaves in conquered territory. Thus, it fell much more comfortably within the president's role as a military leader.

Congress probably had concurrent power over emancipation, either under its specific power to make rules for captures on land or under its more general power to effectuate the conduct of war (implicit in the power to declare war). If Congress had countermanded Lincoln's proclamation, a difficult constitutional problem would have been presented. As it was, Lincoln's action seems relatively unproblematic in terms of the separation of powers.

Merryman AND HABEAS

William H. Seward, the secretary of state, was in charge of military arrests until February 1862, when control was transferred to the War Department. He reputedly told the British ambassador that he had more power than the British monarch and could order the arrest of a citizen anywhere in the country by ringing a little bell on his desk. But under Seward's supervision, the government arrested fewer than nine hundred civilians, a small percentage of the wartime total. Seward was busy with other pressing matters like keeping England out of the war. He also lacked any administrative apparatus for making these arrests. Besides, most disloyal Americans were out of the government's reach at that time. Of those who were arrested, many were in effect enemy aliens—residents of the Confederacy. Only around a hundred of the prisoners lived above the border states in uncontested Union territory.[33]

The eventual number of arrests was in the thousands. After Secretary of War Edwin M. Stanton suspended the writ of habeas corpus in August 1862, apparently under Lincoln's direction, the ensuing arrests were undertaken by petty officials under weak central control. But it was in the South, as the Union began to regain territory, or in the contested portions of border states such as Missouri, that military arrests were most rampant. The number of prisoners who can be identified as Northern (non–border state) residents ran in the hundreds, though they were still a small percentage of the total. Most were probably suspected draft evaders or deserters. Lincoln often intervened on the side of clemency in such cases as reached his desk, but these cases were only the tip of the iceberg.[34]

Detention of the prisoners without any judicial hearing was made possible by the suspension of habeas corpus. Habeas is the traditional common-law writ used to test the legality of detention. The suspension clause (Article I, section 9) provides: "The Privilege of the Writ of Habeas Corpus shall not be suspended, unless when in Cases of Rebellion or Invasion the public safety may require it." Whether or not the military could legally impose punishment on disloyal citizens, the suspension of habeas made it possible at least to detain them for preventive purposes.

The major constitutional issue was whether Congress or the president had the power to suspend the writ. After Congress eventually approved the suspension, this issue was moot. But Lincoln was responsible for the initial suspension of habeas. Until Congress acted to ratify his actions, controversy raged over the existence of any presidential control over habeas.[35]

Habeas was first suspended soon after Sumter, as we saw in chapter 1. After the Baltimore mob blocked the passage of troops to the capital, Lincoln asked his attorney general for advice about his ability to sidestep normal judicial procedures. Bates delegated the question to an assistant, whose answer was not encouraging. Nevertheless, on April 27, Lincoln issued an order suspending the writ of habeas corpus (or rather, authorizing General Scott to do so) along the military line between Philadelphia and Washington. On May 25, John Merryman was arrested for allegedly drilling troops to aid the Confederacy, thus setting the stage for the confrontation with Chief Justice Taney.[36]

The chief justice mounted a powerful challenge to Lincoln's power to suspend the writ. He made three major points. First, the suspension clause is found in Article I, devoted mostly to the legislative power, not in Article II, devoted to the executive power. This placement seemed unlikely for a constraint on the president. Second, after long struggles on behalf of liberty, the English monarch had been completely deprived of the power to suspend the writ. Would the Framers have given the president more draconian powers than those possessed by George III? Third, eminent judicial authorities and commentators such as Chief Justice Marshall and Justice Story had described the suspension power as congressional. Thus, Lincoln's actions contradicted the accepted reading of the clause.[37]

In his July 4 special message to Congress, Lincoln responded to these arguments. It was here that he made his famous argument of necessity, asking whether "all the laws *but one*" were to go unexecuted, "and the government itself go to pieces, lest that one be violated?" But, he went on to say, "it was not believed that this question was presented," for it was "not believed that any law was violated." The Constitution is silent about who has the power to suspend. To vest the suspension power solely in Congress, Lincoln said, would be imprudent: "[A]s the provision was plainly made for a dangerous emergency, it cannot be believed the framers of the instrument intended, that in every case, the danger should run its course, until Congress could be called together; the very assembling of which might be prevented, as was intended in this case, by the rebellion." For the benefit of anyone who remained in doubt, Lincoln added that the attorney general would furnish a more complete analysis in due course.[38]

The attorney general obliged with an opinion filed the next day. Not surprisingly, he upheld the president's power to suspend. Bates argued that under the oath clause as well as the militia act, the president was required to suppress insurrections by use of the militia, the army, and the navy. He must use his discretion in meeting the threat. "If the insurgents assail the nation with an army, he may find it best to meet them with an army, and suppress the insurrection in the field of battle." But "if they employ spies and emissaries, to gather information, to forward rebellion, he may find it both prudent and humane to arrest and imprison them," either to bring them to trial or to hold them in custody until the emergency is past. As to the suspension clause, Bates admitted, "learned persons have differed widely about the meaning of this short sentence, and I am by no means confident that I fully understand it myself." But when the judiciary is unable to maintain public order, the president must step in to deal with the emergency. When the president has called out the military, Bates maintained, it would be absurd to say he must send captured soldiers or spies before any judge who chooses to issue a writ.[39]

Congress ultimately settled the dispute in March 1863 with a statute declaring that the president did have the power to suspend the writ. Under the statute, a military officer could respond to the writ merely by certifying that the person was detained by authority of the president. This language was carefully ambiguous about whether Congress was conferring the power to suspend the writ or merely recognizing its existence in the hands of the president. In the meantime, Lincoln issued a whole series of suspension orders, gradually expanding the scope of the authorization until it covered the entire nation. He was apparently not very enthusiastic about these measures. In a memo on May 17, he said, "Unless the *necessity* for these arbitrary arrests is *manifest,* and *urgent,* I prefer they should cease."[40]

Lincoln's actions, though extraordinary, were not completely unprecedented. In 1777, the Continental Congress had recommended that disloyal persons in Delaware and Pennsylvania be taken into custody. Only later did the Pennsylvania legislature pass a statute approving the measure and indemnifying the state executive. In the meantime, the prisoners had obtained a writ of habeas, which was ignored by their custodian. In a better-known incident, as commanding general in New Orleans, Andrew Jackson had suspended the writ. Not only that, but he imprisoned the judge who had issued it. And when the U.S. attorney went to another judge to secure the first judge's release, Jackson had them arrested as well. When the first judge was finally released, he held Jackson in contempt of court and fined him one thousand dollars, which "Old Hickory" paid out of his own pocket. Years later, Congress ordered the fine repaid with interest, but with no clear indication whether this was an endorsement of his actions or just a charitable act toward an aging hero.[41]

In contrast, on other notable occasions when the writ was suspended, the action was taken by the legislature. This was true in Shays's Rebellion, an uprising that helped prompt the drive toward the 1787 Philadelphia convention. Similarly, it was the state legislature that suspended habeas in the Rhode Island uprising that gave rise to *Luther v. Borden*. But suspending access to civilian courts had been a rare event in American history, and the sparse precedents were relatively uninformative.[42]

The original understanding sheds a limited amount of light on the suspension power. Habeas was introduced as a topic at the Constitutional Convention by Charles Pinckney on August 20, 1787, along with a number of other provisions. His habeas proposal read as follows: "The privileges and benefit of the Writ of Habeas corpus shall be enjoyed in this Government in the most expeditious and ample manner; and shall not be suspended by the Legislature except upon the most urgent and pressing occasions, and for a limited time not exceeding [blank] months." This language would have clearly indicated that the suspension power was vested in Congress.[43]

On August 28, in the debate over the Committee on Detail draft, Pinckney spoke again, "urging the propriety of securing the benefit of the Habeas corpus in the most ample manner." He moved that habeas "should not be suspended but on the most urgent occasions, & then only for a limited time, not exceeding twelve months." A brief discussion took place. Rutledge opposed allowing suspension at all, because he doubted that suspension on a nationwide basis would ever be necessary. Wilson also opposed any suspension power, arguing that the judges could always deny bail. Morris then proposed what became essentially the final language of the suspension clause, with only trivial changes in wording (capitalizing "invasion" and changing "where" to "when"). This discussion, it should be noted, was part of the debate over what was then Article XI, dealing with the federal judiciary. Without explanation, the Committee on Style later moved this language to Article I, which almost entirely deals with Congress. Later, when habeas suspension occasionally came up in the ratification debates, the speakers seemed to assume that the power resided in Congress.[44]

There are three possible interpretations of the suspension power. It either belongs exclusively to Congress or to the president, or concurrently to both. The least plausible of these possibilities is that the president has exclusive power. That view is at least in tension with the constitutional text and with our admittedly limited evidence regarding the original understanding. The location of the clause, in Article I rather than Article II, suggests at least some congressional role. Except for its brief sojourn in the judiciary article, which left the source of the suspension power completely ambiguous, everything else about the drafting and ratification history suggests a connection between Congress and the suspension power. So does the long English struggle to move the power to the legislature, recounted by Taney (but validated by more objective historians). Moreover, the Framers were suspicious of unchecked power. They would have been unlikely to give the president the exclusive, final word about his own power to deprive citizens of their liberty without legal process. This leaves us with the other two possibilities, exclusive congressional power or concurrent power.[45]

A concurrent presidential power would require some source in Article II. If the president does have some constitutional power to suspend habeas, where does he get it? The suspension clause itself limits the power to suspend to certain circumstances rather than serving as a source of suspension authority. It is a "thou shalt not," rather than a "thou mayest." Plainly, suspending habeas would not have been considered an inherent part of the "executive power" granted by the vesting clause of Article II (assuming the vesting clause actually is an independent source of power). The whole thrust of English history had been to move the power to Parliament; it was not a power the king possessed at the time of American independence. Where else? The only plausible answers are the same clauses that authorized Lincoln to take military action against the rebellion—in particular, the power to use military force in response to sudden attacks. If he can supplement the congressional power to declare war by making war on his own in certain circumstances, he presumably can also take other emergency measures needed to meet the same threat, such as declaring martial law or suspending habeas. Or at least he should be able to do so when Congress has not spoken to the contrary in advance of the emergency. Thus, the president's power to make war in response to "sudden attack" is the most plausible source of his authority to suspend habeas in the theater of the ensuing war.[46]

In any event, if prior congressional authorization was needed, it probably did exist. In the special session called by Lincoln, Congress ratified all of his orders relating to the militia or armed forces. Since Lincoln's suspension directive took the form of an authorization to General Scott, this may well have ratified at least his past suspension in cases like *Merryman*. But, even before the special session, Lincoln already probably had whatever congressional authorization he needed, at least for the initial emergency suspension in *Merryman*. This source of authority was the militia act. This theory was adopted in *Ex parte Field*,[47] where the federal circuit court held that the statutes empowering Lincoln to call out the militia also implicitly authorized him to declare martial law, and hence to suspend habeas.

The circuit court's view in *Ex parte Field* was upheld, in effect, in the Supreme Court's later opinion in *Moyer v. Peabody* (the opinion discussed earlier dealing with the violent strike).[48] Although not directly concerned with presidential power, the Court provided a crucial interpretation of the federal statute authorizing the state governor to call out the national guard. The Court emphasized that this statute necessarily allowed him to use deadly force if needed, and therefore also allowed him to detain prisoners if needed to suppress the insurrection. Perhaps not coincidentally, the author of the opinion was Holmes, who had been wounded repeatedly in action during the Civil War. Although it is usually said that the Supreme Court never ruled on the legality of Lincoln's habeas suspension, *Moyer* was the next best thing to a direct holding on point, though delivered years after the fact. In the spring and summer of 1861, the area of insurrection might be said to include Maryland. If so, under *Moyer*, Lincoln clearly would have been empowered to use deadly force to suppress the insurrection. It is hard to quarrel with Holmes's conclusion that the power to detain dangerous individuals goes along with the power to use deadly military force against them.[49]

Thus, emergency habeas suspension, in the face of sudden attack, may well have been implicitly authorized by statute. At worst, it seems to fall in the "twilight zone" of concurrent power under the three-part analysis discussed in the last chapter. Justice Holmes's reasoning in *Moyer,* though addressed to a statutory issue, would apply with equal force to the president's constitutional power as commander in chief. Under the rationale of *Moyer,* that power presumptively includes the ability to suspend habeas where required by military necessity, when the president has congressional authorization to use military force to quell insurrection. Prior interactions between the branches do not speak clearly to the question. But as in the Iranian hostage case, the fact of subsequent congressional approval supports the legality of Lincoln's actions. Once again, later decisions like the hostage case obviously do not prove that Lincoln's actions were valid under the constitutional doctrine of the time. They do show, however, that his views are consistent with our current views of legitimate executive power.[50]

Thus, although the constitutional issue can hardly be considered free from doubt, on balance Lincoln's use of habeas in areas of insurrection or actual war should be considered constitutionally appropriate, at least in the absence of any contrary action by Congress. When the war broke out, given the riots in Baltimore and the threat of secession by Maryland, that state could be considered a site of insurrection, particularly given its proximity to enemy territory and its control over access to Washington. Consequently, suspension of habeas could be justified as an emergency military measure.[51]

This reasoning takes care of the early suspension of the writ that was involved in *Merryman,* but not necessarily of the full scope of the habeas suspension nationally or of the military trials that followed. Some of these actions took place far away from the actual scene of war or insurrection, where the president's power as a military commander was less relevant. Until explicit congressional authorization was provided, the broader suspension was at least suspect constitutionally. Even after Congress authorized suspending habeas, as we will see, the use of military law in the North sometimes went beyond constitutional limits.

MILITARY TRIALS IN THE NORTH

Trials by military commissions, as opposed to preventive detention, were first authorized by Stanton's order of August 8, 1862, suspending habeas. The trials were supervised by Joseph Holt, the judge advocate general, who sometimes reversed convictions based on procedural irregularities. Thus, while lacking the full safeguards of normal criminal trials, these were not merely "kangaroo courts." As we have seen, trials in occupied Southern territory or contested areas of border states probably involved a justifiable application of martial law. Arrests in the North were more problematic. Roughly 5 percent of the military trials—about two hundred—took place in uncontested territory, outside of the South or the border states. Many of these Northern trials involved Confederate citizens or residents of border states, such as Kentuckians caught while trying to head South and join the Confederate army. Others related to draft riots. But some others, like the Vallandigham case considered in the next section, merely involved disloyal speech.[52]

Some of the trials of "civilians" in the North may have been justified by special circumstances. Under an 1827 Supreme Court decision, individuals who refused to serve when called up by the militia were subject to court martial. This ruling might cover draft dodgers. In addition, deserters were clearly subject to military jurisdiction, which inevitably meant some trials of suspected deserters who were in fact civilians. Others, if not technically soldiers, were employed by the military as civilians or were military contractors, who might conceivably fall within a broad understanding of the congressional power over the military.[53]

Furthermore, at least some actions by civilians were subject to military trial, even in the North. During time of war, regardless of the status of the territory involved, the military has jurisdiction to try offenses against the laws of war. These include what we would now call war crimes, as well as spying and sabotage by members of the opposing army not in regular uniform. This rule continued to be recognized in the years after World War II. But these "special cases" did not account for all of the Northern trials. The remaining residue of cases could be justified only on the basis of a sweeping power to try anyone charged with seditious conduct or treason before a military tribunal.[54]

The issue finally reached the Supreme Court after the war was over. Lambdin Milligan was a Peace Democrat (a group that did not think preserving the Union was worth a war). Some Peace Democrats had formed a secret society known as the Order of American Knights, later called the Sons of Liberty. Some members planned raids to release Confederate prisoners or seize army supplies and weapons. Milligan himself was closely associated with one Harrison Dodd, the group's Indiana leader, who was in fact preparing it for armed action. But whether Milligan himself was involved in these paramilitary plans is unclear. At least one recent review of the trial record concludes that the proof was insufficient. Nevertheless, along with some others, Milligan was tried and sentenced to death. (Dodd himself climbed out a window and escaped to Canada.) Some indication exists that Lincoln was planning to pardon the defendants, but after his death, President Andrew Johnson refused to do so. Johnson did, however, eventually commute the sentences to life at hard labor. In the meantime, Milligan had applied for habeas in a federal trial court, which certified the issue to the Supreme Court.[55]

The Court was unanimous in reversing Milligan's conviction but divided about the reasons. All agreed that military trials were impermissible under the circumstances of the case. Four justices, led by Chief Justice Chase, were content to rest the decision on statutory grounds. Justice Davis's majority opinion held, however, that such trials were unconstitutional and could not have been validly authorized by Congress. Davis's opinion contains a rousing paean to the need to maintain constitutional safeguards such as the right to jury trial and an independent judiciary even in wartime. The Constitution, Davis declaimed, "is a law for rulers and people, equally in war and in peace, and covers with the shield of its protection all classes of men, at all times, and under all circumstances." Davis denounced the doctrine that "any of its provisions can be suspended during any of the great exigencies of government." Besides its "pernicious consequences," the doctrine of necessity was based on a false assumption, "for the government, within the Constitution, has all the powers granted to it, which are necessary to preserve its existence; as has been happily proved by the result of the great effort to throw off its just authority."[56]

Justice Davis touched upon some of those legitimate war powers, none of which he found applicable. First, men "wicked enough to counsel their fellow-citizens to resist the measures" of the government in wartime may be arrested and detained without habeas corpus. But this power of detention did not include the power to try and punish the detainees. Second, if in "foreign invasion or civil war, the courts are actually closed, and it is impossible to administer criminal justice according to law," martial law applies "on the theatre of active military operations, where war really prevails." But martial law cannot exist "where the courts are open, and in the proper and unobstructed exercise of their jurisdiction." Martial law is "also confined to the locality of actual war"—Virginia yes, but Indiana no.

A mere threatened invasion is not enough to trigger martial law—the "necessity must be actual and present; the invasion real, such as effectually closes the courts and deposes the civil administration." Third, the case did not present the question of "what rule a military commander, at the head of his army, can impose on states in rebellion to cripple their resources and quell the insurrection." Nor did it involve a person connected with the U.S. military, who would properly be subject to martial law—nor someone connected with the Confederate military, who would be covered by the laws of war.[57]

In short, the trial was of a civilian who was in friendly territory and not charged with war crimes. In the state where Milligan was tried, a federal court also "met, peacefully transacted its business, and adjourned." That court "needed no bayonets to protect it, and required no military aid to execute its judgments." Nor was its loyalty doubtful—it was composed of "judges commissioned during the Rebellion, who were provided with juries, upright, intelligent, and selected by a marshal appointed by the President." In Indiana, "the Federal authority was always unopposed, and its courts always open to hear criminal accusations and redress grievances; and no usage of war could sanction a military trial there for any offence whatever of a citizen in civil life, in nowise connected with the military service." Hence, use of a military tribunal lacked any constitutional justification.[58]

Led by Chief Justice Chase, four justices disagreed with this reasoning, though concurring in the result of the case. Chase relied on the statute ratifying habeas suspension, which required prisoners (other than prisoners of war) to be indicted within twenty days of arrest and subjected to the ordinary criminal process. Because in his view Congress had not authorized, indeed had forbidden, military trials, he considered it unnecessary to decide the constitutional question. But since the majority had reached out to decide the constitutional question, Chase addressed it as well. In his view, Congress's war power allowed it to authorize military trials even where the courts were open. The war power "extends to all legislation essential to the prosecution of war with vigor and success, except such as interferes with the command of the forces and the conduct of campaigns." Congress might well conclude that military trials were needed even where courts were open, because judges and marshals might be "in active sympathy with the rebels, and courts their most efficient allies." In time of "insurrection or invasion, or of civil or foreign war," it was up to Congress to determine "where ordinary law no longer adequately secures public safety and private rights."[59]

Despite the sweeping language early in Justice Davis's opinion, he actually left the extent of military jurisdiction unclear. The general rule is that martial law ends when the courts are "open." Even this general rule seems to have exceptions whose scope is rather unclear: for conquered territory (how long after the occupation?), for persons "connected with" the armed services (does this include civilian employees or contractors?), and for members of the Confederate military (how formal does the connection have to be?). Putting aside these exceptions, the rule itself is less than clear. When are the courts considered to be "open"? This term might mean that martial law applies only when physical danger prevents judges and lawyers from holding court. But the opinion also leaves room for a broader interpretation—that courts are only "open" when staffed by loyal officers, and when their trials take place and their decrees are enforced without the need for military intervention. Under the broader interpretation, Davis really differed from Chase only in degree. Both agreed (in the words of a recent commentator) "that civil courts and juries would yield in the face of military necessity," while Chase (but not Davis) found "the situation in Indiana serious enough to justify a military tribunal."[60]

A little—but only a little—light is shed on the scope of *Milligan* by two World War II cases that applied the decision. The earlier case, *Ex parte Quirin*,[61] upheld a military tribunal's jurisdiction over a group of German soldiers (one an American citizen). The group had been taken by German submarine to the U.S. coast, where they landed, buried their uniforms, and headed inland to conduct a campaign of sabotage. The U.S. courts were, of course, "open and functioning normally." Because they were not in uniform, the German soldiers were classified as spies rather than prisoners of war and were subject to the death penalty. The Court upheld the death sentences for violating the law of war. It distinguished the *Milligan* ruling on the ground that Milligan had been "a citizen twenty years resident in Indiana, who had never been a resident of any of the states in rebellion" and "was not an enemy belligerent either entitled to the status of a prisoner of war or subject to the penalties imposed upon unlawful belligerents." Although the Court did not attempt to define the precise "boundaries of the jurisdiction of military tribunals to try persons according to the law of war," the prisoners in *Quirin* were "plainly within those boundaries," having "entered or after entry remained in our territory without uniform—an offense against the law of war."[62]

The second case, *Duncan v. Kahanamoku,*[63] was decided just after World War II. After Pearl Harbor, martial law had been imposed in Hawaii. The statute governing the territory specifically authorized the use of "martial law" but did not define the term. The statute remained in place long after emergency conditions had ceased. Not just the local courts, but even bars and night clubs were open. But military courts continued to conduct criminal trials of civilians. One of the defendants was a stockbroker who was convicted of embezzling stock belonging to another civilian. The other was a civilian employee at the Navy Yard who got into a brawl with two marine sentries. The decision reversing these military convictions was technically based on the statute governing the territory, not directly on the Constitution. The Court held, however, that Congress intended the statute to operate within the same constitutional limitations that would apply within a state (but not necessarily within a territory). Construing the term "martial law" with *Milligan* and traditional boundaries between civilian and military power in mind, the Court held that the statute did not authorize military trials. A threatened invasion was not enough. Instead, "the civil courts must be utterly incapable of trying criminals or of dispensing justice in their usual manner before the Bill of Rights may be temporarily suspended" (citing *Milligan*).[64]

But as in *Milligan,* the Court blunted this seemingly absolute language with indications of a more pragmatic approach. Some aspects of the opinion suggest that the real problem may have been a lack of military necessity rather than the mere fact that Hawaiian courtrooms were unlocked and open for business in routine civil cases. "[T]here is no question here as to the loyalty of the Hawaiian judiciary or as to the desire and ability of the judges to cooperate fully with military requirements." Furthermore, there was "no evidence of disorder in the community which might have prevented the courts from conducting jury trials." The governor and the chief judge of the territory testified that military trials of civilians were unnecessary. "In short, the Bill of Rights disappeared by military fiat rather than by military necessity." (And the Court at least hinted that this military fiat may have been based on a racist fear of allowing Japanese Americans to serve on juries.) The opinion's concluding paragraph also seems more guarded than its earlier absolutist language. It warns that militarism is "not our way of life" and "is to be used only in the most extreme circumstances." So we must be "on constant guard against an excessive use of any power, military or otherwise, that results in the needless destruction of our rights and liberties." Thus, "There must be a careful balancing of interests." This talk of "extreme circumstances," "excessive" use of power, and "careful balancing" is at odds with the more absolutist language of the opinion.[65]

The best synthesis of the law on the general subject of martial law would probably be something like this. In emergencies—sudden attack or insurrection—the president has the power to suspend the writ of habeas corpus and detain suspects within the general zone of military conflict. Congress has ultimate control over suspension of habeas. The only apparent limitations on Congress are the existence of an invasion or insurrection and of the requisite need to protect public safety. Military trials, as opposed to preventive detentions, are also permissible in time of war, but under narrower circumstances—in the actual theater of war, in occupied hostile territory, or for individuals connected with our own military or the enemy's. Courts clearly must show some deference to military judgment. Nevertheless, they are required to evaluate the plausibility of any claim of military necessity, in light of the facts and of the traditional boundaries between civilian and military authority. In Hawaii, as the events of Pearl Harbor receded, and in Indiana during the Civil War, the claim of military necessity was factually implausible and would have required greatly stretching the recognized boundaries of military jurisdiction.

The existence of any exceptions to the general rule against military trials may seem inconsistent with the language of the Bill of Rights. Provisions such as trial by jury may seem to brook no exceptions. But as the Court explained in *Quirin,* this appearance is misleading. For the originalist, one might respond that this language must be read in light of the general understanding of the time, which recognized the need for martial law during the Revolution. For the textualist, one might respond that the language is susceptible to a narrower reading, so as to exclude cases legitimately within military jurisdiction. And for the rest—those who believe in an evolving or "living" Constitution—we may say that this is in fact what constitutional law has evolved into. Moreover, the current state of the law is consistent with the general rule that constitutional rights—even such vital ones as freedom of speech and freedom from racial discrimination—can be limited where truly necessary to attain a compelling government interest. But perhaps it is just as well that these exceptions are a bit doubtful. Such doubts may not deter the government where the need is truly pressing, but they could help provide a check on reflex authoritarianism.[66]

Assuming that these exceptions are indeed valid, and reading them for all they are worth, the government clearly went too far in cases like *Milligan*. The Constitution does not authorize military trials for civilians in friendly territory who were unconnected in any way with either military. In the trauma of our bloodiest war, a war fought between Americans on American soil, the failure to observe these limits may have been understandable. But these excesses should not serve as a precedent for the future.

Vallandigham AND FREE SPEECH

A small percentage, but still a disturbing number, of Civil War actions taken under military authority impinged on freedom of speech. These actions might have occurred anyway, but were probably encouraged by the absence of the usual procedural safeguards, not to mention the ingrained military attitude toward insubordination and disloyalty.

Free speech issues arose early in the war. Prisoners' records in the early days referred to "treasonable language" and "disloyalty" as grounds for arrest, along with "threatening Unionists" or "inducing desertion." In Cincinnati, a man was arrested for selling stationery with Confederate mottoes. A general in Tennessee enforced a ban on similar items. A dozen of the individuals arrested without legal process were identified as newspaper editors or reporters. One general in Indiana prohibited any criticism of statutes such as those creating the draft or the income tax. Lincoln's proclamation of September 1862 authorized military trials for persons discouraging enlistments. A year later, though, he wrote a Missouri general to caution him against suppressing newspapers or assemblies except "when they may be working *palpable* injury to the Military in your charge."[67]

Lincoln played only a secondary role in the most famous instance of interference with free speech, the *Vallandigham* case. The case arose from an 1863 order by General Burnside, an incompetent whose men had been slaughtered at Fredericksburg. To get him out of the way before any more of his troops were butchered, he was made commanding general of the Department of Ohio. The move did not improve the soundness of his judgment. Burnside's General Order No. 38 proclaimed that the "habit of declaring sympathies for the enemy will not be allowed in this Department." Treason, "express or implied," would not be tolerated. That spring,

over a hundred Union soldiers arrived at the house of Clement Vallandigham in the middle of the night, forced their way into the house, and arrested him for violating Burnside's order. Vallandigham was a well-known
national figure, a former congressman who (like Milligan) was a Peace Democrat. The basis for Vallandigham's arrest was a speech he had given a few
days earlier. In that speech, he had called the war "wicked, cruel, and unnecessary," a war fought for abolitionism rather than to save the Union. He
allegedly said, however, that he would not counsel "resistance to military or
civil law; that was not needed." Instead, he called upon his audience to use
the ballot box to hurl "King Lincoln" from his throne. The military commission found him guilty and ordered his confinement for the duration of
the war. This blunder was a great embarrassment to the administration,
and Lincoln ultimately ordered Vallandigham expelled into Confederate
territory instead of imprisoning him.[68]

In response to protests against Vallandigham's conviction, Lincoln defended the general policy of military arrests in an open letter to some
prominent New York Democrats. He defended the policy on the basis of
public necessity. Early intervention was needed to restrain dangerous individuals before they could commit actual crimes. If this policy had been
pursued earlier, he pointed out, Lee would never have had the chance to
join the Confederate army. And, said Lincoln, "he who dissuades one man
from volunteering, or induces one soldier to desert, weakens the Union
cause as much as he who kills a union soldier in battle." As to Vallandigham, the arrest was not for criticizing the administration or General Burnside, which Lincoln conceded would be wrong. Instead, Vallandigham
"avows his hostility to the war on the part of the Union; and his arrest was
made because he was laboring, with some effect, to prevent the raising of
troops; to encourage desertions from the army, and to leave the rebellion
without an adequate military force to suppress it." "Must I shoot a simple-
minded soldier boy who deserts," asked Lincoln, "while I must not touch a
hair of a wiley agitator who induces him to desert?"[69]

Did Vallandigham's conviction violate the First Amendment? This is a
difficult question to answer because views of the First Amendment have
changed so much over the years. Unlike separation-of-powers doctrine,
current First Amendment doctrine has not merely evolved since the Civil
War; it has essentially sprung into existence out of a legal void. Before and
during the Civil War, freedom of speech was vigorously debated and had

strong defenders. But the Supreme Court did not seriously confront First Amendment issues until about fifty years later, during World War I and its aftermath.

The Court's initial decisions supported the suppression of any speech that conceivably hindered recruiting, the draft, or the war effort generally. In *Schenck v. United States*,[70] the Court upheld a conviction for mailing a leaflet to draft-age men arguing that the draft was unconstitutional. In *Abrams v. United States*,[71] the defendants had published leaflets lambasting the Allies' attempted intervention in the Russian Revolution (which had been intended to bring Russia back into the war). The obvious effect of the leaflets, the Court thought, was to discourage people from buying war bonds or working in defense plants; this was enough to justify the conviction. Even more notably, in *Debs v. United States*,[72] the Court upheld the conviction of a third-party presidential candidate for outspokenly criticizing the war and thereby supposedly hindering recruitment. The World War I–era Court would have had little difficulty in upholding Vallandigham's conviction.

The standard that began to emerge from these cases was the "clear and present danger" test. In a series of famous dissents, Justices Holmes and Brandeis began to press for a more stringent application of this test. Their position seems to be close to Lincoln's insistence to the Missouri general on the need for "palpable injury" as a basis for suppressing speech. Applying this test requires a close understanding of the circumstances, which is difficult at this remove in time. The test would have required the prosecutor to show a clear danger that Vallandigham's speech would have directly harmed the war effort. It seems unlikely, but possible, that such a showing could have been made.[73]

Because the "clear and present danger" test was so fact-based, it provided only uncertain protection to speech. In the Warren Court years, the test was stiffened and given a more objective component. Under *Brandenburg v. Ohio*,[74] a speaker can be punished for inciting illegal action only under narrow circumstances. Such advocacy can be punished only when it is directed to producing imminent lawless action and is likely to produce that result. That is, the speech must be at least fairly explicit in calling for illegal action, and the audience must be primed to respond. It seems very doubtful, based on what we know of the facts, that such a showing could have been made regarding Vallandigham.

Which of these standards should we use to assess the government's actions in the *Vallandigham* case—the relaxed standard adopted sixty years later, the tighter one of seventy-five years later, or the strict one of a century later? If the question is whether Vallandigham's conviction should serve as a precedent today, the answer seems clear. That kind of speech regulation was decisively rejected by the Supreme Court over three decades ago, and was eroded badly several decades earlier. If the question is whether Lincoln acted in knowing violation of constitutional standards, it is hard to hold him responsible for failing to anticipate the views that the Supreme Court itself would not develop until many decades later.

If the question instead is whether Lincoln was "right" about the First Amendment in some objective sense, it is hard to know how to answer. What is the one true meaning of the First Amendment? The text and original intent are both unhelpful here. For one thing, the text only says that "Congress shall make no law," and Lincoln claimed to be acting under his own war powers, not those of Congress. The amendment forbids any abridgement of "the freedom of speech." But unless that term is implausibly taken to mean the unlimited right to communicate anything at all under any circumstances—the right to engage in false advertising or price-fixing agreements, for instance—its meaning is hardly self-defining. And as to the original understanding, little is clear except perhaps a desire to go beyond Blackstone's definition (which banned only prior censorship, not punishment after the fact for harmful speech). Persuasive arguments can be made that the Court's current approach is most consistent with the needs of a free society. But those arguments are based in part on information (like the World War I experience and the excesses of the McCarthy era) unavailable to Lincoln. And even today, in circumstances as dire as those of the Civil War, who can be sure what the courts would do?[75]

Some other restrictions on speech involved clearer constitutional violations. These incidents involved military orders that shut down newspapers, at least temporarily. The most notorious incident involved the *New York World*. Two journalists forged an Associated Press story about a bogus presidential call for drafting four hundred thousand men. (As a signal of desperation by the president, this "news" was supposed to drive up the price of gold, allowing the two men to make a quick profit.) The *World* fell for the stunt and published the story. Suspecting a Confederate plot, Lincoln ordered the arrest of the editors and publishers, as well as the seizure of the premises. This put the newspaper out of business until the order was countermanded.[76]

Shutting down the newspaper violated a core First Amendment rule known as the prior restraint doctrine. The prior restraint doctrine embodies a strong presumption against any prior censorship or closure of the press. For instance, in *Near v. Minnesota,*[77] the Supreme Court chastised a state court in 1931 for enjoining the publication of a newspaper that had violated state law. Punishing illegal publications after the fact is one thing, but preventing the publication in the first place is another and is almost never permissible. The Court did say that the rule against prior restraints was subject to wartime exceptions. An injunction might be in order to prevent "the publication of the sailing dates of transports or the number and location of troops." But while Lincoln may have had good reason to think that the *World* was disloyal and even that it had engaged in a dangerous action in the past, he had no specific information about future misconduct. Moreover, unlike the "clear and present danger" test and related doctrines, prior restraint doctrine is no modern innovation. Rather, as the Court pointed out in *Near,* the doctrine was clearly stated even by Blackstone, well before the Bill of Rights was adopted. In shutting down the paper, Lincoln was invading a core constitutional right, without a clear factual basis or opportunity for a hearing. Consequently, it is hard to quarrel with the conclusion of another member of Lincoln's cabinet, Gideon Welles, who said that seizure of the paper was "hasty, rash, inconsiderate, and wrong, and cannot be defended."[78]

These Civil War intrusions on speech seem excessive. Because interference with free speech during the Civil War was sporadic, it did not damage American liberty nearly as much as it might have. But the very infrequency and arbitrariness of cases like *Vallandigham* strongly suggest that these actions were not truly necessary. This conclusion is reinforced by Lincoln's own misgivings about these actions, even when he felt compelled to defend them. By and large, the army got along just fine without suppressing dissident Northern politicians or newspapers, even during the worst of the Civil War. By comparison, later periods like World War I seem to have involved more systematic, though equally unnecessary, forms of censorship. Lincoln's intuition that free speech should be suppressed only under imperative circumstances was correct, but he failed to effectively hold his subordinates to that standard. In defending them in his letter to Corning, he went too far in condoning invasions of civil liberties.

The verdict on the Lincoln administration's civil liberties record is mixed. Many of the acts denounced as dictatorial—the suspension of habeas at the beginning of the war, emancipation, military trials of civilians in contested or occupied territory—seem in retrospect to have reasonably good constitutional justifications under the war power. Other leaders, faced with half the country in open rebellion, would have gone much farther than Lincoln did. But there were clear excesses, like the treatment of Milligan, Vallandigham, and the *New York World*. Such actions were generally not taken at Lincoln's initiative, but as president, he retained ultimate accountability.

Even if it was unclear at the time that these actions were unconstitutional, it should have at least been clear that they were unnecessary and unjust. But in a war where soldiers were dying not just by the thousands but by the hundreds of thousands, the administration's mixed record on civil liberties is perhaps understandable. Still, we should understand clearly that these were regrettable errors, not reliable precedents. Lincoln's occasional efforts to defend these actions do not bear up under the test of time. Overall, however, given the extremity of the country's situation, Lincoln's record on civil liberties was not at all bad.

CHAPTER 8

The Rule of Law in Dark Times

The relation between the Civil War and the rule of law seems paradoxical. Lincoln's goal was to prove that "among free men, there can be no successful appeal from the ballot to the bullet; and that they who take such appeal are sure to lose their case, and pay the cost." Indeed, he had originally called up the militia in the name of the rule of law, because "the laws of the United States have been for some time past, and now are opposed, and the execution thereof obstructed" by "combinations too powerful to be suppressed by the ordinary course of judicial proceedings." Yet, in defense of the democratic rule of law, as we've seen, Lincoln suspended habeas corpus, instituted military trials, and imposed military government on the South. Seemingly, in the name of restoring democracy and the rule of law, he was willing to trample on both.[1]

We have already considered many of Lincoln's most controversial actions: his unilateral response to secession, suspension of habeas corpus, use of martial law, and Emancipation Proclamation. By and large, we have seen, these were constitutionally defensible. What remains for consideration is Lincoln's view of the relationship between the rule of law and the harsh necessities of war. A leader could easily go astray in coping with this complex and conflicted relationship. But Lincoln had an ability to work his way unflinchingly to the heart of an issue and act accordingly, without self-righteousness or arrogance. It was this that allowed him to navigate the chaos of civil war, finding a viable accommodation between wartime needs and legal principle.

LINCOLN'S EVOLVING VIEW OF THE RULE OF LAW

Long before he was a national figure, Lincoln's first important public address was an 1838 speech on "The Perpetuation of Our Political Institutions." His theme was the rule of law. He began by decrying an increasing tendency toward lawlessness and mob rule. "[B]y instances of the perpetrators of such acts going unpunished, the lawless in spirit, are encouraged to become lawless in practice," while even the law-abiding lose faith in the government. When confidence in law had deteriorated, he feared, some Napoleonic figure might step forth to seize the opportunity. How to guard against this danger? "The answer is simple. Let every American, every lover of liberty, every well wisher to his posterity, swear by the blood of the Revolution, never to violate in the least particular, the laws of the country; and never to tolerate their violation by others."[2]

Lincoln waxed eloquent in this speech about obedience to law. "Let reverence for the laws, be breathed by every American mother, to the lisping babe, that prattles on her lap—let it be taught in schools, in seminaries, and in colleges; . . . let it be preached from the pulpit, proclaimed in legislative halls, and enforced in courts of justice." In short, "[L]et it become the *political religion* of the nation; and let the old and the young, the rich and the poor, the grave and the gay, of all sexes and tongues, and colors and conditions, sacrifice unceasingly upon its altars." He did not mean to say, he hastened to add, that there were no bad laws. Such laws should be repealed. But "still while they continue in force, for the sake of example, they should be religiously observed." Now that the passions of the Revolutionary generation had faded from the scene, patriotic sentiment was no longer enough to maintain the social order. Reason—"cold, calculating, unimpassioned reason"—must "furnish all the materials for our future support and defence." Key among these materials is "a *reverence for the constitution and laws*."[3]

Before *Dred Scott*, Lincoln does not seem to have questioned the role of the courts in maintaining the constitutional order. Indeed, according to a newspaper report, Lincoln had once called on Southerners to seek a judicial ruling on slavery in the territories rather than breaking apart the Union. He was quoted as saying that the Supreme Court "is the tribunal to decide such questions, and we will submit to its decisions; and if you do also, there will be an end of the matter. Will you? If not, who are the disunionists, you or we?" If he did say this, he must have soon regretted it when the Court actually ruled on the issue.[4]

When the *Dred Scott* decision came down, Lincoln promptly rejected the ruling as a definitive resolution of the constitutional issue. He agreed that the Supreme Court's "decisions on Constitutional questions, when fully settled, should control, not only the particular cases decided, but the general policy of the country, subject to be disturbed only by amendments of the Constitution as provided in that instrument itself." "More than this," he added, "would be revolution." But he considered Taney's opinion to have questionable value as precedent, as a matter of common sense and of "the customary understanding of the legal profession." The decision's authority was impaired in several ways. It was made by a divided court and seemingly tainted by partisan bias. It was inconsistent with prior government practice. It was based on historical errors. Even so, if Taney's theory "had been before the court more than once, and had there been affirmed and re-affirmed through a course of years, it then might be, perhaps would be, factious, nay, even revolutionary, to not acquiesce in it as a precedent." But under the circumstances, "it is not resistance, it is not factious, it is not even disrespectful, to treat it [the decision] as not having yet quite established a settled doctrine for the country."[5]

In his "House Divided" speech, Lincoln cast additional aspersions on the opinion. He questioned whether the judges had acted impartially and without regard to politics. The case came to the Court before the election, he observed, but the decision was deferred until afterward, and then the case was set for reargument. The incoming president's inaugural address "fervently exhorted the people to abide by the forthcoming decision, *whatever it might be.*" Then "in a few days" came the Court's ruling. Senator Douglas quickly made a speech endorsing it, and the president also seized an early opportunity for doing so. All of these actions fit together too smoothly to have been unplanned, Lincoln intimated. And was this the end of the Court's campaign for slavery? Perhaps not, he warned. A second *Dred Scott* decision might be in the works, limiting the ability of free states to exclude slaves.[6]

By the First Inaugural, Lincoln's position on *Dred Scott* had fully crystallized. He agreed that the Court's decisions "must be binding in any case, upon the parties to a suit, as to the object of that suit." Although such a decision might be erroneous, "still the evil effect following it, being limited to that particular case, with the chance that it may be over-ruled, and never become a precedent for other cases, can better be borne than could the evils of a different practice." In addition, judicial decisions were "also entitled to very high respect and consideration, in all paralel [*sic*] cases, by all other departments of the government." But the "candid citizen must confess that if the policy of the government, upon vital questions, affecting the whole people, is to be irrevocably fixed by decisions of the Supreme Court, the instant they are made, . . . the people will have ceased, to be their own rulers, having, to that extent, practically resigned their government, into the hands of that eminent tribunal." This was not, he said, an "assault upon the court, or the judges." It was their duty to decide the cases before them, and "it is no fault of theirs, if others seek to turn their decisions to political purposes." Thus, Lincoln seemed to have backed away from the view that well-settled precedents were binding on the country as a whole. But he still insisted on the binding effect of judicial decisions on the parties—even decisions wrongfully returning a person to slavery.[7]

Merryman made even that degree of support for judicial authority seem questionable. Whether Taney was right or wrong in *Merryman,* he did issue an order to the executive branch, and that order was ignored. Wasn't this a violation of Lincoln's obligation to "take care that the laws be faithfully executed"? In his special message to Congress soon afterward, Lincoln defended his actions. Lincoln argued that the "whole of the laws which were required to be faithfully executed, were being resisted, and failing of execution, in nearly one-third of the States." "Must they be allowed to finally fail of execution, even had it been perfectly clear, that by the use of the means necessary to their execution, some single law . . . should, to a very limited extent, be violated?" Stating the question more directly, he asked, "[A]re all the laws, *but one,* to go unexecuted, and the government itself go to pieces, lest that one be violated?" Wouldn't this itself be a violation of the oath? But, Lincoln continued, he did not think this dilemma was actually presented, because he believed that he did have the power to suspend habeas corpus. He was apparently unfazed either by Taney's opinion to the contrary or by the impropriety of violating a court order.[8]

As he took office, Lincoln also may have been reevaluating the centrality of law in general. In an unpublished fragment, thought to have been written before the First Inaugural, he emphasized the centrality of the Declaration of Independence rather than such legal institutions as the Constitution or the Union. Without these legal institutions, "we could not have attained the result; but even these, are not the primary cause of our great prosperity." Rather, "There is something back of these, entwining itself more closely about the human heart. That something, is the principle of 'Liberty to all.'" The principle of liberty "was *the* word . . . which has proved an 'apple of gold' to us." In contrast, the "*Union,* and the *Constitution,* are the *picture* of *silver,* subsequently framed around it." The picture was made to preserve and adorn the apple. "The *picture* was made *for* the apple—*not* the apple for the picture." Hence, the Declaration's proclamation of liberty was primary, and the law came second.[9]

Thus, Lincoln's thought seemed to shift over the course of his career—from acceptance of Supreme Court precedents as the ultimate constitutional authority to merely giving them "high respect and consideration," and from obedience even to unjust judicial decrees to outright defiance. Seemingly, Lincoln had gone from absolute obedience to law to a willingness to violate the law whenever necessary. Some aspects of this apparent evolution were real. But as we will see, in other respects, Lincoln's views actually remained more balanced than they may appear.

Dred Scott AND THE LIMITS OF JUDICIAL AUTHORITY

In recent years, the Supreme Court has considered itself the definitive interpreter of the Constitution. In contrast to Lincoln's mature view, the Court now seems to view its decisions as fixing the meaning of the Constitution for the whole country. The Court's assertion of authority has not gone unchallenged by critics.

The Court's most prominent pronouncement regarding its role came in *Cooper v. Aaron*.[10] The case involved Southern resistance to racial integration after *Brown v. Board of Education*. The Court's opinion was unique—not only unanimous but individually signed by each justice to emphasize the Court's unity. The Court asserted that its pronouncements were "the supreme law of the land," binding all state officials under the supremacy clause. Under *Marbury v. Madison,* the Court said, it was not only authorized to interpret the Constitution, it also was "supreme in the exposition" of the Constitution. As the Court put it, *Marbury* "declared the basic principle that the federal judiciary is supreme in the exposition of the law of the Constitution, and that principle has ever since been respected by this Court and the Country as a permanent and indispensable feature of our constitutional system."[11]

More recently, another important decision emphasized the Court's authority to settle divisive national issues. The issue in *Planned Parenthood v. Casey*[12] was whether to overrule *Roe v. Wade*.[13] The Court was closely divided, with the balance of power held by Justices O'Connor, Kennedy, and Souter. In a lengthy joint opinion explaining their views, the three said that *Roe* was entitled to an extraordinary level of respect, even beyond the normal Supreme Court precedent. "Where, in the performance of its judicial duties, the Court decides a case in such a way as to resolve the sort of intensely divisive controversy reflected in *Roe* and those rare, comparable cases, its decision has a dimension that the resolution of the normal case does not carry." This dimension is present "whenever the Court's interpretation of the Constitution calls the contending sides of a national controversy to end their national division by accepting a common mandate rooted in the Constitution." Although these cases are rare, "when the Court does act in this way, its decision requires an equally rare precedential force to counter the inevitable efforts to overturn it and to thwart its implementation." For backing down would appear to be "a surrender to political pressure, and an unjustified repudiation of the principle on which the Court staked its authority in the first instance." Overruling *Roe* would cause "both profound and unnecessary damage to the Court's legitimacy, and to the Nation's commitment to the rule of law."[14]

The Court's claim to be the final authority on the meaning of the Constitution has been vigorously challenged, not least by occupants of the White House. The dispute has existed since early in our history. In his campaign to eliminate the Bank of the United States, for instance, Andrew Jackson was unmoved by the Supreme Court's unequivocal holding that the bank was constitutional. He insisted that the executive and legislative branches have as much right to interpret the Constitution in the exercise of their own powers as the Supreme Court does in the exercise of its powers. Thomas Jefferson was even more outspoken. Jefferson "den[ied] the right they [judges like Marshall] usurp of exclusively explaining the constitution." If the judges had this right, vis-à-vis the other branches of government, the Constitution would be self-defeating. "For intending to establish three departments, co-ordinate and independent, that they might check and balance one another, it has given, according to this opinion, to one of them alone, the right to prescribe rules for the government of the others, and to that one too, which is unelected by, and independent of the nation." If judges had the final word over its meaning, the Constitution would be "a mere thing of wax in the hands of the judiciary, which they may twist and shape into any form they please." In Jefferson's view, "[E]ach department is truly independent of the others, and has an equal right to decide for itself what is the meaning of the constitution in the cases submitted to its action; and especially, where it is to act ultimately and without appeal."[15]

The debate has continued among modern scholars. Much of the scholarship on the subject opposes judicial supremacy—though it is unclear whether this is because of the actual weight of the arguments or merely because the Court's critics feel more strongly motivated to write about the subject. Three main arguments are made against judicial supremacy.

Along the lines sketched by Jefferson, the first argument against judicial supremacy invokes the separation of powers. The key concept here is that the three branches are supposed to be coordinate and independent. Members of each have taken an oath to support the Constitution. Consequently, each branch must make its own independent judgment about the meaning of the Constitution. In particular, the president's duty to take care that the laws be faithfully executed requires that he determine for himself what the laws actually require. The Court is also entitled to decide constitutional questions, but its precedents are not binding on the other branches.[16]

The second argument is based on the nature of the judicial role. When the Supreme Court decides a case, its opinions are intently scrutinized by the press as well as by lawyers. It is those opinions that are studied in classes in law schools. But the core function of courts is not to issue opinions. Historically, many Anglo-American courts have decided cases without written opinions, either with an oral statement from the bench or no explanation at all (especially in the case of trial courts). What all courts do, however, is issue judgments—dismissing lawsuits, awarding damages, enjoining illegal conduct, or at the appellate level, reversing or affirming the trial court. It is these judgments that are the real business of the courts. Judicial opinions are merely explanations of the judge's reasons, and are no more "the law" than the statement a president may issue when he signs a bill. Only the judgment is the legally operative act. The opinion is not itself a legally operative act, though it is significant because it helps predict how the court will rule in later cases. Consequently, though the court's *judgment* may bind other branches, its *opinion* is no more binding than a press release.[17]

The third argument is based on the need for dialogue about critical constitutional issues. Everyone, including the justices, agrees that the Supreme Court is not infallible. (Otherwise, there would be no dissenting opinions!) If society is completely bound by the Court's opinions, dialogue about constitutional issues is cut off the moment the Court issues a ruling. Among other flaws, this deprives the Court of the opportunity to reconsider its views—complete deference toward its views means that no future cases will come before the Court raising the same issue. It is healthier for the three branches of government to pursue their own diverse constitutional views, leaving it to the system of checks and balances to maintain an overall equilibrium.[18]

Besides questioning each of these claims, supporters of judicial supremacy offer two major arguments of their own. Their first argument stresses the importance of having some authoritative method for settling disputes. Critics of judicial supremacy seem sanguine about the possibility of a series of constitutional crises, in which branches of the government go head to head over constitutional issues. But one of the key functions of courts is to provide a peaceful, orderly method of resolving disputes. Yes, the Constitution does divide powers among independent branches, so as to maintain democracy and prevent tyranny. But the Constitution was supposed to be a scheme for effective government, not merely unending political debate. Some authoritative method is needed to resolve disputes about the meaning of the Constitution. Without such a dispute resolution mechanism, the Constitution cannot succeed in its efforts to "establish Justice, insure domestic Tranquility, . . . promote the general Welfare, and secure the Blessings of Liberty."[19]

The second major argument for judicial supremacy emphasizes the unique strength of courts as interpreters of the Constitution. One obvious reason is the Court's relatively nonpolitical position. To say that the Court always stands above politics is an exaggeration, but the justices, unlike politicians, do not have to keep a constant eye on reelection. If the point of having a written Constitution is to provide a check on the political process, this check should not itself be at the whim of political forces. This argument is all the more powerful when we deal with the Bill of Rights, which limits majority rule. Allowing politicians rather than judges to interpret the Bill of Rights would be leaving the fox to guard the henhouse. In addition, unlike presidents or members of Congress, judges are specifically chosen for their legal expertise. And the judicial process is uniquely designed as a forum of principle rather than politics, with its presentation of opposing arguments, its deliberative qualities, and its mandate for reasoned explanation of decisions.[20]

Does the president have a legal duty to follow the rulings of the Supreme Court? The arguments on both sides seem to have some merit. We may make some progress by clarifying the question. One reason for the confusion is that the term *legal duty* covers a multitude of different situations, in terms of the variety of law involved, the type of duty, and the strength of the duty. A common-law judicial opinion is "law," but not in quite the same way as a statute. A duty may be "legal" in several different senses. And even where a legal duty of some kind does exist, it might be overridden in special circumstances. The debaters on judicial supremacy have not always been careful in drawing these distinctions.

We can make a start in clarifying the debate by distinguishing between two types of legal duties. In the narrower sense, a legal duty exists when the law provides an injured person with a legal remedy against the actor. Thus, a doctor has a duty to use reasonable care and obtain informed consent from patients; breach of this duty results in an award of damages for malpractice. In this narrow sense, a legal duty is the flip side of a legal right—someone has a duty to refrain from conduct if and only if the conduct would violate someone else's enforceable legal rights.

In a broader sense, however, a legal duty exists whenever a law-abiding citizen would refrain from certain conduct, regardless of whether the duty is owed to any particular person or whether any legal remedy exists. In this sense, a juror has a legal duty to follow the judge's instructions rather than acquitting the defendant for other reasons. If the jury chooses to acquit in violation of the law, there is no remedy: the acquittal must stand and the jurors cannot be sanctioned. So in the narrower sense, jurors have no legal duty to obey the judge's instructions. Nevertheless, law-abiding jurors would generally do so, thus recognizing a legal duty in the broader sense. In extreme cases, however, jurors might reasonably conclude that their general duty to follow instructions is trumped by more urgent considerations.

These distinctions may seem abstruse, but the basic point is a simple one. If a presidential action is subject to review by the courts, and he knows in advance how they will rule on the case, respect for the legal process means that he should comply in advance. For the executive to rely on his own contrary view of the law is merely to delay the inevitable, to no one's good and to the cost of any individual whose legal rights have been invaded. When a presidential action is not subject to review by the courts, he still owes the Supreme Court's views a respectful hearing, but he need not accept the Court's general pronouncements about legal principles.[21]

In the narrower sense, it seems clear that the Supreme Court's interpretations of the Constitution sometimes *can* create legal duties on the part of the executive branch. For instance, the police have a duty to provide *Miranda* warnings—their failure to do so will result in the exclusion of the confession. Other forms of police misconduct may result in an award of damages, like the failure to obtain a search warrant when the Supreme Court has said that one is necessary. These rules of constitutional law create defined duties toward specific persons backed by legal remedies. They create legal duties much like those of tort, contract, and property law. They are part of federal law—of the "supreme law of the land"—just as state court rulings are part of a state's law. In determining whether the defendant violated the plaintiff's rights under state law, we would think it bizarre for a federal court to ignore a state supreme court's interpretation of its own state constitution. We would rightly regard that interpretation as itself part and parcel of state law. The same is true of Supreme Court rulings as a part of federal law: within their scope of application, they define legal rights and duties under federal law.[22]

Lincoln might well have been faced with the narrower issue of enforcing legal rights arising out of *Dred Scott.* If a slave in the same position as Scott had escaped into Illinois, and Lincoln were called upon to execute the Fugitive Slave Act, he would have been violating his legal duty to the owner if he refused to act because of his disagreement with the Court's interpretation of the law. Or at least this is true if we assume that *Dred Scott* in fact settled the judiciary's view of the issue. Given the degree of division within the Court, the confusing multiple opinions, and the analytical weakness of Taney's opinion, *Dred Scott* arguably was not a definitive judicial resolution of the issue, as Lincoln himself argued in his Springfield speech about the case. So long as the law was unsettled, Lincoln—like any other legal actor—was free to take his chances about the final resolution by the courts. But if the rule had been well settled, so that individuals had clearly defined legal rights, then Lincoln would have been bound to respect those rights.

But a presidential action, though logically at odds with the Supreme Court's vision of the Constitution, may not violate any legal duty in this narrower sense. For example, if Congress passed a territorial slave code in conformity with *Dred Scott,* no one would have any conceivable legal remedy if Lincoln vetoed the statute. The veto would not violate anyone's legal rights. Similarly, if Lincoln pardoned someone who helped Scott escape, again he would be violating no one's rights. As with a juror's vote to acquit, a pardon or a veto is subject to no judicial remedies and does not violate anyone's rights. Still, such a pardon or veto might sometimes be thought to reflect a disrespect for "the law," and hence violate a "legal duty" in the broader sense.[23]

When we consider the narrower sense of legal duty, the argument for judicial supremacy is at its strongest. By hypothesis, we are dealing with situations in which the courts would ultimately rule in favor of the aggrieved individual and provide a remedy. Deciding specific legal claims about the rights of individuals is the core function of the courts, and at most a peripheral function of the executive. In this setting, judicial supremacy is strongly bolstered by the need for effective settlement of conflicts and the superior institutional design of the courts for deciding legal disputes. Knowing how a court will ultimately resolve a specific dispute within its competence, a president should not evade the legally inevitable outcome. For the president to drag his heels in this situation or frustrate the legal process is at best an effort to exploit unfairly the delays and inefficiencies of the court system. To do so would be just as lawless as a judge indefinitely postponing the trial of a clear-cut case because he disagreed with the prosecutor's decision to file it.

The certainty of executive execution of the law, including rules of law articulated by the courts, is important both for the security of individual rights and for the supremacy of federal law. If every disagreement with judicial interpretation were viewed as an excuse for executive noncompliance, the rule of law could hardly function. Individuals need to be assured of compliance. The system could not work effectively if enforcement depended on the executive's agreement with judicial reasoning.

When we think of legal duty in the broader sense, however, the argument for judicial supremacy is weaker. Where enforceable legal rights are not involved, the need for executive compliance is less pressing. On the other hand, the arguments against judicial supremacy have real bite here. If presidents and legislatures must *always* accept the Supreme Court's views as dogma, even when their actions do not in themselves violate anyone's legal rights, then judicial supremacy does conflict with other important norms. Such an extreme form of judicial supremacy would curtail the independence of the other branches of government and would cut off dialogue about constitutional issues completely. Such a strong form of judicial supremacy is also unnecessary to effectuate the core judicial function of defining and enforcing individual rights and duties.

This does not mean that presidents should freely ignore judicial interpretations of the Constitution, even when the president's action would not violate anyone's legal rights as defined by the courts. The arguments for judicial supremacy are not strong enough to dictate complete abdication to the courts in such situations, but they are strong enough to provide grounds for deference to judicial opinions. Even if the president disagrees with the Court's viewpoint, it may be wise to defer. Many issues, even constitutional issues, are simply not significant enough to justify keeping them "in play." Even as to more important issues, deference to the courts may be wise because it is important for the government to speak with one voice, or simply because courts are better designed institutionally to engage in constitutional interpretation than the executive. After all, the Justice Department does not have the benefit of adversary presentations, is inevitably subject to political pressures, and has no special mandate to represent the interest of the politically powerless. The need for settled interpretation is particularly strong regarding structural issues, so that everyone has the same understanding of the "rules of the game."

Lincoln was wrong if he meant to say that, in executing his duties under specific statutes such as the Fugitive Slave Act, he would ignore judicial rulings such as *Dred Scott.* Or at least, he was wrong about his obligations under the law. Whether he had the *moral* right to ignore *Dred Scott,* the Fugitive Slave Act, or the Constitution itself on the subject of slavery, is another question. To say that the law requires something, does not necessarily exclude civil disobedience. But Lincoln himself clearly did not embrace civil disobedience on the slavery issue. If Lincoln meant to ignore all judicial interpretations in carrying out his law enforcement duties as president, the South would have had a valid complaint, because Lincoln would be systematically violating the legal rights of individual Southerners.

If Lincoln meant instead that he would sign legislation banning slavery in the territories, this action would violate no one's legal rights. The constitutionality of such legislation was subject to legitimate dispute, and the legal process would offer protection against any actual violation of legal rights under the statute. Ultimately, the statue might prove constitutionally unenforceable, but that does not make signing it illegal. Normally, a president might properly defer to the Supreme Court's interpretations even in this setting, but not here. The arguments for deferring to the Court's views, even when the president is taking actions outside the judiciary's reach, were particularly weak with regard to *Dred Scott.* The importance of the slavery issue far outweighed the value of settling constitutional disputes efficiently, and the decision itself was so deeply flawed as to be entitled to little respect in its own right. In short, even under a view which is fairly favorable toward judicial supremacy, Lincoln would have been right to say that *Dred Scott* did not end legitimate debate about the issue of slavery and the territories.

Merryman AND THE LIMITS OF OBEDIENCE

Despite the disagreement about judicial supremacy, almost everyone agrees about one point: the president must enforce the judgments of the federal courts in specific cases, right or wrong. As James Madison said when he refused a governor's request to block enforcement of a federal decree, the president "is not only unauthorized to prevent the execution of a Decree sanctioned by the Supreme Court" but is "especially enjoined by statute to carry into effect such decree, where opposition be made to it." He concluded that he had "no legal discretion" in the matter. With a single notable exception, constitutional scholars concur with Madison.[24]

Lincoln's action in *Merryman* seems inconsistent with this consensus. True, he believed that Taney's view of the suspension power was wrong. But Taney did issue an order to produce Merryman, backed later by a contempt citation. Right or wrong, shouldn't Lincoln and his subordinates have complied with these orders? Even if it was illegal, Lincoln's action might arguably have been justified on the basis of necessity—his "all the laws but one" argument. But he believed this defense was not ultimately required. Was his action legal?

Lincoln's action might suggest that he thought he had the general power to second-guess judicial orders. The argument in favor of such a presidential power has been pressed with great ingenuity, relying on the postulate that each coordinate branch of government is independent within its own realm. Thus, if the president may interpret the Constitution independently when he is considering whether to veto a bill, he should have the power to interpret the Constitution independently when he is exercising his duty to execute the laws. Judicial decrees are not self-executing; they often require the intervention of an executive officer such as a marshal. The president, then, must have the power to determine whether a decree is valid, in order to determine whether it is part of the law he must "faithfully execute" or contrary to that law.[25]

This argument for executive nullification has not been well received, even among scholars generally hostile to judicial supremacy. Critics point out that *Merryman* is the only known instance where the president has actually disobeyed a court order merely because he disagreed with it. They also argue that "the available historical materials . . . at least suggest that judgments are absolutely binding. . . . [J]udgments have always been thought of as final *between* the judicial department and the political departments." A contrary view would undermine the judiciary's position as a coordinate department, effectively reducing it to a mere adviser to the president, who would have the final say about the disposition of lawsuits. The "judicial power" would not amount to much if judgments could be overruled at will by the other branches. And the practical consequences are at least potentially chaotic, threatening a constitutional crisis any time the Court rules against the government in litigation. In this respect, executive nullification has similar vices to Calhoun's theory of state nullification.[26]

The argument for executive nullification is based on the president's admitted right to make independent constitutional judgments in connection with vetoes, pardons, and similar actions. This is a non sequitur. The ability of the president to follow his own constitutional views in issuing a pardon or veto follows simply from the fact that this action does not violate a legally enforceable duty to any individual. But a judgment *does* create a right to enforcement on behalf of the beneficiary. Moreover, the validity of the judgment does not depend on the correctness of the court's decision. A judgment based on an error of law is still an enforceable legal judgment. Otherwise, having a judgment would mean nothing, since any time enforcement was sought, the whole case could be reopened.

If we reject executive nullification, we seem to have left Lincoln in a precarious position. Notably, however, he did not feel called upon to offer a separate legal defense of his defiance of Taney's order, much less defend executive nullification generally. Instead, he seems to have assumed that if the suspension of the writ was valid, he was entitled to ignore Taney's order. Before we deem his actions lawless, we should at least consider the possibility that Lincoln's assumption was correct.

At first blush, this assumption seems contrary to the basic rule about court judgments: a judgment's validity generally is completely unrelated to its correctness. Once an injunction is issued, it must be obeyed even if it was erroneous. A legal error in entering the injunction is no defense to a contempt citation. This is true even if the injunction violates a constitutional right. For instance, a court order that violates the First Amendment normally must be obeyed until it is set aside on appeal. Similarly, if a judgment is entered in one state, another state must recognize that judgment as valid without inquiring into the merits of the case. Hence, even if Taney was wrong, his order was entitled to obedience. The incorrectness of Taney's view on the merits would be no defense in a contempt hearing. Similarly, if Taney had then issued a damage award to Merryman, as he might have done in an action for false imprisonment, that judgment would have been enforceable in any other court in the Union, regardless of the underlying merits. In lawyer's jargon, the judgment is immune from collateral attack. In plainer language, it acquires a life and validity of its own, disconnected from the legal and factual claims that gave birth to it.[27]

But there is an important exception. A court that lacks the power to hear a case—lacks jurisdiction over the defendant or over the subject matter of the case—cannot give itself jurisdiction by fiat. The court's judgment is open to attack on the basis of lack of jurisdiction. If the executive was cited for contempt in such a case, he could argue that the order was void. If a damage award was entered, he could resist enforcement on the basis of lack of jurisdiction. If Taney did not merely make an error of law, but proceeded in the absence of jurisdiction, his order would create no legal obligation. That at least was the traditional rule applying at the time. Today a more pragmatic approach might be taken. Under this more pragmatic approach, a legal obligation may be created by a judgment, even in the absence of jurisdiction, if no important policy is infringed by doing so.[28]

It probably goes too far to say that the president can always make his own independent determination of whether a court had jurisdiction. If the jurisdictional issue has been fully litigated between the parties, the loser should not have the right to "appeal" to the president. Also, not every jurisdictional issue is significant enough to justify a presidential refusal to enforce a judgment. For example, when jurisdiction is based on the parties' being citizens of different states, Congress has required that the amount in controversy must exceed a certain sum. A judicial error in this regard clearly would not be a valid basis for the president to decline enforcement. (Similarly, the question of whether a case could be brought directly before the Supreme Court or only by appeal from a lower court, the issue in *Marbury v. Madison,* clearly does not seem earthshaking enough to justify noncompliance.) But if the court's exercise of judicial power is a clear usurpation of authority over a case that it has no colorable claim to be hearing, or if the court's claim of jurisdiction invades some critical constitutional policy, then the president may not be obligated to obey. Regard for checks and balances should make us reluctant to go much beyond such extraordinary cases. But when a court acts without jurisdiction at the expense of critical constitutional values, presidential noncompliance coheres with our normal understanding of the binding effects of judicial decrees.

Whether we take the traditional approach and speak of jurisdiction, or a pragmatic approach based on constitutional policy, the question is ultimately the same: how drastic an effect does habeas suspension have on the courts? Does it merely require them, on the merits, to reject the petition if they find that the suspension is valid? Or does it render them utterly powerless to go forward after being notified of the situation, so that the executive is excused from paying any further attention to the proceedings?

Arguably, a valid suspension of the writ does eliminate the court's very power to proceed. This was apparently Congress's view in the Habeas Corpus Act, which confirmed the suspension. The jurisdictional view is also supported by Taney's comment in another case. When a state court received a habeas petition from a federal prisoner, Taney did not merely say that granting relief had been erroneous. Instead, he said, when state judges learn that a petitioner is held in federal custody, "they can proceed no further." Thus, when habeas runs into a paramount federal interest, something more than ordinary legal error is involved if the court does not desist.[29]

This jurisdictional view of suspension also fits the purpose of suspending the writ. Suspension takes place only when needed to preserve the public safety during invasion or insurrection. Thus, by definition, we are dealing with dire emergencies. It would be a considerable burden on the officers who are seeking to cope with the emergency if they were required to attend to habeas litigation. Habeas proceedings would require them to produce prisoners before a potentially disloyal tribunal and to engage in litigation over the validity of their actions. It also would introduce the possibility of release with or without bail. All of this would be highly disruptive to efforts to cope with the emergency. Thus, a plausible argument can be made that during a suspension, the executive not only has a valid legal defense that the habeas court should accept, but he is entitled to ignore any order to appear or to produce or release the prisoner. As precedent for this, one might refer to the Revolutionary War officer's action, apparently accepted by the Framers, of ignoring a state habeas petition on instructions from the Continental Congress. Essentially, on this view, during suspension, a writ of habeas corpus means little more than a purported writ of harum scarum. Both are nullities.[30]

The strongest argument against the jurisdictional view of suspension is that in practice it would leave the executive as the sole judge of whether the writ was validly suspended. This is true only to a limited extent. After the insurrection is over, the officer might be liable for damages if the detention was unwarranted. The law of the time did not recognize any good faith defense to a damage action based on an illegal official act. Moreover, Congress has the final word about habeas and could intervene to end the suspension. Thus, the president would not be completely unchecked. Still, allowing the president to ignore an adverse ruling about the validity of the suspension is undoubtedly dangerous. The counterargument is that it is more dangerous to require compliance with erroneous judicial rulings regarding suspension, during extreme emergencies like the outbreak of the Civil War.[31]

Under this analysis, Lincoln's action in *Merryman* would not stand for any general right to disobey judicial decrees. It would stand only for a limited right to disobey decrees when the judge lacked the sheer power to issue a binding order. If this jurisdictional analysis is rejected, however, we should concede that Lincoln's action was unlawful. It is fruitless to argue for a general power of executive nullification. Lincoln himself did not even offer this defense, and history speaks strongly against it. Instead, we are thrown back on the necessity defense that he did in fact offer.

"ALL THE LAWS BUT ONE"

Some of Lincoln's initial acts were unconstitutional even under the relatively favorable view of his powers taken in this book. At least his unauthorized expansion of the regular army and disbursement of funds fall into this category. Disobedience of Taney's order may fall into the same category, unless that order was a nullity. There may well have been other unlawful actions. For example, Lincoln's suspension of habeas in areas removed from any hint of insurrection arguably went beyond his emergency powers to respond to sudden attack. And of course, none of the constitutional arguments in favor of Lincoln's actions during the war are incontestable. Some would argue that nearly everything Lincoln did in those early days was unconstitutional. Thus, to a smaller or greater extent, we are forced to consider Lincoln's claim that otherwise unlawful actions were justified by necessity. At first blush, it seems that Lincoln was claiming to stand above the law in dealing with the emergency.

Lincoln's invocation of necessity was not unprecedented. According to Jefferson, a "strict observance of the written laws is doubtless *one* of the high duties of a good citizen, but it is not the *highest.*" Rather, Jefferson claimed, the "laws of necessity, of self-preservation, of saving our country when in danger, are of higher obligation." For to "lose our country by a scrupulous adherence to written law, would be to lose the law itself, with life, liberty, property and all those who are enjoying them with us; thus absurdly sacrificing the end to the means." Thus, Jefferson observed, when Washington besieged Yorktown, "he leveled the suburbs, feeling that the laws of property must be postponed to the safety of the nation." Likewise, if the president learned of an opportunity to acquire Florida for the United States while Congress was not in session to appropriate the funds, shouldn't he nevertheless act "to have secured the good to his country, and to have trusted to their justice for the transgression of the law?" (This discretion does not belong to low-level officials, however, but only in those "who accept of great charges, to risk themselves on great occasions, when the safety of the nation, or some of its very high interests are at stake.") For an "officer is bound to obey orders; yet he would be a bad one who should do it in cases for which they were not intended, and which involved the most important consequences."[32]

Earlier, Jefferson had taken a similar position in connection with the Louisiana Purchase. He thought that the Constitution did not authorize the federal government to acquire new territory except through a constitutional amendment. Thus, the "Executive in seizing the fugitive occurrence which so much advances the good of their country, have done an act beyond the Constitution." Similarly, the "Legislature in casting behind them metaphysical subtleties, and risking themselves like faithful servants, must ratify & pay for it, and throw themselves on their country for doing for them unauthorized what we know they would have done for themselves had they been in a situation to do it." Jefferson compared these necessary but unlawful acts to a guardian making an advantageous, but unauthorized, land purchase on behalf of his ward. When the ward came of age, the guardian would have to say, "I did this for your good; I pretend to no right to bind you: you may disavow me, and I must get out of the scrape as I can: I thought it my duty to risk myself for you."[33]

Jefferson's argument was that a president must sometimes go *beyond* the law, but he did not argue that the president's action was *above* the law. Circumstances might make an unlawful action necessary for the good of the nation, but the president remained answerable for the violation of the law. He must then depend on absolution or else face the legal consequences.

Jefferson followed the classic liberal approach to the problem of emergency decisions. The executive had a moral duty to respond to grave emergencies, despite legalities, but necessity was not a legal defense for his actions. Even actions taken in good faith could result in damages or other sanctions such as impeachment, unless Congress ratified the action and shielded the executive, usually by indemnifying him from any damage award. Thus, the executive always remained answerable for his conduct to Congress, the legal system, and the people. The maxim that "necessity knows no law" was foreign to classic liberal thought.[34]

Lincoln's defense of his arguably illegal actions fell into two parts. First, he argued that his actions, "whether strictly legal or not," were taken in response to public demand and a public necessity, "trusting, then as now, that Congress would readily ratify them." Second, he argued that actions such as suspending habeas, even if illegal, were not inconsistent with his oath to "take care that the laws be faithfully executed." Here, Lincoln argued that he lacked the ability to execute *all* of the laws. Instead, he was faced with the choice between violating a "single law" to a "very limited extent," or seeing every law "failing of execution, in nearly one-third of the States." Thus, his oath required him to choose the lesser of the two evils in terms of observance of the law. It is here that he posed the famous question, "[A]re all the laws, *but one,* to go unexecuted, and the government itself, go to pieces, lest that one be violated?" He continued with another question: "[W]ould not the official oath be broken, if the government should be overthrown, when it was believed that disregarding the single law, would tend to preserve it?"[35]

In short, on careful reading, Lincoln was not arguing for the *legal* power to take emergency actions contrary to statutory or constitutional mandates. Instead, his argument fit well within the classic liberal view of emergency power. While unlawful, his actions could be ratified by Congress if it chose to do so ("trusting, then as now, that Congress would readily ratify them"). The actions were also morally consistent with his oath of office ("would not the official oath be broken . . . ?").

Congress did respond with legislation ratifying the president's military actions. Later, it augmented its support of the president with an immunity statute. An 1863 statute provided that "any order of the president, or under his authority, made at any time during the existence of the present rebellion, shall be a defence in all courts to any action or prosecution . . . for any search, seizure, arrest, or imprisonment." The statute also gave the defendant the power to remove state litigation to federal court and provided a two-year statute of limitations (even if the case remained in state court) for any action brought against an officer acting "under color of" presidential or congressional authority.[36]

The Supreme Court upheld this statute in *Mitchell v. Clark*.[37] When the Civil War began, the Court explained, no legal authority had existed to deal with dangerous, disloyal individuals, thus requiring officials to take extralegal action. "For most of these acts there was constitutional power in congress to have authorized them, if it had acted in the matter in advance." In addition, perhaps "in a few cases, for acts performed in haste and in the presence of an overpowering emergency, there was no constitutional power anywhere to make them good." The Court had no doubt about the validity of the statute: "That an act passed after the event, which, in effect, ratifies what has been done, and declares that no suit shall be sustained against the party acting under color of authority, is valid, so far as congress could have conferred such authority before, admits of no reasonable doubt." For "[t]hese are ordinary acts of indemnity passed by all governments when the occasion requires it."[38]

This immunity covered most of Lincoln's actions. The transfer of money to private hands, the expansion of the military, and the suspension of habeas, all were well within the power of Congress. Congress did not, however, have power to authorize military trials of civilians in the North in cases such as *Milligan*. Here, however, the officers responsible could rely for protection on the statute of limitations and the opportunity to remove any suit against them to federal court. Thus, in the end, Congress ratified as much of the executive's actions as it could, excusing the lack of prior authorization, and tried to ensure a fair legal procedure for dealing with the remaining cases. Nowhere was there any thought that necessity alone gave the president an exemption from the legal consequences of violating statutory or constitutional requirements. Lincoln does not seem to have claimed such legal immunity. Nor did he claim that pressing circumstances overrode the "take care" duty to follow the law. He merely observed that he was faced with the utter impossibility of full compliance and had to choose the lesser of two evils. We tend to read his statements differently, as if they claimed more, only because we no longer see them in their original context.

AFTERWORD *The Lessons of History*

 The Civil War was a crisis without parallel in our nation's history. When Lincoln took office in March 1861, the lower South had declared independence and rejected federal authority. Lincoln's predecessor had announced that he had little if any power to respond. Others argued that secession was constitutional. Forts in Florida and South Carolina were in danger of being taken by force, and others were already in Southern hands. In the meantime, Lincoln had only the skeleton of a national government behind him. When the war came just a few weeks later, he had to take unprecedented action, hastily mustering a military force, suspending habeas corpus, and commencing a formal state of war with a blockade. Much of this was done without congressional authority.

It may seem that Lincoln violated the rule of law in his effort to vindicate the legal order. Much of this apparent paradox dissolves on closer examination, partly because most of his actions were indeed lawful, and partly because the rule of law is not an inflexible concept. Yet, a subtler paradox persists. The rule of law is usually contrasted with the "rule of men." But at least in a time of crisis, maintaining the ideals of the rule of law depends in a crucial way on the character and courage of a society's leaders.

As we have seen, most of what Lincoln did, then and later, was in fact constitutional. He was correct that secession was unconstitutional, a revolutionary act rather than a legitimate exercise of state sovereignty. He was also correct that, in actual areas of war or insurrection, he had emergency power to suspend habeas and impose martial law. This is not to say that everything he did was constitutional. Military jurisdiction was extended beyond constitutional bounds in the North; money was spent and the military expanded without the necessary authority from Congress; and freedom of speech was sometimes infringed. Not a perfect record, but a creditable one, under incredibly trying circumstances.

What are we to learn from this, in a world far removed from Lincoln's? Lincoln himself was doubtful that history could answer the questions that confronted him. "The dogmas of the quiet past," he said, "are inadequate to the stormy present." Rather, "[a]s our case is new, so we must think anew, and act anew." So perhaps it is best to begin with what we should *not* learn from the Civil War experience.[1]

Viewing Lincoln's actions, it is tempting to take the wrong lessons. Lincoln's presidency does not stand for the proposition that on great occasions, great men rise above the law. Lincoln did not claim that public necessity gave him any immunity from the demands of the law. He felt compelled to act without congressional authority. But he did not deny that this put him at risk if Congress failed to back him up. His actions, even if taken without specific congressional authority, were rarely contrary to the will of Congress. Instead, he primarily acted in the gray area of congressional silence, where the modern Supreme Court has usually recognized the legitimacy of presidential initiative. His unilateral response to Fort Sumter also does not stand for a general presidential power to take the nation to war without congressional approval. Large parts of the country were already under the control of a hostile power which had initiated the conflict by firing on the U.S. military. Lincoln's response fell within the acknowledged power of the president to respond to sudden attack, and did not require him to claim a broader power to initiate hostilities at will.

Nor, by and large, does the Civil War provide any general warrant for abandoning constitutional protections in times of crisis. Most of Lincoln's emergency actions fell within a much narrower power to suspend the normal legal process in the actual vicinity of war or insurrection, where the authority of the government was challenged by forces too strong for the conventional legal system to control. This narrower power was still subject to abuse, with unnecessary harm to civil liberties, but it was confined to areas where force had already displaced law as the operative principle. The fact that Lincoln acted under narrower powers does not disprove the existence of broader ones, but it does not support them either.

If these are the wrong lessons to learn, what are the right ones? Two lessons in particular stand out.

The first concerns the uses of history in constitutional interpretation. Modern-day originalists parse the constitutional debates and legal sources of the Framing era, looking for clues about the meaning of specific phrases in the Constitution. What they miss is the history that was lived by the Framers. Men such as Madison and Hamilton had lived through dangerous times. They had learned, the hard way, that it is only "united we stand." They had seen firsthand both the need for strong government and the need to protect liberty. If we seek to understand their handiwork, it will not do to separate their words and ideas from the struggles of their times.

Lincoln's form of nationalism remains relevant for us today. Midway through the writing of this book came a brutal and frightening reminder that peace and security can never be taken wholly for granted. In interpreting the very real role of the states in the constitutional scheme, we must not forget that the *primary* purpose of the Constitution was not to enshrine state sovereignty but to create "a more perfect Union." As Lincoln recognized, the Constitution was an exercise in nation building. The Framers did construct checks and balances; they did respect the prerogatives of state governments; they did not expect the federal government to be all-powerful. During times of peace and prosperity, it is easy to remember these qualifications, but to forget the overriding purpose of creating a central government strong enough to ensure the nation's security and prosperity. When times are easy, we may come to regard federal power as an embarrassment and a threat. It is only when we come to hard times—like those of the Framers—that we recall why we really need a federal government.

The second lesson derives from Lincoln himself. This lesson involves the indispensable role of character in times of crisis. In a grave emergency, it is easy to lose our way. In retrospect, it may be easy to identify the nature of the real threat and diagnose the necessary response. In the crisis itself, it is all too easy to flounder, unsure of which way to go. This must have been especially true in 1861 for an inexperienced and untested president, faced with an unprecedented national crisis while coping with an unstable political base. In the end, the war imposed a human cost beyond anyone's desires or expectations. Lincoln held firm throughout the storm.[2]

But, in a terrible crisis, failing to do what is necessary is only one of the risks. The other risk is that a zealous reaction to necessity will trample everything else underfoot. In any emergency, some people will see the need to take harsh actions. Others will fear that individual rights and needs will be crushed in the rush to save the nation. Lincoln was extraordinary because he could see both at once. Unlike many of his critics, he could see that the times demanded extraordinary measures. Unlike many of his subordinates, he could maintain a sense of perspective about these measures and their human costs. He could also keep clearly in mind that the long-term goal was not merely to crush the rebellion but to save the nation as a bastion of liberty. Thus, Lincoln never flinched from stern measures but he never forgot the need to keep the juggernaut in check. In his ability to combine ruthless pragmatism and a deep fidelity to principle, he may have been unique.

A moral philosopher has defined courage as "the duty to defend or pursue what is important to us in the face of obstacles that make this difficult or dangerous, although neither futile nor suicidal." This requires a moral judgment about the seriousness of the danger. Moral judgment is also needed to "steer us between the twin dangers of timidity and overzealousness, of doing too little to uphold our commitments and of rushing headlong into extravagance." Judgment of this kind is needed, we are told, even under the extreme conditions of the battlefield. This form of courage—unshakable determination, combined with a shrewd sense of reality—was Lincoln's greatest source of strength.[3]

Lincoln's character is thrown into bolder relief by contrast with some of the other key actors of the time. Buchanan was weak and irresolute, aware of the need to preserve the Union but unable to convert this perception into meaningful action. Most of the time, he was a pawn of his circle of advisers. Many of Lincoln's generals were too timid on the battlefield, but too quick to use their authority over the civilian populace. They lacked Lincoln's ability to discern which restrictions on civilians were necessary and which exacted an unnecessary human cost.

Finally, there was Lincoln's great judicial adversary, Chief Justice Taney. Although not a bad man by any means, Taney was arrogant and rigid. His *Merryman* opinion was deliberately written so as to weaken the president as much as possible. It was not just that he ruled against Lincoln on the habeas issue, but he went out of his way to undermine any claim of emergency power of any kind. Taney even seemed oblivious to the existence of the emergency itself, as if the unrest in Maryland were merely a routine law enforcement problem. He failed to realize the relevance of his own experiences with Andrew Jackson or of his own opinion in *Luther v. Borden,* both of which should have given him a clearer view of presidential authority. To top it all off, he failed to give the government a genuine opportunity to be heard, mocked Lincoln for failing to observe his oath of office, and widely publicized his opinion in order to undermine the administration. A judge with a little less self-righteousness and a little more humility might still have ruled against Lincoln, but he would not have overreached so badly. It was much the same arrogance that lead Taney to think he could settle the slavery issue single-handedly with his *Dred Scott* opinion.

It was Lincoln's character—his ability, judgment, courage, and humanity—that brought the Union through the war with the Constitution intact. It was as much dumb luck as anything else that placed Lincoln in the White House in this critical time. To expect another Lincoln would be foolish. Nor should the legal system be designed on the assumption that all leaders will have his qualities. Even the wisest rulers must be restrained by law. But no matter how many checks and balances and protections we build into the system, we must keep in mind Hamilton's admonition. "Sir, when you have divided and nicely balanced the departments of government; when you have strongly connected the virtue of your rulers with their interest; when, in short, you have rendered your system as perfect as human forms can be—you must place confidence; you must give power." In the end, all power can be abused, so we must take the risk of putting confidence in those who exercise power. This is as much true of generals and justices as it is of presidents. We had best take care that, like Lincoln, they are worthy of our trust.[4]

Notes

INTRODUCTION

1. J. G. Randall, *Constitutional Problems under Lincoln*, rev. ed. (Urbana: University of Illinois Press, 1951; originally published in 1926).

CHAPTER 1

1. David Detzer, *Allegiance: Fort Sumter, Charleston, and the Beginning of the Civil War* (New York: Harcourt, 2001), 108–36, 269–70, 308, 317. Detzer provides a good blow-by-blow account of events in South Carolina, though less information about developments in Washington.

2. David Potter, *The Impending Crisis, 1848–1861* (New York: Harper and Row, 1976), 583. Potter's book is indispensable reading on the background of the war.

3. See Detzer, *Allegiance*, 320.

4. Message to Congress in Special Session, July 4, 1861, in *The Collected Works of Abraham Lincoln*, ed. Roy P. Basler (New Brunswick, N.J.: Rutgers University Press, 1953–55), 4:426.

5. See Potter, *Impending Crisis*, 18–23, 53–62, 88–89, 108, 113–16.

6. The issue of slavery in the territories and its political effects are discussed in more detail in chapter 4. For a recent, comprehensive treatment by a historian, see Michael A. Morrison, *Slavery and the American West: The Eclipse of Manifest Destiny and the Coming of the Civil War* (Chapel Hill: University of North Carolina Press, 1997).

7. See Potter, *Impending Crisis*, 132–37; Allan Nevins, *The Emergence of Lincoln*, vol. 2, *Prologue to Civil War, 1859–1861* (New York: Charles Scribner's Sons, 1950), 30–31, 115, 488–89; Kenneth M. Stampp, *The Imperiled Union: Essays on the Background of the Civil War* (Oxford: Oxford University Press, 1980), 237; Allan Nevins, *The Emergence of Lincoln*, vol. 1, *Douglas, Buchanan, and Party Chaos* (New York: Charles Scribner's Sons, 1950), 229–304.

8. See Potter, *Impending Crisis*, 158–59, 199–224, 297–325; Allan Nevins, *Ordeal of the Union: A House Dividing, 1852–1857* (New York: Charles Scribner's Sons, 1947), 1:78–159, 301–46; Kenneth M. Stampp, *America in 1857: A Nation on the Brink* (Oxford: Oxford University Press, 1990), 144–81, 257–331 (comprehensive treatment of the Kansas dispute); Nevins, *Douglas, Buchanan, and Party Chaos*, 253 ("I wish you to remember . . .").

9. 60 U.S. 393 (1857). For an intriguing reexamination of the background of the case, see Lea VanderVelde and Sandhya Subramanian, "Mrs. Dred Scott," 106 *Yale Law Journal* 1033 (1997).

10. Don E. Fehrenbacher's book, *The Dred Scott Case: Its Significance in American Law and Politics* (Oxford: Oxford University Press, 1978), is a classic treatment of the historical context, legal complexities, decisional process, and impact of the case. It is more readily available in an abridged paperback, *Slavery, Law, and Politics: The Dred Scott Case in Historical Perspective* (Oxford: Oxford University Press, 1981). Another useful treatment is Paul Finkelman, *Dred Scott v. Sandford: A Brief History with Documents* (Boston: Bedford Books, 1997), which also contains excerpts from the long, meandering opinions and reprints the responses of Northern and Southern papers to the decision. For a brief introduction to the case and its effects, see Richard H. Sewell, *A House Divided: Sectionalism and Civil War, 1848–1865* (Baltimore: Johns Hopkins University Press, 1988), 57–61. A biting legal critique of the opinion can be found in David P. Currie, *The Constitution in the Supreme Court: The First Hundred Years, 1789–1888* (Chicago: University of Chicago Press, 1985), 263–72. Currie views the opinion as a "disreputable performance" (272). He adds that the "variety of feeble, poorly developed, and unnecessary constitutional arguments suggests, if nothing else, a determination to reach a predetermined conclusion at any price" (272). Lincoln's reactions to the opinion are discussed in chapter 8.

11. See Stampp, *Imperiled Union,* 228–44; Nevins, *Prologue to Civil War,* 113–15, 125–30, 178–80; Potter, *Impending Crisis,* 381–84.

12. "A House Divided": Speech at Springfield, Illinois, June 16, 1858, in *Collected Works,* 2:61–62. For a comprehensive view of Lincoln's thinking during this period, see Don E. Fehrenbacher, *Prelude to Greatness: Lincoln in the 1850s* (Stanford, Calif.: Stanford University Press, 1962), 22–25, 70–120.

13. First Debate with Stephen A. Douglas at Ottawa, Illinois, August 27, 1858, in *Collected Works,* 3:16, 29 ("my equal and the equal of Judge Douglas"), 152 ("eradicating the light of reason"). For further discussion of Lincoln's views on race and slavery, see David Herbert Donald, *Lincoln* (New York: Simon and Schuster, 1995), 176, 180–81, 633–34.

14. Speech at Peoria, Illinois, October 16, 1854, in *Collected Works,* 2:274.

15. See Potter, *Impending Crisis,* 407–16, 427–30, 439–40, 442–47; Nevins, *Prologue to Civil War,* 209–28, 272–76, 288–90.

16. Stampp, *America in 1857,* 15–45 (sectional differences), 110 ("centrality of the slavery issue in the sectional conflict"); Stampp, *Imperiled Union,* 194–98 (cultural and economic differences); James M. McPherson, *Battle Cry of Freedom: The Civil War Era* (Oxford: Oxford University Press, 1988), 7–8, 38–41, 91–100, 241, 253; Sewell, *A House Divided,* 5–9, 68–72. For more on the importance of the slavery issue to the decision to secede, see chapter 5.

17. Nevins, *Prologue to Civil War,* 318–28, 359, 417, 433.

18. Nevins, *Douglas, Buchanan, and Party Chaos,* 61–67; Potter, *Impending Crisis,* 535 ("More often than not," Buchanan "allowed himself to be governed by the collective will of his cabinet, in which southern views tended to predominate").

19. Nevins, *Prologue to Civil War,* 342–54; Potter, *Impending Crisis,* 517–22. In chapter 5, I will analyze in detail the contrasting views of Lincoln and Buchanan about the federal government's authority to use force against seceding states.

20. Nevins, *Prologue to Civil War,* 367–68, 375, 376–78, 390–91, 395–96, 398; Potter, *Impending Crisis,* 526–45; Phillip Shaw Paludan, *The Presidency of Abraham Lincoln* (Lawrence: University Press of Kansas, 1994), 59–65.

21. J. G. Randall, *Lincoln the President,* vol. 1, *Springfield to Gettysburg* (1945; reprint, Cambridge, Mass.: Da Capo Press, 1997), 293–95.

22. First Inaugural Address–Final Text, March 4, 1861, in *Collected Works,* 4:262–70, 271.

23. Randall, *Springfield to Gettysburg,* 307–8.

24. Potter, *Impending Crisis,* 570–82; Stampp, *Imperiled Union,* 181–86; Donald, *Lincoln,* 279–94.

25. Allan Nevins, *The War for the Union,* vol. 1, *The Improvised War, 1861–1862* (1959; reprint, New York: Konecky and Konecky, 1971), 67–68.

26. Donald, *Lincoln,* 296–97.

27. Nevins, *Improvised War,* 89–91.

28. See ibid., 78–79; Randall, *Springfield to Gettysburg,* 363.

29. Nevins, *Improvised War,* 81–87.

30. Carl B. Swisher, *The Taney Period, 1836–1864,* vol. 5 of *The Oliver Wendell Holmes Devise History of the Supreme Court of the United States* (New York: Macmillan, 1974), 842–54. Presidential authority to suspend habeas is analyzed in chapter 7, while Lincoln's willingness to defy Taney's order is discussed in chapter 8.

31. Paludan, *Presidency of Abraham Lincoln,* 71; Randall, *Springfield to Gettysburg,* 374–75. The constitutionality of these actions is analyzed in chapter 6.

32. Letter to Winfield Scott, April 25, 1861, in *Collected Works,* 4:344. Later that summer, however, General McClellan did arrest several Maryland legislators under circumstances that still remain somewhat mysterious. See Mark E. Neely Jr., *The Fate of Liberty: Abraham Lincoln and Civil Liberties* (Oxford: Oxford University Press, 1991), 16–18.

33. Message to Congress in Special Session, July 4, 1861, in *Collected Works,* 4:426 ("no choice . . ."), 427 ("this giant insurrection"), 428 ("strictly legal"), 434 ("all the laws but one," "sovereignty," "older than any of the States").

34. Ibid., 438 ("people's contest"), 441 ("having thus chosen our course").

35. A fuller discussion of the extent and justifiability of the arrests can be found in chapter 7.

36. Neely, *Fate of Liberty,* 27 (President Pierce), 54–55 (Illinois doctor), 58 (the Iowa editor), 64 ("stars and stripes").

37. Ibid., 64–65.

38. For an extensive discussion of the "dictatorship" thesis, see Herman Belz, *Abraham Lincoln, Constitutionalism, and Equal Rights in the Civil War Era* (New York: Fordham University Press, 1998), 17–35. On the rarity of politically motivated arrests, see Neely, *Fate of Liberty*, 133, 137–38. For an engaging treatment of the reelection campaign, see John C. Waugh, *Reelecting Lincoln: The Battle for the 1864 Presidency* (New York: Crown, 1997).

39. For a thoughtful analysis of the various threads of the rule of law ideal, see Richard H. Fallon Jr., " 'The Rule of Law' as a Concept in Constitutional Discourse," 97 *Columbia Law Review* 1 (1997).

40. William Sherman to Salmon P. Chase, August 11, 1862, in *Sherman's Civil War: Selected Correspondence of William T. Sherman, 1860–1865*, ed. Brooks Simpson and Jean Berlin (Chapel Hill: University of North Carolina Press, 1999), 269 ("When one nation is at war . . ."); William Sherman to John Sherman, November 24, 1862, id., 336–37 (Being at war . . ."); William Sherman to John Sherman, September 9, 1863, id., 540 ("Agitators & theorists"); William Sherman to Joseph Hold, April 6, 1864, id., 615 ("Spies and guerrillas . . .").

41. William Sherman to Thomas Ewing, June 7, 1862, ibid., 239 ("supremacy of *Written* Law"); William Sherman to John M. Schofield, May 28, 1865, id., 907 ("People of this Country . . .").

42. Message to Congress in Special Session, July 4, 1861, in *Collected Works*, 4:426.

CHAPTER 2

1. See Forrest McDonald, *States' Rights and the Union: Imperium in Imperio, 1776–1876* (Lawrence: University Press of Kansas, 2000), 193–94 ("sublime moral principle"). For further discussion of sovereignty, see my review of McDonald's book, "E Pluribus Unum?" 18 *Constitutional Commentary* 243 (2001).

2. For a discussion of the various types of sovereignty, see Stephen D. Krasner, *Sovereignty: Organized Hypocrisy* (Princeton, N.J.: Princeton University Press, 1999), 9–25.

3. *U.S. Term Limits, Inc. v. Thornton*, 514 U.S. 779 (1995).

4. Ibid., 803, 822 (internal quotations and citations omitted); Robert V. Remini, *Daniel Webster: The Man and His Time* (New York: W. W. Norton, 1997), 379.

5. *U.S. Term Limits*, 514 U.S. at 846, 849 (Thomas, J., dissenting).

6. Ibid., 846–47 n. 1. The constitution of the Confederate States of America was more explicit in adopting Thomas's theory, referring to itself as a creation of the states, "each state acting in its sovereign capacity." See Ralph Stein, "The South Won't Rise Again but It's Time to Study the Defunct Confederacy's Constitution," 21 *Pace Law Review* 395, 402 (2001).

7. *U.S. Term Limits*, 514 U.S. at 848–49. As Kathleen Sullivan points out, Thomas's dissent embraced the "constitutional ontology" of the Southern nullificationists like Calhoun, though it "did not go as far as to advocate state nullification." Kathleen M. Sullivan, "Dueling Sovereignties: *U.S. Term Limits, Inc. v. Thornton*," 109

Harvard Law Review 78, 98–99 (1995). For a more sympathetic view of Thomas's opinion, see Robert F. Nagel, "The *Term Limits* Dissent: What Nerve," 38 *Arizona Law Review* 843 (1996). For an overview of Calhoun's views, see Richard Hofstadter, *The American Political Tradition* (New York: Vintage, 1954), 68–92. Calhoun's views are discussed extensively in chapter 3.

8. *U.S. Term Limits,* 514 U.S. at 839–42 (Kennedy, J., concurring).

9. 527 U.S. 706 (1999).

10. Ibid., 715.

11. Jack N. Rakove, "Making a Hash of Sovereignty, Part I," 2 *Green Bag* 2d 35, 37 (1998) (quoting Blackstone). Blackstone's sovereign was supposed to exercise unlimited authority. Such a concept of sovereignty does not fit American government. In theory, the ultimate ability to make law resides in those empowered to amend the Constitution—a coalition consisting of supermajorities within Congress and among the states. But this supercoalition plays no role in the day-to-day operations of either level of government, and has acted fewer than twenty times in our history. Thus, the sovereignty of the "constitution makers" has mostly been theoretical rather than practical, and has nothing to do with critical decisions such as war and peace. The legislators who have the ability to form such a supercoalition are themselves controlled by the electorate and restricted in all other activities by the Constitution. As a practical matter, then, no identifiable group actually exercises unrestricted authority. Thus, whatever may be true of other societies, the concept of domestic sovereignty has limited descriptive value in the American context.

12. For example, Paul and Mary might currently be in possession of Blackacre, while Bill has an easement to use a private road across the property, Jill has the right to take possession when Paul and Mary die, and Fred owns the mineral rights. Asking which of these people "owns" Blackacre is not a meaningful question. At least in the American context, sovereignty is also a bundle of sticks. Various people in and out of the state and federal government have different powers. Asking who is the true American sovereign is something like asking whether Paul, Mary, Bill, Jill, or Fred is the one true owner of Blackacre.

13. On Lincoln's views, see Message to Congress in Special Session, July 4, 1861, in *The Collected Works of Abraham Lincoln,* ed. Roy P. Basler (New Brunswick, N.J.: Rutgers University Press, 1953–55), 4:434–35; James M. McPherson, *Battle Cry of Freedom: The Civil War Era* (Oxford: Oxford University Press, 1988), 247–48; Michael Kammen, *A Machine That Would Go of Itself: The Constitution in American Culture* (New York: Alfred A. Knopf, 1986), 109 (reprinting a Civil War–era constitutional catechism); Kenneth M. Stampp, *The Era of Reconstruction, 1865–1877* (New York: Alfred A. Knopf, 1965), 25–27. A forceful argument for the nationalist view can be found in Richard B. Morris, "The Forging of the Union Reconsidered: A Historical Refutation of State Sovereignty over Seabeds," 74 *Columbia Law Review* 1056 (1974).

14. This theory was endorsed, for example, by the majority in the *Term Limits* case. See *U.S. Term Limits, Inc. v. Thornton,* 514 U.S. 779, 803 (1995). See also Charles Fried, "The Supreme Court 1994 Term—Foreword: Revolutions?" 109 *Harvard Law Review* 13, 22–23 (1995) (stressing the "discontinuity" between the Constitution and previous governmental arrangements); Akhil Reed Amar, "Of Sovereignty and Federalism," 96 *Yale Law Journal* 1425, 1460 (1987). The quoted passages from the *Federalist* can be found in *The Federalist Papers,* ed. Isaac Kramnick (New York: Penguin, 1987); Federalist 22 (Hamilton), 177, 184; Federalist 46 (Madison), 297, 300, 301. For a recent restatement of Amar's view explicitly contrasting his position with Lincoln's, see Akhil Reed Amar, "The David C. Baum Lecture: Abraham Lincoln and the American Union," 2001 *University of Illinois Law Review* 1109, 1120–23.

15. Remini, *Daniel Webster,* 377 (quoting Calhoun: "I go on the ground . . ."). See Amar, "Of Sovereignty and Federalism," 1452, 1520 nn. 108–9; Stampp, *Era of Reconstruction,* 25; McPherson, *Battle Cry of Freedom,* 240; David M. Potter, *The Impending Crisis, 1848–1861* (New York: Harper and Row, 1976), 479.

16. John C. Calhoun, *A Discourse on the Constitution and Government of the United States,* in *Union and Liberty: The Political Philosophy of John C. Calhoun,* ed. Ross M. Lence (Indianapolis: Liberty Fund, 1992), 82, 116–17, 127.

17. See Daniel A. Farber and Suzanna Sherry, *A History of the American Constitution* (St. Paul, Minn.: West Publishing, 1990), 39, 48.

18. For discussions by recent historians, see Richard B. Morris, *The Forging of the Union, 1781–1789* (New York: Harper and Row, 1987), 55–59; Samuel H. Beer, *To Make a Nation: The Rediscovery of American Federalism* (Cambridge, Mass.: Belknap Press of Harvard University Press, 1993), 197–202, 236, 248–55, 314–15, 320–28; Gordon S. Wood, *The Creation of the American Republic, 1776–1787* (Chapel Hill: University of North Carolina Press, 1969), 344–89, 524–36. The evolution of the concept of the Union between the founding and the Civil War is traced in Paul C. Nagel, *One Nation Indivisible: The Union in American Thought, 1776–1861* (Oxford: Oxford University Press, 1964). On the practical legal implications of the sovereignty issue, see Forrest McDonald, *Novus Ordo Seclorum: The Intellectual Origins of the Constitution* (Lawrence: University Press of Kansas, 1985), 146, see also 235 (on the "multilingual" nature of the Framers' political philosophy).

19. See Jack N. Rakove, *Original Meanings: Politics and Ideas in the Making of the Constitution* (New York: Alfred A. Knopf, 1996), 163; Douglas G. Smith, "An Analysis of Two Federal Structures: The Articles of Confederation and the Constitution," 34 *San Diego Law Review* 249, 261–68 (1997).

20. See Beer, *To Make a Nation,* 1–12, 196–202, 314–25.

21. McDonald, *States' Rights,* 4, 8–9, 236 n. 3 ("thirteen real compacts"); Robert Middlekauff, *The Glorious Cause: The American Revolution, 1763–1789* (Oxford: Oxford University Press, 1982), 321, 323 (Rhode Island).

22. See McDonald, *States' Rights,* 10; Beer, *To Make a Nation,* 164, 197, 199–202, 419 n. 20 ("exercise of every kind of authority"); Rakove, *Original Meanings,* 164.

23. See Rakove, *Original Meanings,* 100, 164–66; Beer, *To Make a Nation,* 202.

24. See Merrill Jensen, *The Articles of Confederation: An Interpretation of the Social-Constitutional History of the American Revolution, 1774–1781* (Madison: University of Wisconsin Press, 1940), 160–76.

25. See ibid., 160–76; James Madison, *Vices of the Political System of the United States* (April 1787), in *Writings,* ed. Jack Rakove (New York: Library of America, 1999), 69, 74.

26. Rakove, *Original Meanings,* 168.

27. Joseph Story, *Commentaries on the Constitution of the United States: With a Preliminary Review of the Constitutional History of the Colonies and States, before the Adoption of the Constitution* (Boston: Little and Brown, 1851), 1:238–39, 247. In most states the critical language was "we . . . do assent to, and ratify the said constitution." Massachusetts' and New Hampshire's ratification documents put it a bit differently: "acknowledging, with grateful hearts, the goodness of the Supreme Ruler of the universe in affording the people of the United States, in the course of his providence, an opportunity, . . . peaceably, without force or surprise, of entering into an explicit and solemn compact with each other, by assenting to, and ratifying a constitution . . . [we] assent to, and ratify the said constitution." In addition, the Virginia ratification refers to the federal government's powers as "being derived from the people of the United States."

28. For the complete text of the letter and a fuller discussion of its significance, see Daniel A. Farber, "The Constitution's Forgotten Cover Letter: An Essay on the New Federalism and the Original Understanding," 94 *Michigan Law Review* 615, 627 (1995) (citing Letter of the President of the Federal Convention to the President of Congress [Sept. 17, 1787], in Charles C. Tansill, ed., *Documents Illustrative of the Formation of the Union of the American States* 1003 [Washington, D.C.: GPO, 1927]).

29. The quoted passage from the *Federalist* is from Federalist 33 (Hamilton), 223, 225.

30. The Washington letter also suggests that the convention thought of the United States as having some kind of existence as an entity, rather than being merely a concatenation of smaller units. The letter refers to the "friends of our country," as if "we" already shared a common country. Later, the letter adds that "consolidation of our Union" is "the greatest interest of every true American," which again implies that a union already exists (but needs strengthening) and that Americans are in some sense already unified. Similarly, the fifth paragraph expresses the hope that the Constitution will "promote the lasting welfare of that country so dear to us all," rather than saying "those countries so dear to each of us." Farber, "The Constitution's Forgotten Cover Letter," 627–28.

31. *U.S. Term Limits,* 514 U.S. at 839–40 (Kennedy, J., concurring).

32. The *Federalist* passage can be found in Federalist 39 (Madison), 254, 255–57.

33. 17 U.S. 316, 403–05 (1819).

34. "To the formation of a league, such as was the confederation, the state sovereignties were certainly competent." But, Marshall continued, "when 'in order to form a more perfect union,' it was deemed necessary to change this alliance into

an effective government, possessing great and sovereign powers, and acting directly on the people, the necessity of referring it to the people, and of deriving its powers directly from them, was felt and acknowledged by all" (ibid., 404). Thus, Marshall clearly rejected the idea that the federal government enjoyed less sovereignty than the state governments or derived its powers from them. Whether residual sovereignty was still held by the people of the individual states is unclear, depending on whether we stress Marshall's rejection of the people's being "one common mass" or read him merely to say that American people are united but can only "*act* in their states."

35. See Rakove, "Making a Hash of Sovereignty, Part I," 41 ("everywhere and nowhere"); Jack N. Rakove, "Making a Hash of Sovereignty, Part II," 3 *Green Bag* 2d 51 (1999). The *Federalist* passage can be found in Federalist 39 (Madison), 254, 259.

36. See Alexander Hamilton to James Duane, Sept. 3, 1780, in *The Founders' Constitution,* ed. Philip B. Kurland and Ralph Lerner (Chicago: University of Chicago Press, 1987), 1:150–53 (summarizing complaints about Congress's lack of powers under the Articles); Morris, *Forging of the Union,* 269 ("rally of nationalists"); Wood, *Creation of American Republic,* 526 ("it was precisely an absorption of all the states").

37. Drew R. McCoy, *The Last of the Fathers: James Madison and the Republican Legacy* (Cambridge: Cambridge University Press, 1989), 127.

38. See H. Jefferson Powell, "The Oldest Question of Constitutional Law," 79 *Virginia Law Review* 633, 656 (1993); Gary Lawson, "The Rise and Rise of the Administrative State," 107 *Harvard Law Review* 1231, 1234 (1994) ("Leviathan"); E. James Ferguson, *The Power of the Purse: A History of American Public Finance, 1776–1790* (Chapel Hill: University of North Carolina Press, 1961), xiv–xvi, 111–12.

39. *McCulloch,* 17 U.S. at 316, 405, 421, 428.

40. These political developments are discussed in McDonald, *States' Rights,* 97–163.

CHAPTER 3

1. This schism and its constitutional dimensions are reviewed in David McGowan, "Ethos in Law and History: Alexander Hamilton, *The Federalist,* and the Supreme Court," 85 *Minnesota Law Review* 755 (2001).

2. On the emergence of partisan politics, see Stanley Elkins and Eric McKitrick, *The Age of Federalism: The Early American Republic, 1788–1800* (Oxford: Oxford University Press, 1993), 257–302; James Roger Sharp, *American Politics in the Early Republic: The New Nation in Crisis* (New Haven, Conn.: Yale University Press, 1993).

3. Elkins and McKitrick, *Age of Federalism,* 590–92. For a thorough treatment of the controversy, see James Smith, *Freedom's Fetters: The Alien and Sedition Laws and American Civil Liberties* (Ithaca, N.Y.: Cornell University Press, 1956).

4. Sharp, *American Politics,* 44.

5. Ibid., 194–95; Merrill D. Peterson, *The Jefferson Image in the American Mind* (Oxford:

Oxford University Press, 1960), 56–57 (on the publication of the draft and Calhoun's reaction).

6. Kentucky Resolutions of 1798 and 1799, in Jonathan Elliot, *The Debates in the Several State Conventions* (Philadelphia: J. B. Lippincott Co., 1891), 4:540, 544. On the difference between Jefferson and Madison regarding the precise nature of the federal compact, see H. Jefferson Powell, "The Principles of '98: An Essay in Historical Retrieval," 80 *Virginia Law Review* 689, 717–18 (1994).

7. Sharp, *American Politics,* 197, 199–206.

8. Virginia Resolutions Against the Alien and Sedition Acts, Dec. 21, 1798, in James Madison, *Writings,* ed. Jack Rakove (New York: Library of America, 1999), 589; Sharp, *American Politics,* 204–5 (arming state); David P. Currie, *The Constitution in Congress: The Federalist Period, 1789–1801* (Chicago: University of Chicago Press, 1997), 272 ("as the frog said").

9. The State of Rhode Island and Providence Plantations to Virginia, Feb. 1799, in *State Documents on Federal Relations: The States and the United States,* ed. Herman Ames (Cambridge, Mass.: Da Capo Press, 1970), 17, 25–26 (paginated within section "Interpretation of the Constitution during the First Two Decades").

10. Madison, Report on the Alien and Sedition Acts, in *Writings,* 610–11, 613–14.

11. Ibid., 659.

12. See Saul Cornell, *The Other Founders: Anti-Federalism and the Dissenting Tradition in America, 1788–1828* (Chapel Hill: University of North Carolina Press, 1999), 241–43; Adrienne Koch, *Jefferson and Madison: The Great Collaboration* (Oxford: Oxford University Press, 1964), 197–98 ("But determined . . .").

13. Forrest McDonald, *States' Rights and the Union: Imperium in Imperio, 1776–1876* (Lawrence: University Press of Kansas, 2000), 43 ("almost sacred"); Elkins and McKitrick, *Age of Federalism,* 691–711, 719–26; Currie, *Constitution in Congress,* 269 ("if you were wondering") (Ross Barnett was a segregationist governor who resisted a federal decree).

14. G. Edward White, *The Marshall Court and Cultural Change, 1815–1835,* abridged ed. (Oxford: Oxford University Press, 1991), 37–75.

15. 18 Va. 1 (1814). The Reporter noted that this opinion, "being in all respects the most important and interesting case in the volume, is inserted first, although not first in order of time as to its decision." The lasting significance of this provision (section 25) of the Judiciary Act is discussed in Charles Warren, *The Supreme Court in United States History* (Boston: Little, Brown, 1922), 1:13–17.

16. It is no coincidence that this case involved land titles. Representatives of Virginia and Kentucky had already voiced strong opposition to federal judicial supremacy, for fear that federal courts would be unsympathetic to property interests in those two states. See Warren, *The Supreme Court,* 1:219. The writ of error procedure is described in White, *Marshall Court,* 165, 169.

17. 18 Va. at 4–9 (Cabell, J.) (emphasis omitted). Cabell rejected the argument that appellate jurisdiction was needed to preserve the integrity of the federal system.

Giving finality to state supreme court rulings would not be disruptive, he argued, because Congress could provide for pretrial transfer of all cases presenting federal questions into federal court. Hence, cases involving federal issues would be heard in state court only if Congress decided to leave them there or if plaintiffs chose the state forum, in which case they ought to abide by the state judiciary's decisions.

18. 18 Va. at 10–12 (Brooke, J., concurring); id. at 19, 21 (Roane, J., concurring). The third concurring judge thought it clear that the Constitution's reference to the Supreme Court's appellate jurisdiction must relate only to Congress's authority to establish lower federal courts, not to appeals from state courts, id. at 32 (Fleming, J., concurring).

19. *New York v. United States,* 505 U.S. 144, 178–79 (1992). For a cogent refutation of the Court's argument, see Evan H. Caminker, "State Sovereignty and Subordinacy: May Congress Commandeer State Officers to Implement Federal Law?" 95 *Columbia Law Review* 1001, 1022–60 (1995).

20. *Martin v. Hunter's Lessee,* 14 U.S. 304, 324–28 (1816). According to Story, the Constitution's grant of federal jurisdiction over multistate disputes shows that the Framers were concerned about the objectivity of state judges. Otherwise, they would not have provided federal jurisdiction to protect outsiders from potentially biased state courts. Even apart from this concern, Story said, there was a pressing need for national uniformity in interpreting the Constitution. The power to transfer cases from state to federal trial courts, which the Virginia court had invoked as a cure for these evils, was no answer. Such a transfer was technically an exercise of appellate jurisdiction anyway, and besides, could not be used in criminal cases or where the federal issue did not appear in the complaint. Id. at 338–50. For an analysis of Story's opinion, agreeing with the result (but not all of the reasoning) from a textualist/originalist perspective, see David P. Currie, *The Constitution in the Supreme Court: The First Hundred Years, 1789–1888* (Chicago: University of Chicago Press, 1985), 91–96.

21. 19 U.S. 264 (1821).

22. Warren, *Supreme Court,* 546–47 (quoting Jefferson's correspondence). Jefferson's spelling has been slightly modernized in the text.

23. 19 U.S. at 380, 387–89. Nor was the Eleventh Amendment a barrier, Marshall said, because it was only designed to allow states to avoid paying debts to outsiders, and did not cover a writ of error. The *Cohens* holding was reaffirmed in *McKesson Corp. v. Division of ABT,* 496 U.S. 18, 26–28 (1990). Current Eleventh Amendment doctrine is quite intricate, though the Supreme Court's appellate jurisdiction over state criminal cases is now beyond question. For an accessible overview, see Erwin Chemerinsky, *Federal Jurisdiction,* 2d ed. (Boston: Little, Brown, 1994), 367–419.

24. 19 U.S. at 413–14, 416, 418.

25. Warren, *Supreme Court,* 546–47, 552–57.

26. 22 U.S. 738 (1824).

27. Warren, *Supreme Court,* 526, 528–29. During the litigation, the Ohio legislature passed another law, depriving the bank of any right to sue in the state courts and of any protection from state officers. Id. at 536.

28. The defendants conceded that state officers might be liable for damages. Or, as Marshall put it, they "expressly waive the extravagant proposition, that a void act can afford protection to the person who executes it, and admits the liability of the defendants to the plaintiffs, to the extent of the injury sustained, in an action at law." But an injunction, they argued, would involve the state itself more directly. 22 U.S. at 839, 846.

29. Ibid., 847–48, 857–58. A suit for damages might be brought against the state official enforcing such a law, Marshall admitted, but this might be too little and too late to do any good. *Osborn* partially anticipated the Court's best-known decision on injunctions against state officers, *Ex parte Young,* 209 U.S. 123 (1908). The Court in the latter case relied on *Osborn* in upholding the power of federal courts to enjoin constitutional violations by state officials. See id. at 150, 166. *Ex parte Young* did go further than *Osborn,* however, insofar as it upheld an injunction against a state attorney general bringing suit on the state's behalf in its own courts.

30. 19 U.S. 598 (1821).

31. After all, Johnson argued, in *Marbury v. Madison* and other cases, the Supreme Court had held that the writ was unavailable to the federal courts. Would anyone seriously maintain that this was among the reserved powers of the states simply because it had not been vested in the federal courts? Whatever questions might be raised about the supremacy of the federal government in other contexts, "no one has ever contested its supreme right to dispose of its own property in its own way." 19 U.S. at 598, 604–5.

32. Gerald Gunther, ed., *John Marshall's Defense of McCulloch v. Maryland* (Stanford, Calif.: Stanford University Press, 1969), 195 ("no national existence," "nation composed of states"), 203 ("act of a single party," "arguments founded on leagues"), 211 ("whole owes to its parts," "great objects"). The debate with the Virginians may have sharpened Marshall's views. See R. Kent Newmyer, "John Marshall, *McCulloch v. Maryland,* and the Southern States' Rights Tradition," 33 *John Marshall Law Review* 875, 877 (2000).

33. See Merrill D. Peterson, *The Great Triumvirate: Webster, Clay, and Calhoun* (Oxford: Oxford University Press, 1987), 170–75; White, *Marshall Court,* 267.

34. Peterson, *Great Triumvirate,* 175–78.

35. William W. Freehling, *The Road to Disunion: Secessionists at Bay, 1776–1854* (Oxford: Oxford University Press, 1990), 1:213–52.

36. John C. Calhoun, *Exposition and Protest,* in *Union and Liberty: The Political Philosophy of John C. Calhoun,* ed. Ross M. Lence (Indianapolis: Liberty Fund, 1992), 363–64.

37. Robert Middlekauff, *The Glorious Cause: The American Revolution, 1763–1789* (Ox-

ford: Oxford University Press, 1982), 120, 124–26, 150–56; Keith E. Whittington, *Constitutional Construction: Divided Powers and Constitutional Meaning* (Cambridge, Mass.: Harvard University Press, 1999), 93 (Madison), 95–96 (Clay). For a thorough treatment of the constitutional arguments, see David P. Currie, *The Constitution in Congress: The Jeffersonians, 1801–1829* (Chicago: University of Chicago Press, 2001), 283–89.

38. Freehling, *Road to Disunion,* 1:276–77.

39. Peterson, *Great Triumvirate,* 193 (Calhoun "never at a loss for principle").

40. Fort Hill Address, July 26, 1831, in *Correspondence of John C. Calhoun,* ed. J. Franklin Jameson (New York: D. Appleton and Co., 1856), 59–94.

41. See Richard E. Ellis, *The Union at Risk: Jacksonian Democracy, States' Rights, and the Nullification Crisis* (Oxford: Oxford University Press, 1987), 75–76.

42. Ellis, *Union at Risk,* 78.

43. Andrew Jackson, Proclamation, Dec. 10, 1832, in James D. Richardson, *A Compilation of the Messages and Papers of the Presidents, 1789–1897* (Washington, D.C.: Government Printing Office, 1896), 3:1211.

44. Ibid., 3:1219; Ellis, *Union at Risk,* 86, 88 ("when a faction").

45. See Ellis, *Union at Risk,* 94, 180–81. Opinions differ about who "won" in the nullification crisis. See Donald B. Cole, *The Presidency of Andrew Jackson* (Lawrence: University Press of Kansas, 1993), 178–80.

46. Richard Hofstadter, *The American Political Tradition* (New York: Vintage, 1954), 74. Hofstadter provides a masterful sketch of Calhoun. For a more detailed discussion of Calhoun's views and his role in the nullification crisis, see William W. Freehling, *Prelude to Civil War: The Nullification Controversy in South Carolina, 1816–1836* (Oxford: Oxford University Press, 1965), 2–3, 132–44, 154–59, 208, 290–92, 354–55.

47. John C. Calhoun, *A Discourse on the Constitution and Government of the United States,* in *Union and Liberty,* 72, 108–9, 115.

48. Federalist 82 (Hamilton), in *The Federalist Papers,* ed. Isaac Kramnick (New York: Penguin, 1987), 458–61.

49. Calhoun, *Discourse,* 158, 162–63, 166–67, 271. It does not seem to have occurred to Calhoun that the party system would also give national politicians a powerful interest in preserving state government on behalf of their local allies. See Larry Kramer, "Understanding Federalism," 47 *Vanderbilt Law Review* 1485, 1522–42 (1994).

50. Calhoun, *Discourse,* 92–96.

51. Ibid., 223–24. According to Calhoun, Congress had no power to subordinate state judges to the Supreme Court. On a plain reading of Article III of the Constitution, Calhoun argued, the appellate jurisdiction of the Supreme Court only extends over the lower federal courts. Appellate jurisdiction would imply a position of inferiority, which contradicts the fundamental principle that the states and the federal government are coequal and coordinate. By logical implication,

that same nefarious principle of federal supremacy would allow transfer of state criminal and civil trials to federal court, exemption of federal officers from state court jurisdiction, and even federal habeas for state prisoners. What would be left of the reserved powers of the states? (id., 226–33).

52. Ibid., 241–42, 247.

53. Ibid., 185–87.

54. Ibid., 191–99.

55. Ibid., 211–12. Calhoun placed the burden of using the amendment power on the federal government rather than the dissident state for two reasons. First, in a contest between a limited government and one with indefinite reserved rights, the burden of proof is on the government with limited powers (the federal government). Second, since the federal government represents a national majority, only it has realistic prospects of invoking the amendment power, while the dissenting individual state cannot hope to do so (id., 208–11).

56. Ibid., 269–77.

57. See Drew R. McCoy, *The Last of the Fathers: James Madison and the Republican Legacy* (Cambridge: Cambridge University Press, 1989), 135, 140, 147, 150–62 ("impenetrable stupidity" is at p. 152). McCoy's excellent book provides a vivid portrait of Madison in old age and of his long struggle to defend his legacy against nullifiers such as Calhoun.

58. Letter from James Madison to Edward Everett, August 28, 1830, in Madison, *Writings*, 842–45.

59. Ibid.

60. Letter from James Madison to William Cabell Rives, March 12, 1833, in *Writings*, 863–64.

61. Madison to Everett, 847–48.

62. Ibid.

63. Letter from James Madison to Nicholas P. Trist, May, 1832, in *Writings*, 860.

64. Madison to Everett, 850–52.

65. Madison to Trist, 860. After Madison died, Calhoun was true to the logic of his constitutional theory. He unsuccessfully opposed on constitutional grounds a law authorizing the federal government to purchase the Madison papers. McCoy, *Last of the Fathers*, 163–70.

CHAPTER 4

1. See David M. Potter, *The Impending Crisis, 1848–1861* (New York: Harper and Row, 1976), 152–76; David Herbert Donald, *Lincoln* (New York: Simon and Schuster, 1995), 167–85; James M. McPherson, *Battle Cry of Freedom: The Civil War Era* (Oxford: Oxford University Press, 1988), 121–30; Richard H. Sewell, *A House Divided: Sectionalism and Civil War, 1848–1865* (Baltimore: Johns Hopkins University Press, 1988), 42–53.

2. Speech at Peoria, Illinois, on October 16, 1854, in *The Collected Works of Abraham*

Lincoln, ed. Roy P. Basler (New Brunswick, N.J.: Rutgers University Press, 1953–55), 2:255, 275–76.

3. Daniel A. Farber and Suzanna Sherry, *A History of the American Constitution* (St. Paul, Minn.: West Publishing, 1990), 253–58; Don E. Fehrenbacher, *The Slaveholding Republic: An Account of the United States Government's Relations to Slavery* (Oxford: Oxford University Press, 2001), 278–91; Potter, *Impending Crisis,* 36–43.

4. Farber and Sherry, *History of the American Constitution,* 257–58.

5. Fehrenbacher, *Slaveholding Republic,* 301–4; Allan Nevins, *The Emergence of Lincoln,* vol. 1, *Douglas, Buchanan, and Party Chaos, 1857–1859* (New York: Charles Scribner's Sons, 1950), 7–10; Kenneth M. Stampp, *America in 1857: A Nation on the Brink* (Oxford: Oxford University Press, 1990), 35–36, 113–18, 122–24.

6. Allan Nevins, *The Emergence of Lincoln,* vol. 2, *Prologue to Civil War, 1859–1861* (New York: Charles Scribner's Sons, 1950), 30–32, 149–59, 281–82, 455; Potter, *Impending Crisis,* 458–70 (describing Southern nationalism).

7. McPherson, *Battle Cry of Freedom,* 56–57, 195–98; Fehrenbacher, *Slaveholding Republic,* 291–92; Stampp, *America in 1857,* 101, 110, 113–17.

8. See Nevins, *Prologue to Civil War,* 204–23, 268–72 (describing the Charleston Convention, its breakdown, and the nomination of Breckinridge). For other accounts of the Charleston Convention and its aftermath, see McPherson, *Battle Cry of Freedom,* 213–16; and Potter, *Impending Crisis,* 407–15.

9. Nevins, *Prologue to Civil War,* 176–77, 211, 227, 285.

10. Ibid., 318–28.

11. Ibid., 330–34 (quoting Rhett).

12. Potter, *Impending Crisis,* 477 ("monolithic, closed system"); Sewell, *House Divided,* 77–78 ("grossly insulted"). A sympathetic postal service had previously closed the Southern mails to antislavery papers and pamphlets.

13. *Power of the President in Executing the Laws,* 9 Op. Att'y Gen. 516–24 (Nov. 20, 1860).

14. James Buchanan, Message of the President of the United States, Cong. Globe, 36th Cong., 2d Sess., Appendix 1-4 (Dec. 3, 1860) (hereafter *Annual Message*); Fehrenbacher, *Slaveholding Republic,* 304 ("confession of national impotence"). Some readers may find it easier to access President Buchanan's speech on-line, at http://www.presidency.ucsb.edu/sou_pages/buchanan4su.html.

15. The text of the declaration is excerpted in Kenneth M. Stampp, ed., *The Causes of the Civil War* (New York: Simon and Schuster, 1991), 60–62. For discussion of the South Carolina Ordinance of Secession and those of the other seceding states, see Mark E. Brandon, *Free in the World: American Slavery and Constitutional Failure* (Princeton, N.J.: Princeton University Press, 1998), 192–98.

16. McPherson, *Battle Cry,* 272–73; Potter, *Impending Crisis,* 498–513.

17. Jefferson Davis, Message of April 29, 1861, to the Provisional Congress, in *The Messages and Papers of Jefferson Davis and the Confederacy, Including Diplomatic Correspondence, 1861–1865,* ed. James D. Richardson (New York: Chelsea House–Robert Hector, 1966), 1:63–65.

18. Ibid., 65–68.

19. Ibid., 68–69.

20. Alexander Stephens, *A Constitutional View of the Late War between the States* (Philadelphia: National Publishing Co., 1868–70), 1:295, 480, 491, 496. On the influence of Stephens's views, see William Davis, *The Union That Shaped the Confederacy: Robert Toombs and Alexander H. Stephens* (Lawrence: University Press of Kansas, 2001), 242–44.

21. Jefferson Davis, Inaugural Address of the President of the Provisional Government, February 18, 1861, in Richardson, *Messages and Papers,* 32–33; First Inaugural Address–Final Text, March 4, 1861, in *Collected Works,* 4:264–65. For an extensive analysis of Lincoln's inaugural, see Harry V. Jaffe, *A New Birth of Freedom: Abraham Lincoln and the Coming of the Civil War* (Lanham, Md.: Rowman and Littlefield, 2000), 189–97, 268–71. Lincoln's argument received scholarly support from a leading twentieth-century constitutional scholar in Edward S. Corwin, "National Power and State Interposition, 1787–1861," 10 *Michigan Law Review* 535 (1911–12).

22. First Inaugural Address–Final Text, March 4, 1861, in *Collected Works,* 4:264–65.

23. Ibid., 267–68.

24. Chapters 2 and 3 review that history.

25. *U.S. Term Limits, Inc. v. Thornton,* 514 U.S. 779, 846–50 (1995) (Thomas, J., dissenting).

26. *U.S. Term Limits,* 514 U.S. at 847–50.

27. The idea of a New England secession is not wholly fanciful. At various times in the nineteenth century, the idea was raised, with varying degrees of seriousness. See Forrest McDonald, *States' Rights and the Union: Imperium in Imperio, 1776–1876* (Lawrence: University Press of Kansas, 2000), 69–70, 152; Brandon, *Free in the World,* 182–86.

28. See E. Allan Farnsworth, *Contracts,* 2d ed. (Boston: Little, Brown, 1990), 480–82.

29. Buchanan, *Annual Message,* 2; James Madison to William Cabell Rives, Mar. 12, 1833, in *Writings,* ed. Jack N. Rakove (New York: Library of America, 1999), 864.

30. See David M. Golove, "Treaty-Making and the Nation: The Historical Foundations of the Nationalist Conception of the Treaty Power," 98 *Michigan Law Review* 1075, 1143–44 (2000). It is not clear how Madison squared these assertions with the obvious fact that England had indeed agreed to cede part of its "territory"— namely, the United States. But then, America had only been a possession, not a true part of the British nation.

31. See *Ableman v. Booth,* 62 U.S. 506 (1858). Madison's views on nullification are discussed in chapter 3.

32. Federalist 40 (Madison), in *The Federalist Papers,* ed. Isaac Kramnick (New York: Penguin, 1987), 259–63; Farber and Sherry, *History of the American Constitution,* 40 ("a Treaty only," "in the most exceptional form").

33. *U.S. Term Limits,* 514 U.S. at 801–3.

34. James Madison to Nicholas P. Trist, Dec. 23, 1832, in Madison, *Writings,* 861–62.
35. Ibid.
36. See *Texas v. White,* 74 U.S. 700, 725 (1868).
37. For criticisms of the "more perfect Union" argument, see David P. Currie, *The Constitution in the Supreme Court: The First Hundred Years, 1789–1888* (Chicago: University of Chicago Press, 1985), 311–12; Kenneth M. Stampp, *The Imperiled Union: Essays on the Background of the Civil War* (Oxford: Oxford University Press, 1980), 5–11. See Currie, *Constitution in the Supreme Court,* 313, for an elaboration on the supremacy clause argument. Story's explanation of the meaning of *constitution* is found in Joseph Story, *Commentaries on the Constitution of the United States: With a Preliminary Review of the Constitutional History of the Colonies and States, before the Adoption of the Constitution* (Boston: Little and Brown, 1851), 225–29, 233–37. On the English-Scottish Union and its relevance, see Akhil Reed Amar, "The David C. Baum Lecture: Abraham Lincoln and the American Union," 2001 *University of Illinois Law Review* 1109, 1124.
38. For an in-depth description of these casual references, see Stampp, *Imperiled Union,* 12–20.
39. Buchanan, *Annual Message,* 2.
40. James Madison to Alexander Hamilton, July 20, 1788, in Madison, *Writings,* 408.
41. Federalist 40, 260 ("a firm national government") (emphasis omitted); Buchanan, *Annual Message,* 2 ("mere voluntary association"); David McGowan, "Ethos in Law and History: Alexander Hamilton, *The Federalist,* and the Supreme Court," 85 *Minnesota Law Review* 755, 795, 817–19, 860–64 (2001) (discussing the general views of Madison, Hamilton, and Washington). The compact clause, which requires congressional approval for agreements between states, even if those agreements raise no other constitutional problem, also bespeaks a fear that states might combine at the expense of the Union.
42. James Madison to Edward Everett, Aug. 28, 1830, in *Writings,* 844–45 ("ultima ratio").
43. James Madison to Mathew Carey, July 27, 1831, in *Writings,* 858–59.
44. Federalist 40, 263; Federalist 22, 180. Madison pointed to a recent instance of such "inflexible opposition given by a *majority* of one sixtieth of the people of America"—an episode he said was "still fresh in the memory and indignation of every citizen who has felt for the wounded honor and prosperity of his country."

CHAPTER 5
1. James Buchanan, Message of the President of the United States, Cong. Globe, 36th Cong., 2d Sess., Appendix 3 (Dec. 3, 1860) (hereafter *Annual Message*). Buchanan also pointed to what would turn out to be a real difficulty when he asked, "Suppose such a war should result in the conquest of a State: how are we to govern it afterwards?" This was a problem that later plagued both Congress and the president during Reconstruction.

2. James M. McPherson, *Drawn with the Sword: Reflections on the American Civil War* (Oxford: Oxford University Press, 1996), 56–57; James M. McPherson, *Battle Cry of Freedom: The Civil War Era* (Oxford: Oxford University Press, 1988), 662 (Pickett's charge), 735 (Cold Harbor), 856 (Southern death toll); Geoffrey C. Ward, *The Civil War: An Illustrated History* (New York: Alfred A. Knopf, 1998), 121 (Grant on Shiloh), 293 (Spotsylvania).

3. Ward, *Illustrated History,* 121, 161–62, 224, 231, 289, 303.

4. Buchanan, *Annual Message,* 3.

5. *Power of the President in Executing the Laws,* 9 Op. Att'y Gen. 516, 524 (Nov. 20, 1860).

6. 505 U.S. 144 (1992).

7. Ibid., 180, 188. The facts were, of course, a far cry from the secession crisis. In response to the difficulty of finding disposal sites for low-level radioactive waste from hospitals and other facilities, Congress passed a statute in 1985 at the behest of the state governments. The statute provided various incentives for states to provide such disposal sites. The Court upheld all of these incentives but one. The flawed provision required states to adopt certain legislation regarding the waste or to "take title" to the waste themselves. This, the Court held, was unacceptable "commandeering" of the state legislature. Justice O'Connor quoted Federalist 20 to the effect that "a sovereignty over sovereigns, a government over governments, a legislation for communities, as contradistinguished from individuals, as it is a solecism in theory, so in practice it is subversive of the order and ends of civil policy." Relying on Federalist 39, she concluded that the Constitution " 'leaves to the several States a residuary and inviolable sovereignty' reserved explicitly to the States by the Tenth Amendment."

8. Ibid., 164–66. The New Jersey Plan is reprinted in appendix B of Daniel A. Farber and Suzanna Sherry, *A History of the American Constitution* (St. Paul, Minn.: West Publishing, 1990), 420. Similarly, the Virginia Plan called for a congressional power "to call forth theforce [*sic*] of the Union agst. any member of the Union failing to fulfill its duty under the articles thereof" (id., 415–16).

9. 521 U.S. 898 (1997).

10. Ibid., 919.

11. For critiques of the Court's use of history, see the *Printz* dissent, 521 U.S. at 945–53 (Stevens, J., dissenting), and Evan H. Caminker, "State Sovereignty and Subordinacy: May Congress Commandeer State Officers to Implement Federal Law?" 95 *Columbia Law Review* 1001 (1995).

12. Federalist 16 (Hamilton), in *The Federalist Papers,* ed. Isaac Kramnick (New York: Penguin, 1987), 154–55.

13. Ibid., 155.

14. The quoted statements are from David McGowan, "Ethos in Law and History: Alexander Hamilton, *The Federalist,* and the Supreme Court," 85 *Minnesota Law Review* 755, 791, 793–94 (2001). McGowan argues persuasively that Hamilton would

have been most unlikely to concur with Justice Scalia's opinion in *Printz* (857–74).

15. See Edward S. Corwin, "National Power and State Interposition, 1787–1861," 10 *Michigan Law Review* 535, 542 (1911–12) (quoting Aug. 30 debates).

16. Federalist 43, 282.

17. *McCulloch v. Maryland,* 17 U.S. 316 (1819).

18. Corwin, "National Power and State Interposition," 541–42 (quoting Aug. 20 debates).

19. James Madison to Nicholas P. Trist, in *Writings,* ed. Jack Rakove (New York: Library of America, 1999), 863.

20. Declaration of the Causes of Secession, in *The Causes of the Civil War,* ed. Kenneth M. Stampp (New York: Simon and Schuster, 1991), 60, 62; Jefferson Davis, Inaugural Address of the President of the Provisional Government, Feb. 18, 1861, in James D. Richardson, *The Messages and Papers of Jefferson Davis and the Confederacy, Including Diplomatic Correspondence, 1861–1865* (New York: Chelsea House–Robert Hector, 1966), 1:33.

21. McPherson, *Battle Cry of Freedom,* 240–41.

22. Forrest McDonald, *States' Rights and the Union: Imperium in Imperio, 1776–1876* (Lawrence: University Press of Kansas, 2000), 205.

23. James Ostrowski, "Was the Union Army's Invasion of the Confederate States a Lawful Act? An Analysis of President Lincoln's Legal Arguments against Secession," in *Secession, State, and Liberty,* ed. David Gordon (New Brunswick, N.J.: Transaction Publishers, 1998), 161.

24. First Inaugural Address–Final Text, March 4, 1861, in *The Collected Works of Abraham Lincoln,* ed. Roy P. Basler (New Brunswick, N.J.: Rutgers University Press, 1953–55), 4:267, 269.

25. Allan Nevins, *The Emergence of Lincoln,* vol. 2, *Prologue to Civil War, 1859–1861* (New York: Charles Scribner's Sons, 1950), 332, 465.

26. Charles B. Dew, *Apostles of Disunion: Southern Secession Commissioners and the Causes of the Civil War* (Charlottesville: University Press of Virginia, 2001), 11–14. After the war, Stephens claimed unconvincingly to have been misquoted (15–16).

27. Ibid., 39–44.

28. Ibid., 77–79.

29. McPherson, *Battle Cry of Freedom,* 241 ("What were these rights?"); Don E. Fehrenbacher, *Constitutions and Constitutionalism in the Slaveholding South* (Athens: University of Georgia Press, 1989), 56 (abolitionism's "stamp of possession"); Nevins, *Prologue to Civil War,* 470–71.

30. First Inaugural Address–Final Text, March 4, 1861, 4:268–69; McPherson, *Drawn with the Sword,* 195–206.

31. Don E. Fehrenbacher, *The Slaveholding Republic: An Account of the United States Government's Relations to Slavery* (Oxford: Oxford University Press, 2001), 16.

32. "Spot" Resolutions in the United States House of Representatives, December 22, 1847, in *Collected Works,* 1:421.

33. Speech in the United States House of Representatives: The War with Mexico, Jan. 12, 1848, in *Collected Works,* 1:438–39.

34. Steven Yates, "When Is Political Divorce Justified?" in *Secession, State, and Liberty,* ed. Gordon, 37, 63.

35. For Lincoln's view, see Message to Congress in Special Session, Jan. 12, 1848, in *Collected Works,* 4:437. On the state of Southern sentiment, see David M. Potter, *The Impending Crisis, 1848–1861* (New York: Harper and Row, 1976), 494–50, 557–58; McPherson, *Battle Cry of Freedom,* 235–39.

36. First Inaugural Address–Final Text, Mar. 4, 1861, 4:267–68.

37. The arguments against providing a constitutional right to secede are explored in Cass R. Sunstein, "Constitutionalism and Secession," 58 *University of Chicago Law Review* 633 (1991). A thoughtful argument for a limited secession right can be found in Alan Patten, "Democratic Secession from a Multinational State," 112 *Ethics* 558 (2002). Patten's argument would not, however, support secession by the South.

38. For a discussion of the place of *ex ante* binding agreements in democratic theory, see Stephen Holmes, *Precommitment and the Paradox of Democracy,* in *Constitutionalism and Democracy,* ed. Jon Elster and Rune Slagstad (Cambridge: Cambridge University Press, 1988), 195.

39. *Reference re Secession of Quebec,* 2 S.C.R. 217, 264, 267–73 (1998).

40. Ibid., 284–87. For a thoughtful appraisal of the opinion, see Sujit Choudry and Robert Howse, "Constitutional Theory and the Quebec Secession Reference," 13 *Canadian Journal of Law and Jurisprudence* 1 (2000).

41. First Inaugural Address–Final Text, Mar. 4, 1861, 4:269–70. For further discussion of how the Article V amendment process might have provided a constitutional mechanism for secession, see Akhil Reed Amar, "The David C. Baum Lecture: Abraham Lincoln and the American Union," 2001 *University of Illinois Law Review* 1109, 1114–15.

42. On the efforts of secession advocates to foreclose meaningful debate, see Nevins, *Prologue to Civil War,* 319–28. "Fire-eaters" opposed calls for a Southern-wide convention to decide on secession, where they feared they would be outvoted, as they had been in 1850. See Potter, *Impending Crisis,* 486. The constitutionality of secession is discussed in chapter 4.

43. For an optimistic view, see Richard H. Shryock, "What Price Union?" in *Causes of the Civil War,* ed. Stampp, 71–74.

44. First Inaugural Address–Final Text, March 4, 1861, 4:265–66, 271.

CHAPTER 6

1. The dictatorship charge is discussed briefly in chapter 1 and more extensively in chapter 7.

2. James M. McPherson, *Battle Cry of Freedom: The Civil War Era* (Oxford: Oxford University Press, 1988), 271–74; Philip Paludan, *The Presidency of Abraham Lincoln*

(Lawrence: University Press of Kansas, 1994), 66 (probable Southern reaction to resupply expedition); Kenneth Stampp, *The Imperiled Union: Essays on the Background of the Civil War* (Oxford: Oxford University Press, 1980), 184–86.

3. McPherson, *Battle Cry of Freedom,* 274 (Douglas quote), 313 (preparedness).

4. Proclamation Calling Militia and Convening Congress, Apr. 15, 1861, in *The Collected Works of Abraham Lincoln,* ed. Roy P. Basler (New Brunswick, N.J.: Rutgers University Press, 1953–55), 4:331–32; David Donald, *Lincoln* (New York: Simon and Schuster, 1995), 296 (period of militia service); John G. Nicolay and John Hay, *Abraham Lincoln: A History* (New York: Century Co., 1917), 4:88 (blockade and Davis's privateering order).

5. Donald, *Lincoln,* 297–99; Allan Nevins, *The War for the Union,* vol. 1, *The Improvised War, 1861–1862* (1959; reprint, New York: Konecky and Konecky, 1971), 79 (General Scott's defense plan). As we will see in chapter 7, habeas was eventually suspended nationwide.

6. Donald, *Lincoln,* 301; Paludan, *Lincoln Presidency,* 69, 71; Proclamation Calling for 42,034 Volunteers, May 3, 1861, in *Collected Works,* 4:353–54; Stephen B. Oates, *With Malice toward None: The Life of Abraham Lincoln* (New York: New American Library, 1977), 252 (disloyal bureaucracy); Nevins, *Improvised War,* 167–68 (Chase's role); J. G. Randall, *Constitutional Problems under Lincoln,* rev. ed. (Urbana: University of Illinois Press, 1951), 37 n. 15 (names of New Yorkers). For Lincoln's explanation of the use of private channels for funds, see To the Senate and House of Representatives, May 26, 1862, in *Collected Works,* 5:242–43.

7. Message to Congress in Special Session, July 4, 1861, in *Collected Works,* 4:425.

8. Ibid., 428–29.

9. Forrest McDonald, *The Presidency: An Intellectual History* (Lawrence: University Press of Kansas, 1994), 280, 283 (size of White House staff; status of attorney general), 320 (chief clerks).

10. Paludan, *Lincoln Presidency,* 27; Michael F. Holt, *The Rise and Fall of the American Whig Party: Jacksonian Politics and the Onset of the Civil War* (Oxford: Oxford University Press, 1999), 17, 25.

11. *Ex parte Merryman,* 17 Fed. Cas. 144 (Case No. 9,487).

12. *Youngstown Sheet & Tube Co. v. Sawyer,* 343 U.S. 579, 585–90 (1952).

13. A useful collection of materials bearing on presidential power can be found in Peter M. Shane and Harold H. Bruff, *Separation of Powers Law: Cases and Materials* (Durham, N.C.: Carolina Academic Press, 1996). The history of Article II is summarized in Charles C. Thach Jr., *The Creation of the Presidency, 1775–1789* (Baltimore: Johns Hopkins University Press, 1923).

14. See Daniel A. Farber and Suzanna Sherry, *A History of the American Constitution* (St. Paul, Minn.: West Publishing, 1990), 81–98.

15. Ibid., 79–81; Martin S. Flaherty, "The Most Dangerous Branch," 105 *Yale Law Journal* 1725, 1771 (1996) (powers of New York governor), 1775 ("what strikes anyone"), 1807 (quoting Madison letter to Jefferson on "mere shades of difference").

16. Steven G. Calabresi and Saikrishna B. Prakash, "The President's Power to Execute the Laws," 104 *Yale Law Journal* 541, 559, 578 (1994).

17. Flaherty, "Most Dangerous Branch," 1790 ("no such generally understood bundle existed"), 1792 ("cryptic phrase"); Calabresi and Prakash, "The President's Power," 629 ("meaningless"); Lawrence Lessig and Cass Sunstein, "The President and the Administration," 94 *Columbia Law Review* 1 (1994) (distinguishing between executive departments and other administrators); A. Michael Froomkin, "Still Naked after All These Words," 88 *Northwestern University Law Review* 1420 (1994) (critiquing Calabresi's views).

18. *Youngstown Sheet & Tube,* 343 U.S. 579, 634–35 (1952) (Jackson, J., concurring).

19. On the conflicting values involved in assessing executive power, see Geoffrey P. Miller, "The Unitary Executive in a Unified Theory of Constitutional Law: The Problem of Interpretation," 15 *Cardozo Law Review* 201 (1993) (energy versus avoidance of faction); Flaherty, "Most Dangerous Branch," 1802–4 (energy, accountability, and balance); Peter L. Strauss, "Formal and Functional Approaches to Separation-of-Powers Questions—A Foolish Inconsistency?" 72 *Cornell Law Review* 488, 523–24 (1987) (balance versus accountability).

20. McDonald, *The Presidency,* 238–39 (neutrality debate), 219–20 (removal debate); Calabresi and Prakash, "The President's Power," 652–53; Jack N. Rakove, *Original Meanings: Politics and Ideas in the Making of the Constitution* (New York: Alfred A. Knopf, 1996), 245. Based on a careful review of the House proceedings, David Currie concludes that "there was no consensus" about whether the president got his power to remove the secretary of state from the Constitution or from Congress. See David P. Currie, "The Constitution in Congress: The First Congress and the Structure of Government, 1789–1791," 2 *University of Chicago Law School Roundtable* 161, 200–201 (1995). Currie points out that the secretary of Treasury, who today is considered the epitome of an executive officer, was originally in part designated as an agent of Congress, with no complaint from anyone, including Alexander Hamilton—that devotee of executive power who would soon be the first Treasury secretary (202).

21. Federalist 37 (Madison), in *The Federalist Papers,* ed. Isaac Kramnick (New York: Penguin, 1987), 244–45. The argument for this evolutionary understanding of the separation of powers is made in Peter Spiro, "Treaties, Executive Agreements, and Constitutional Method," 79 *Texas Law Review* 961, 1009–34 (2001).

22. McDonald, *The Presidency,* 232 (D.C.), 236 (neutrality proclamation), 257 (gunboats), 264 (squadron sent to Tripoli).

23. Henry P. Monaghan, "The Protective Power of the Presidency," 93 *Columbia Law Review* 1, 8 (1993).

24. The quotes are from Monaghan, "Protective Power," 2 (Wilson), 7 (Nixon).

25. This and the following two paragraphs are based on the careful review of the debate in George Winterton, "The Concept of Extra-constitutional Executive Power in Domestic Affairs," 71 *Hastings Constitutional Law Quarterly* 1 (1979).

26. *Youngstown Sheet & Tube,* 343 U.S. at 634–35. Recall that the case involved Presi-

dent Truman's emergency seizure of the steel mills to protect vital production during the Korean War.

27. Ibid., 635–38.

28. Ibid., 640–46.

29. 453 U.S. 654 (1981).

30. Ibid., 661–62.

31. Ibid., 661, 669, 675–80, 687–88.

32. *Luther v. Borden,* 48 U.S. 1, 45 (1849). For background on the evolution of the militia statutes, including their aggressive interpretation by Fillmore and Pierce, see Edward S. Corwin, *The President: Office and Powers, 1787–1957,* 4th ed. (New York: New York University Press, 1957).

33. The phrase is from Monaghan's insightful article, "The Protective Power of the Presidency." Monaghan may overstate the case against recognizing any broader inherent presidential power in emergencies, but he convincingly makes the case that at least the protective power is firmly grounded.

34. 135 U.S. 1 (1890).

35. Ibid., 60 ("incontrovertible principle," quoting *Ex parte Siebold,* 100 U.S. 371, 395 (1879)), id. at 61 ("or it is no government," quoting *Siebold*), id. at 65 (protection of the mails), id. at 65–66 (protection of national forests). As an alternative holding, the Court suggested that the action might have been justified under a statute giving marshals and their deputies the same powers as sheriffs have under state law. Id. at 68–69.

36. 158 U.S. 564 (1895).

37. Ibid., 581–82.

38. *United States v. Midwest Oil Co.,* 236 U.S. 459, 467, 469, 472–74 (1915).

39. See Monaghan, "Protective Power," for a persuasive defense of this position.

40. Federalist 23, 185 (Hamilton); Federalist 41, 267 (Madison).

41. Jefferson once diverted an appropriation to provide military funding during a tense dispute with England, successfully requesting congressional approval afterward. See Corwin, *The President,* 400 n. 58.

42. Message to Congress in Special Session, July 4, 1861, in *Collected Works,* 4:429.

43. Paludan, *Lincoln Presidency,* 82.

44. Proclamation of Blockade, Apr. 27, 1861, in *Collected Works,* 4:346; Proclamation of a Blockade, Apr. 19, 1861, *Collected Works,* 4:338.

45. See Henry Wheaton, *Elements of International Law,* 6th ed. (Boston: Little, Brown, 1855), 504, 507, 535–36, 553, 577, 581, 587; Theodore D. Woolsey, *Introduction to the Study of International Law, Designed as an Aid in Teaching, and in Historical Studies* (New York: Charles Scribner's Sons, 1870), 325 ("exceedingly annoying"). It is sometimes suggested that Lincoln might have simply closed Southern ports as ports of entry, but Woolsey, at least, seems to doubt whether neutrals would have been obliged to respect what would amount to a purely paper blockade (275).

46. 67 U.S. 635 (1862). For a critique of the majority opinion, see David P. Currie, *The*

Constitution in the Supreme Court: The First Hundred Years (Chicago: University of Chicago Press, 1985), 273–75 (finding the opinion "unimpressive" but agreeing with the result).

47. The alarmed "observer" was Richard Dana. See Randall, *Constitutional Problems,* 52 n. 5. On the considerable confusion over whether the Union was suppressing a mere insurrection or waging a war (or both), see Randall, *Constitutional Problems,* 59–73. For unusually thoughtful and articulate presentations of the issues regarding the war power, see Abraham D. Sofaer, *War, Foreign Affairs, and Constitutional Power: The Origins* (Cambridge, Mass.: Ballinger, 1976); John Hart Ely, *War and Responsibility: Constitutional Lessons of Vietnam and Its Aftermath* (Princeton, N.J.: Princeton University Press, 1993); Abraham D. Sofaer, "The Power over War," 50 *University Miami Law Review* 33 (1995). A good overview can be found in Phillip R. Trimble, *International Law: United States Foreign Relations Law* (New York: Foundation Press, 2002), 192–259.

48. *Prize Cases,* 67 U.S. at 668–69.

49. Ibid., 669–71, 674. The description of the rights of belligerents in a civil war seems to be correct, though the American Civil War may have been the last real application of the doctrine. See Yair M. Lootsteen, "The Concept of Belligerency in International Law," 166 *Military Law Review* 109 (2000). For an earlier decision applying the doctrine, see *The Santissima Trinidad,* 20 U.S. 283, 336–37 (1822) (according belligerent rights to one party in a civil war, even though the United States did not recognize that government).

50. *Prize Cases,* 67 U.S. at 682, 687–97. Note that Chief Justice Taney joined the dissent, thereby agreeing that the president's use of force was lawful and also that a formal state of war existed after mid-July.

51. James Madison, *Notes on Debates in the Federal Convention of 1787,* indexed ed. (Athens: Ohio University Press, 1984), 476.

52. Pub. L. No. 93-148, 87 Stat. 555 (1973), as codified at 50 U.S.C. §§ 1541 et seq; Harold Koh, *The National Security Constitution* (New Haven, Conn.: Yale University Press, 1990), 39–40 (ineffectiveness of War Powers Resolution); Ely, *War and Responsibility,* 48–52 (failure of Congress to enforce resolution). The troops at Fort Sumter were of course in danger of attack even earlier, but they were already on the spot. Lincoln had not "introduced" them into a situation where hostilities were imminent. The resolution is designed to limit the president's ability to take provocative or offensive action, not to require him to surrender existing positions—let alone U.S. territory—when threatened by force.

CHAPTER 7

1. See Paul Finkelman, "Civil Liberties and the Civil War: The Great Emancipator as Civil Libertarian," 91 *Michigan Law Review* 1353, 1365 (1993) (draft evaders considered already in military, therefore subject to military trial), 1372 (small number of arrests for expression of opinion in North), 1376 ("not just a few or 'several'

editors were arrested"). The numerical estimates are found in Mark E. Neely Jr., *The Fate of Liberty: Abraham Lincoln and Civil Liberties* (Oxford: Oxford University Press, 1991), 127–38. Neely, who exhaustively researched the original records, contends that traditional estimates undercounted the total number of prisoners but greatly overestimated the number of true political prisoners. For a lively account of some of the most notable cases, see William H. Rehnquist, *All the Laws but One: Civil Liberties in Wartime* (New York: Alfred A. Knopf, 1998). The classic treatment of the legal issues is J. G. Randall, *Constitutional Problems under Lincoln,* rev. ed. (Urbana: University of Illinois Press, 1951).

2. Finkelman, "Civil Liberties and the Civil War," 1367; Harold Hyman, *A More Perfect Union: The Impact of the Civil War and Reconstruction on the Constitution* (New York: Random House, 1973), 96 n. 37 (number of federal judges, etc.).

3. Dean Sprague, *Freedom under Lincoln* (Boston: Houghton Mifflin, 1965), 157–58 (Lincoln as arbitrator), 303 (Lincoln's regret for arrests).

4. Randall, *Constitutional Problems,* 171.

5. Neely, *Fate of Liberty,* 32–48.

6. Phillip Shaw Paludan, *The Presidency of Abraham Lincoln* (Lawrence: University Press of Kansas, 1994), 234–35; James M. McPherson, *Battle Cry of Freedom: The Civil War Era* (Oxford: Oxford University Press, 1998), 552 (chamber pot incident).

7. See Abraham D. Sofaer, "Emergency Power and the Hero of New Orleans," 2 *Cardozo Law Review* 233, 241–43 (1981); Edward S. Corwin, *The President: Office and Powers, 1787–1957,* 4th ed. (New York: New York University Press, 1957), 545 n. 15.

8. 48 U.S. 1 (1849).

9. Ibid., 45–46. For extensive background on *Luther,* see William M. Wiecek, *The Guarantee Clause of the Constitution* (Ithaca, N.Y.: Cornell University Press, 1972), 84–129.

10. 212 U.S. 78 (1909).

11. Ibid., 84–85.

12. 327 U.S. 304 (1946).

13. Ibid., 313–14, 319. The Court's holding was anticipated by John P. Frank, *"Ex parte Milligan v. The Five Companies:* Martial Law in Hawaii," 44 *Columbia Law Review* 639 (1944) (arguing that *Milligan* required the Court to review the existence of any military necessity for closing the courts). As we will see, the Court drew similar distinctions in the *Milligan* case immediately after the Civil War.

14. *Duncan,* 327 U.S. at 336–37 (Stone, C.J., concurring).

15. 287 U.S. 378 (1932).

16. Ibid., 399–400.

17. 100 U.S. 158 (1879).

18. Ibid., 164–65, 169–70. See also *Coleman v. Tennessee,* 97 U.S. 509, 517 (1878) (right to govern territory of enemy is an incident of war; Union soldier could not be tried under state law for murder committed during occupation even if guilty of violating military law); Case of James Weaver—Reconstruction Laws, 13 Op.

Att'y. Gen. 59 (1869) (upholding validity of military trial of a Texas civilian for murder). The issue of military rule in the South is treated in detail in Randall, *Constitutional Problems,* 215–38. An earlier relevant precedent is *Cross v. Harrison,* 57 U.S. 164 (1853), upholding the authority of the executive branch to institute a government in California, acting as a belligerent over conquered or ceded territory. Id. at 190, 193. Recent critics of the use of military tribunals acknowledge the strong case for their legitimacy in conquered territory. See Neal Katyal and Laurence Tribe, "Waging War, Deciding Guilt: Trying the Military Tribunals," 111 *Yale Law Journal* 1259, 1293–95 (2002).

19. *Reid v. Covert,* 354 U.S. 1, 33–34 (1957).

20. On due process and preventive detention, see *United States v. Salerno,* 481 U.S. 739, 746–50 (1987). In *Salerno,* the Court said that it had "repeatedly held that the Government's regulatory interest in community safety can, in appropriate circumstances, outweigh an individual's liberty interest. For example, in times of war or insurrection, when society's interest is at its peak, the Government may detain individuals whom the government believes to be dangerous." The Court cited Justice Holmes's opinion in *Moyer v. Peabody,* 212 U.S. 78 (1909) as well as *Ludecke v. Watkins,* 335 U.S. 160 (1948) (said to approve "unreviewable executive power to detain enemy aliens in time of war"). On the nonapplicability of the criminal procedure provisions of the Bill of Rights to cases within military jurisdiction, see *Ex parte Quirin,* 317 U.S. 1 (1942) (no right to jury trial for nonuniformed German saboteurs landing in the United States).

21. The touchstone for martial law is military necessity. The longer an area remained under Union control, as a general matter, the harder it was to say that military security required martial law. Thus, at some point, other justifications for Reconstruction actions were required—or in the lingo of the time, one could not say indefinitely that the South remained "in the grasp of war."

22. The shift in Republican sentiment is discussed in McPherson, *Battle Cry of Freedom,* 495–97. On the precarious Union position in the critical slaveholding border states at the beginning of the war, see id., 284–97. For Lincoln's proposals, see Message to Congress, Mar. 6, 1862, in *The Collected Works of Abraham Lincoln,* ed. Roy P. Basler (New Brunswick, N.J.: Rutgers University Press, 1953–55), 5:144–46; Appeal to Border State Representatives to favor Compensated Emancipation, July 12, 1862, in *Collected Works,* 5:317–19; Address on Colonization to a Deputation of Negroes, Aug. 14, 1862, in *Collected Works,* 5:370–75; Annual Message to Congress, Dec. 1, 1862, in *Collected Works,* 5:518–37.

23. On the evolution of Lincoln's thinking, see David Donald, *Lincoln* (New York: Simon and Schuster, 1995), 125–30, 164–66, 362–76; Paludan, *Presidency of Abraham Lincoln.* On the foreign policy dimension, see McPherson, *Battle Cry of Freedom,* 552–57, 567. See id., 306, 564–66, 769, for a discussion of the use of black soldiers, and id., 837, for the Confederate move toward emancipation at the very end of the war.

24. Preliminary Emancipation Proclamation, in *Collected Works,* 5:433–36; Final

Emancipation Proclamation, in *Collected Works*, 6:28–31. As evidence that the constitutionality of Lincoln's proclamation is still controversial, see Sanford Levinson, "The David C. Baum Memorial Lecture: Was the Emancipation Proclamation Constitutional? Do We/Should We Care What the Answer Is?" 2001 *University of Illinois Law Review* 1135.

25. Letter to Horace Greeley, Aug. 22, 1862, in *Collected Works*, 5:388–89 ("What I do about slavery . . ."); Letter to James C. Conkling, Aug. 26, 1863, in *Collected Works*, 6:408 ("invests its commander-in-chief, with the law of war"). Lincoln had previously rejected an emancipation effort by General Fremont as *"purely political,* and not within the range of *military* law, or necessity." Fremont, he had said, had the right to seize and use slaves where needed for military purposes, "but when the need is past, it is not for him to fix their permanent future condition." That must be decided "by law-makers, and not by military proclamations." Letter to Orville H. Browning, Sept. 22, 1861, in *Collected Works*, 4:531–33. On the validity of the proclamation, see Randall, *Constitutional Problems*, 371–85.

26. Henry Wheaton, *Elements of International Law*, 6th ed. (Boston: Little, Brown, 1855), 416–21. See also Burrus Carnahan, "Lincoln, Lieber, and the Laws of War: The Origins and Limits of the Principle of Military Necessity," 92 *American Journal of International Law* 213, 226–27 (1998).

27. 78 U.S. 268 (1870).

28. Ibid., 306–7.

29. 97 U.S. 594, 605 (1878).

30. 87 U.S. 387, 391 (1874).

31. Ibid., 393–94.

32. See *Lucas v. South Carolina Coastal Council*, 505 U.S. 1003 (1992). Moreover, the so-called property interest in the slave was not "taken" by the government for public use. Instead, it was completely extinguished. Finally, the property interests existed only under state laws. Given that there were no valid state governments in operation in the South (in the Union view), property rights created under their laws had something less than granite solidity.

33. Neely, *Fate of Liberty*, 19 (the "little bell"), 23–24 (Seward), 27 (Northern arrests). The "little bell" story may be apocryphal.

34. Ibid., 53–58 (Aug. 1862), 75–92 (Southern arrests), 116–18 (Lincoln's role), 123–38 (arrest statistics).

35. See Neely, *Fate of Liberty*, 107–10. This is not to say that all of the arrests were unproblematic, just that the remedy of habeas corpus was unavailable. There were some serious abuses, such as a persistent strain of anti-Semitism in many arrest decisions as well as occasional physical abuse of prisoners. As with other abuses, the problem was not Lincoln but his underlings. On Lincoln's rejection of anti-Semitic actions by subordinates, see Eric L. Muller, "All the Themes but One," 66 *University of Chicago Law Review* 1395, 1419–24 (1999). Lincoln's religious tolerance was also reflected in his attitude toward Quakers. See Letter to Eliza Gurney, Sept. 4, 1864, in *Collected Works*, 7:535–36.

36. See Neely, *Fate of Liberty*, 4, 10–11; Letter to Winfield Scott, Apr. 27, 1861, in *Collected Works*, 4:347. For more background on the case, see chapter 1. An excellent short summary of the habeas dispute can be found in John Sharer, "Power, Idealism, and Compromise: The Coordinate Branches and the Writ of Habeas Corpus," 26 *Emory Law Journal* 149 (1977).

37. *Ex parte Merryman*, 17 Fed. Cas. 144 (C.C.D. Md. 1861) (Case No. 9,487).

38. Message to Congress in Special Session, July 4, 1861, in *Collected Works*, 4:430–31.

39. Suspension of the Privilege of the Writ of Habeas Corpus, 10 Op. Att'y Gen. 74 (1861). Bates also suggested that the president and his subordinates are immune from judicial orders, a particularly unpersuasive argument in the habeas context. Such an immunity would defeat the whole purpose of the writ.

40. An Act Relating to Habeas Corpus, and Regulating Judicial Proceedings in Certain Cases, 12 Stat. 755 (March 3, 1863). On the various orders suspending habeas, see Neely, *Fate of Liberty*, 7–9, 11, 51–53, 56. For texts of the 1861 suspension orders, see *Collected Works*, 4:364 (Florida, on May 10), 414 (June 20, as to one Major Chase, accused of treason), 419 (from Washington to New York, July 2), 554 (from Bangor, Maine, to Washington, October 14). The disapproving memo is Memorandum: Military Arrests, circa May 17, 1861, in *Collected Works*, 4:372.

41. See Corwin, *The President*, 454 n. 15 (the Washington episode); Sofaer, "Emergency Power and the Hero of New Orleans," 233. The state courts were also indignant at Jackson's high-handed actions. See *Jefferson v. Duncan*, 3 Mart. (o.s.) 530, 6 Am. Dec. 675 (1815).

42. See Wiecek, *The Guarantee Clause of the U.S. Constitution*, 31 (Shays's Rebellion); *Luther v. Borden*, 48 U.S. 1, 8 (1849) (Dorr's rebellion).

43. See James Madison, *Notes of Debates in the Federal Convention of 1787*, indexed ed. (Athens: Ohio University Press, 1984), 486.

44. See ibid., 541 (Aug. 28 debate); Daniel A. Farber and Suzanna Sherry, *A History of the American Constitution* (St. Paul, Minn.: West Publishing, 1990), 426 (Art. 11 of Committee on Detail Draft), 430 (Article I of Committee on Style draft); William F. Duker, *A Constitutional History of Habeas Corpus* (Westport, Conn.: Greenwood Press, 1980), 133–35 (ratification history).

45. Duker, *Constitutional History*, is the most comprehensive history of the writ. For the argument in favor of exclusive legislative power, see "Developments in the Law: Federal Habeas Corpus," 83 *Harvard Law Review* 1038, 1263–65 (1970).

46. See Duker, *Constitutional History*, 144–46 (suggesting that the president's power to repel sudden attacks includes habeas suspension). The Wisconsin Supreme Court in an 1863 decision rejected any general presidential power to suspend habeas. But it also acknowledged the "right of a military commander to refuse obedience when justified by the exigencies of war," and the "*ipso facto* suspension which takes place wherever martial law actually exists" (which the court remarked that Chief Justice Taney "seems to have overlooked"). *In re Kemp*, 16 Wis. 382, 391 (1863) (Dixon, C.J.); see also id. at 399 (Cole, J.) (martial law displaces civil authority "[i]n places where hostilities exist"); id. at 407 (Paine, J.) (comman-

der in war zone may disregard habeas writ or other writs, where he has seized individuals or property by reason of military necessity). All three judges agreed, and quite properly so, that suspending the writ in Wisconsin did not fall within this power within any stretch of the imagination.

47. 9 Fed. Cas. 1 (C.C.D. Vt. 1862) (No. 4,761).

48. 212 U.S. 78 (1909).

49. On the 1861 statute as an endorsement of the previous suspension of habeas, see Randall, *Constitutional Problems,* 128–29.

50. The Iranian hostage case is also relevant in another respect. It indicates that, under appropriate circumstances, presidential emergency power includes the ability to suspend the prosecution of civil claims, despite statutes giving the courts jurisdiction over such claims.

51. The primary purpose of the suspension was to keep the military reinforcement route to the capital open. See Neely, *Fate of Liberty,* 9.

52. Neely, *Fate of Liberty,* 53 (1862 order), 162–63 (Holt's role), 173–75 (number and nature of cases). The issue of military trials has recently reemerged. See President George W. Bush, Military Order of Nov. 13, 2001–Detention, Treatment, and Trial of Certain Non-Citizens in the War against Terrorism, 66 Fed. Reg. 57833 (2001).

53. On the use of court martial for militia who refused to serve, see *Martin v. Mott,* 25 U.S. 19, 33–34 (1827). The use of court martial for individuals connected with, but not members of, the military was later curtailed in *Reid v. Covert,* 354 U.S. 1 (1957) (barring trials of civilian dependents abroad in peacetime).

54. On trials for violations of the laws of war, see *Ex parte Yamashita,* 327 U.S. 1 (1946) (trial for war crimes); *Ex parte Quirin,* 317 U.S. 1 (1942) (nonuniformed German saboteurs landing in the United States).

55. See Rehnquist, *All the Laws,* 82–85, 89–103. According to Rehnquist, Dodd was the "kingpin of a conspiracy that was planning an uprising," in which at least one of the other defendants was clearly involved, but the "evidence as to Milligan" and two others "tails off dramatically." In addition, Rehnquist contends, the tribunal should not have heard evidence of disloyal speeches by Milligan. See id. at 101–2. For additional information about the litigation, see Charles Fairman, *Reconstruction and Reunion, 1864–88, Part I,* vol. 6 of *The Oliver Wendell Holmes Devise History of the Supreme Court of the United States* (New York: Macmillan, 1971), 192–207.

56. *Ex parte Milligan,* 71 U.S. 2, 120–21 (1866).

57. Ibid., 125–27.

58. Ibid., 121–22.

59. Ibid., 135, 139–42 (Chase, C.J., concurring in the judgment).

60. David P. Currie, *The Constitution in the Supreme Court: The First Hundred Years* (Chicago: University of Chicago Press, 1985), 292. *Milligan* was intensely controversial, denounced on one side as pro-Southern—a second *Dred Scott* decision—

and praised on the other as a great victory for liberty. See Fairman, *Reconstruction and Reunion,* 214–37. Fairman believes that the opinion impaired the Court's standing and spurred party leaders toward more radical measures (237). He also views Davis's opinion as a reaction to the government's "lawless brief" and its sweeping claims of unlimited executive power, filed by "an Attorney General of cloudy judgment" (236).

61. 317 U.S. 1 (1942).

62. Ibid., 45–46. For an argument that *Quirin* should be read narrowly or reconsidered entirely, at least on the issue of congressional authorization, see Katyal and Tribe, "Waging War, Deciding Guilt," 1290–92. For background on the case, see Gary Cohen, "The Keystone Kommandos," *Atlantic Monthly* 289 (2002): 46.

63. 327 U.S. 304 (1945).

64. *Duncan v. Kahanamoku,* 327 U.S. 304, 328–30 (1946).

65. Ibid., 328, 333–35.

66. The textualist argument might run along the following lines: The Sixth Amendment right to jury trial refers to "criminal prosecution," and the Fifth Amendment's right against self-incrimination refers to "any criminal case." These may exclude cases within legitimate military jurisdiction, as the Court argued in *Quirin.* The indictment requirement of the Fifth Amendment explicitly excludes "cases arising in the land or naval forces." Note that the question is where the case "arises," not the identity of the defendant; otherwise the amendment would say "except for persons in the land or naval forces." Perhaps a case "arises" within the military if it is legitimately within military power during wartime.

67. Neely, *Fate of Liberty,* 27, 48 ("palpable injury"), 137 (political or speech-related arrests exceptional); Michael Kent Curtis, "Lincoln, Vallandigham, and Anti-war Speech in the Civil War," 7 *William and Mary Bill of Rights Journal* 105, 120 (1998) (the Indiana general's order).

68. Curtis, "Lincoln, Vallandigham, and Anti-war Speech," 107, 112–14, 119, 122–24, 131–33. The Supreme Court refused to hear Vallandigham's appeal for technical jurisdictional reasons. *Ex parte Vallandigham,* 68 U.S. 243 (1864). Burnside also stupidly closed the *Chicago Times,* an action that Lincoln revoked (Curtis, "Lincoln, Vallandigham, and Anti-war Speech," 132–34).

69. Letter to Erastus Corning and Others, June 12, 1863, in *Collected Works,* 6:264–66.

70. 249 U.S. 47 (1919).

71. 250 U.S. 616 (1919). For more background on the case, including a survey of World War I–era repression of dissidents, see Richard Polenberg, *Fighting Faiths: The Abrams Case, the Supreme Court, and Free Speech* (Ithaca, N.Y.: Cornell University Press, 1987).

72. 249 U.S. 211 (1919).

73. The test further evolved in Justice Holmes's dissents in *Abrams v. United States,* 250 U.S. 616 (1919), and *Gitlow v. New York,* 268 U.S. 652 (1925), along with Justice Brandeis's stirring concurrence in *Whitney v. California,* 274 U.S. 357 (1927). The

Court as a whole had moved to this position during the depression years. See *De Jonge v. Oregon,* 299 U.S. 353 (1937); *Herndon v. Lowry,* 301 U.S. 242 (1937).

74. 395 U.S. 444 (1969).

75. For a brief overview of the original understanding of the First Amendment and the subsequent development of thinking about free speech, see Daniel A. Farber, *The First Amendment* (New York: Foundation Press, 1998), 1–17, 57–72.

76. Neely, *Fate of Liberty,* 104–5. Secretary of State Seward had been the strongest advocate of these actions.

77. 283 U.S. 697 (1931). The prior restraint doctrine is discussed in more detail in Farber, *First Amendment,* 46–49.

78. Neely, *Fate of Liberty,* 104; *Near v. Minnesota,* 283 U.S. 697, 716 (1931). Further information about the incident can be found in Mark E. Neely Jr., *The Union Divided: Party Conflict in the Civil War North* (Cambridge, Mass.: Harvard University Press, 2002), 111–17.

CHAPTER 8

1. Proclamation Calling Militia and Convening Congress, April 15, 1861, in *The Collected Works of Abraham Lincoln,* ed. Roy P. Basler (New Brunswick, N.J.: Rutgers University Press, 1953–55), 4:331–32; Letter to James C. Conkling, August 26, 1863, in *Collected Works,* 6:410 ("appeal from the ballot to the bullet").

2. Address before the Young Men's Lyceum of Springfield, Illinois, Jan. 27, 1838, in *Collected Works,* 1:108, 111–12.

3. Id. at 112, 115.

4. The newspaper's report is quoted in *Selected Speeches and Writings,* ed. Don E. Fehrenbacher (New York: Library of America, 1991), 488, note to p. 211, lines 24–26. Lincoln later questioned this account. In his brief campaign autobiography, Lincoln said in reference to this speech that he did not remember whether he said anything about a Supreme Court decision. If he did speak on the subject, "he thinks he could not have expressed himself as represented." Autobiography Written for John L. Scripps, June 1860, in *Collected Works,* 4:67.

5. Speech at Springfield, Illinois, June 26, 1857, in *Collected Works,* 2:401.

6. "A House Divided": Speech at Springfield, Illinois, June 16, 1858, in *Collected Works,* 2:462–63, 466–67. Lincoln was right that there had been collusion if not conspiracy: Justice Grier had been in close communication with President Buchanan while the case was under consideration. See Paul Finkelman, *Dred Scott v. Sandford: A Brief History with Documents* (Boston: Bedford Books, 1997), 46–47. Finkelman believes that Lincoln's fear of a "second *Dred Scott*" was also not altogether unfounded. Id., 47–49. For further discussion of *Dred Scott,* see chapter 1.

7. First Inaugural Address, March 4, 1861, in *Collected Works,* 4:268.

8. Message to Congress in Special Session, July 4, 1861, in *Collected Works,* 4:430 (discussing *Ex parte Merryman,* 17 Fed. Cas. 144 (C.C.D. Md. 1861) (Case No. 9,487)).

9. Fragment on the Constitution and the Union, circa January 1861, in *Collected Works,* 4:168–69.

10. 358 U.S. 1, 17–18 (1954). For additional background on the case, see Daniel A. Farber, "The Supreme Court and the Rule of Law: *Cooper v. Aaron* Revisited," 1982 *University of Illinois Law Review* 387.

11. 347 U.S. 483 (1954).

12. 505 U.S. 833 (1992).

13. 410 U.S. 113 (1973) (holding that women have a fundamental, constitutionally protected, right to seek an abortion during the first two trimesters of pregnancy).

14. Id. at 836, 866–67.

15. Letter from Thomas Jefferson to Judge Spencer Roane, September 6, 1819, in Thomas Jefferson, *Writings* (New York: Library of America, 1984), 1426–27; Robert V. Remini, *The Life of Andrew Jackson* (New York: Penguin Books, 1988), 228.

16. This argument is made with particular force and clarity in Michael Stokes Paulsen, "The Most Dangerous Branch: Executive Power to Say What the Law Is," 83 *Georgetown Law Journal* 217, 228–62 (1994).

17. See Edward A. Hartnett, "A Matter of Judgment, Not a Matter of Opinion," 74 *New York University Law Review* 123 (1999); Thomas W. Merrill, "Judicial Opinions as Binding Law and as Explanations for Judgments," 15 *Cardozo Law Review* 43 (1993).

18. On the checks and balances side of the argument, see Paulsen, "The Most Dangerous Branch," 321–42; Gary Lawson and Christopher D. Moore, "The Executive Power of Constitutional Interpretation," 81 *Iowa Law Review* 1267, 1329–30 (1996). On the fear that judicial supremacy will cut off constitutional dialogue, see Robert F. Nagel, "A Comment on Democratic Constitutionalism," 61 *Tulane Law Review* 1027 (1987); Mark Tushnet, "The Supreme Court, The Supreme Law of the Land, and Attorney General Meese: A Comment," 61 *Tulane Law Review* 1017 (1987).

19. The argument based on the settlement function is most fully developed in Larry Alexander and Frederick Schauer, "On Extrajudicial Constitutional Interpretation," 110 *Harvard Law Review* 1359 (1997), and Larry Alexander and Frederick Schauer, "Defending Judicial Supremacy: A Reply," 17 *Constitutional Commentary* 455 (2000).

20. See Alexander and Schauer, "Defending Judicial Supremacy," 473–78; Burt Neuborne, "The Binding Quality of Supreme Court Precedent," 61 *Tulane Law Review* 991, 999–1000 (1987).

21. In the first situation, contrary action would be an invasion of an individual's legal rights; in the second situation, no individual has a legally enforceable right at stake. Or, to put it another way, presidential noncompliance would violate a legal duty (an invasion of someone's rights backed by a legal remedy), and in the other instance, it violates only a political duty of mutual respect between the branches of government.

22. This argument is developed more extensively in Farber, "The Supreme Court and the Rule of Law," 403–11. In more technical terms, it is the holding rather than any dictum that gives rise to legal rights.

23. Similarly, no one's legal rights are violated if a president vetoes financial aid for state busing because he disagrees with the Court's desegregation rulings. Such actions violate no one's legal rights and have no legal remedy. Yet one might consider these actions, like jury nullification, to show a disrespect for the law and a failure to live up to the ideal of the law-abiding citizen, and in that sense perhaps to violate a legal duty (at least in the absence of exigent circumstances).

24. See Paulsen, "The Most Dangerous Branch," 309 (quoting Madison); Michael Stokes Paulsen, "The Merryman Power and the Dilemma of Autonomous Executive Branch Interpretation," 15 *Cardozo Law Review* 81, 95 (1993) (consensus about enforcement of judgments; Paulsen himself is an exception).

25. See Paulsen, "The Most Dangerous Branch," 276–88. Paulsen recognizes two exceptions: except where validly suspended, the president must obey a writ of habeas corpus, and he must not overturn jury verdicts (under the Sixth Amendment's jury trial clause). Id., 288–92.

26. Merrill, "Judicial Opinions as Binding Law," 46 (*Merryman* is "only reported instance" of such presidential behavior and "today regarded as an aberration"); Lawson and Moore, "The Executive Power of Constitutional Interpretation," 1319–20. Lawson and Moore make a small concession to executive nullification. They argue that the president can "refuse to enforce a judgment only in extreme circumstances: only for constitutional error, and only when that error is 'so clear that it is not open to rational question.'" Moreover, they contend, the president can refuse to enforce a judgment of liability, but he cannot "affirmatively act to infringe private rights in the face of a judgment of no liability." Id., 325–26. For an extensive discussion of the power of the other branches over final court judgments, see *Plaut v. Spendthrift Farm, Inc.,* 514 U.S. 211 (1995).

27. For a First Amendment example, see *Walker v. City of Birmingham,* 388 U.S. 307 (1967) (upholding contempt citation for violating an injunction that admittedly violated the First Amendment). But *Walker* does not apply when the state court clearly lacked jurisdiction or the order is unconstitutional on its face. See *In re Providence Journal Co.,* 820 F. 2d 1342 (1st Cir. 1986); *Procter & Gamble Co. v. Bankers Trust Co.,* 78 F. 3d 219 (6th Cir. 1996).

28. See *Kalb v. Feuerstein,* 308 U.S. 433, 438, 440 (1940); *United States v. U.S. Fidelity & Guar. Co.,* 309 U.S. 508 (1940); David Shapiro, *Civil Procedure: Preclusion in Civil Actions* (New York: Foundation Press, 2001), 25–32. On the injunction aspect, see *In re Green,* 369 U.S. 689 (1962) (state injunction can be collaterally attacked if preempted by federal law); *United States v. Mine Workers of America,* 330 U.S. 258, 289–95 (1947) (when jurisdiction to issue injunction was in doubt, trial court could issue order to preserve status quo, since court had jurisdiction over subject matter and person of defendant). There is an exception today where the jurisdiction issue was "fully and fairly litigated and finally decided" in the original court (see *Durfee v. Duke,* 375 U.S. 106, 111 (1963)), but this was not true in *Merryman.* As Shapiro points out, the traditional rule was quite clear: a judgment without sub-

ject matter jurisdiction was a nullity (*Preclusion,* 26). The modern cases have lurched away from that position, but probably continue to regard such a judgment as void where a clear need exists to respect the "immunity of a sovereign entity" or the authority of another forum with exclusive jurisdiction. Id. at 28.

29. *Ableman v. Booth,* 62 U.S. 506, 523 (1858).

30. On the duty to produce the body of the prisoner (thus the name of the writ), see William F. Duker, *A Constitutional History of Habeas Corpus* (Westport, Conn.: Greenwood Press, 1980), 5–6.

31. The absence of any good faith defense for officers at this time is illustrated by *The Apollon,* 22 U.S. 362 (1824).

32. Letter from Thomas Jefferson to John B. Colvin, September 20, 1810, in *Writings,* 1231–33. Similarly, Jefferson defended the decision to send Aaron Burr and his comrades to Washington for trial, although Burr was entitled by statute to a trial in the territory where he was captured. "The danger of their rescue, of their continuing their machinations, the tardiness and weakness of the law, . . . salvation of the city, and of the Union itself, which would have been convulsed to its centre, had that conspiracy succeeded; all these constituted a law of necessity and self-preservation, and rendered the *salus populi* supreme over the written law." Id. at 1233.

33. Letter from Thomas Jefferson to John C. Breckinridge, August 12, 1803, in *Writings,* 1138–39.

34. See Jules Lobel, "Emergency Power and the Decline of Liberalism," 98 *Yale Law Journal* 1385, 1390–97 (1989).

35. Message to Congress in Special Session, July 4, 1861, in *Collected Works,* 4:429–30.

36. An Act relating to Habeas Corpus, and regulating Judicial Proceedings in Certain Cases, ch. 81, §§ 4 & 7, 12 Stat. 755 (1863).

37. *Mitchell v. Clark,* 110 U.S. 633 (1884).

38. Id., 640.

AFTERWORD

1. Annual Message to Congress, Dec. 1, 1862, in *The Collected Works of Abraham Lincoln,* ed. Roy P. Basler (New Brunswick, N.J.: Rutgers University Press, 1953–55), 5:537.

2. For some important reflections on the relationship between constitutionalism and public character, see David McGowan, "Ethos in Law and History: Alexander Hamilton, *The Federalist,* and the Supreme Court," 85 *Minnesota Law Review* 755, 819–27, 835–39, 886–98 (2001).

3. See Charles E. Larmore, *Patterns of Moral Complexity* (Cambridge: Cambridge University Press, 1987), 6–7 ("the duty to defend," "steer us between"); Mark J. Osiel, *Obeying Orders: Atrocity, Military Discipline, and the Law of War* (New Brunswick, N.J.: Transaction Publishers, 1999), 247–61 (on military courage); Isaiah Berlin, *The Sense of Reality: Studies in Ideas and Their History* (London: Chatto and Win-

dus, 1996), 35. As Berlin says, there "is no substitute for a sense of reality"—a useful reminder for lawyers and judges in particular, since they are trained to the manipulation of categories and symbols. Although eschewing use of the term *courage,* the most recent study of Lincoln's character stresses his independent judgment, prudence, and resolution, all closely related to the concept of moral courage used here. See William Lee Miller, *Lincoln's Virtues: An Ethical Biography* (New York: Alfred A. Knopf, 2002), 34–44, 74–79, 222–30, 407, 489–90.

4. Alexander Hamilton, Address before the New York State Ratifying Convention, June 27, 1788, quoted in McGowan, "Ethos in Law and History," 793.

Index

Abrams v. United States, 172

Adams, John, 35

Alden v. Maine, 28

Alien and Sedition Acts, 46

"all the laws but one," 18, 158, 179, 192–95. *See also* rule of law

American constitutional discourse, 80–81, 198; constitutional interpretation, 1–2, 125; "living Constitution" theory, 125, 135–36, 169; Madison's views, 39, 126; originalism, 62–65, 94, 197–98; textualism, 82, 126–27, 229n. 66

American Revolution, 30, 33, 35–36, 101–2, 105, 148, 159–60, 191

Anderson, Robert, 7, 13, 116, 132

Antietam, battle of, 92, 153

appointments clause, 124

appropriations clause, 137

Article I, 18, 40, 98, 100, 136–37, 142, 155. *See also* Congress

Article II, 102, 121–26, 137, 142; specific grants of power, 121, 155, 161–62; vesting clause, 123–24, 128, 130. *See also* executive power

Article III, 54, 58, 62–65, 68, 69, 100, 212–13n. 51. *See also* federal courts

Article IV, 86, 98–99

Article V, 31, 38–39, 66, 77, 84, 86, 111–12, 213n. 55, 219n. 41

Article VII, 31, 39, 87–89. *See also* Constitution, ratification of

Articles of Confederation, 36–38, 77, 79, 82, 84–85, 89, 94–95

Bank of the United States, 39, 42–43, 46, 55–56, 119, 181

Bill of Rights. *See specific amendments*

Black, Hugo, 120, 130, 152

blockade of South, 17, 117, 138–43

Booth, John Wilkes, 7

Brandenburg v. Ohio, 172

Brown, John, 11

Brown v. Board of Education, 180

Buchanan, James, 10, 13–14, 75–76, 83, 87–88, 92, 94

Calhoun, Andrew, 103

Calhoun, John C., 2, 9, 28, 31–32, 45, 59, 62–66, 69, 212–13n. 51, 213nn. 55, 65. *See also* nullification

Chase, Salmon, 166–67

citizenship, 10, 27–28

civil liberties. *See* free speech; military arrests/detention; military trials

Civil War, 1, 92–93, 112–14; origins of, 9–15, 102–5

Clay, Henry, 9, 59

Cohens v. Virginia, 53–55

Cold Harbor, battle of, 93

commander-in-chief clause, 129, 154

commerce clause, 40, 58, 89, 134

compact clause, 40, 77, 216n. 41

compact theory, 32, 34, 45, 47–49, 57, 59, 64, 67, 81–85, 207n. 30. *See also* sovereignty

Compromise of 1850, 9

Confederate States of America: as belligerent power, 140–41, 145, 147–48,

Confederate States of America
(*continued*)
151, 155, 166; constitution of, 77,
204n. 6; formation of, 13, 76–77. *See
also* secession
Confiscation Acts, 155–56
Congress: control over appropriations,
18, 137; ratification of presidential
acts, 118, 130–32, 137–38, 158–59,
194–95. *See also* Article I
conspiracy, 72, 178, 230n. 6
Constitution, power to interpret: by
courts, 23, 48–49, 51, 54, 57–58, 84,
178–79, 186; by president, 181, 184–
87; by states, 21, 47–48, 57–58, 65,
78, 84, 89–90. *See also* American constitutional discourse
Constitution, ratification of, 31, 39,
85–91, 124, 207n. 27
Constitutional Convention, official letter to Congress, 37–38, 40, 207n. 30
Continental Congress, 34–35, 159. *See
also* Articles of Confederation
Cooper v. Aaron, 180
Crittenden compromise, 14
Cunningham v. Neagle, 133–34, 228n. 50

Dames & Moore v. Regan, 131–32
Davis, David, 165–67
Davis, Jefferson, 13, 77–78, 81, 101–2,
107, 116–17
Debs v. United States, 172
Debs, In re, 134
Declaration of Independence, 11, 35,
79, 101–2, 179. *See also* American
Revolution
"Declaration of the Causes of Seces-
sion," 76, 101
Democratic party, 9–10, 46, 72, 74, 138
Dorr's rebellion (Rhode Island), 148–
49, 160
Douglas, Stephen, 9, 11, 71, 74, 116,
178

Dow v. Johnson, 151
Dred Scott v. Sandford, 10, 178–79, 185,
200, 202n. 10, 230n. 6
due process clause, 131, 149, 152, 225n.
20
Duncan v. Kahanamoku, 149–50, 168–69

Eleventh Amendment. *See* sovereign
immunity
Emancipation Proclamation, 102, 152–
57
emergency powers, 127–32, 161–62,
165. *See also* executive power; free
speech; military arrests/detention;
military trials
enemy aliens. *See* military arrests/de-
tention; seizure of property
executive power, 19, 75–76, 119, 121–
43, 156–57; emergency powers and,
133–36, 139–42, 161–62; "Goldilocks" principle, 125; Justice Jackson's analysis of, 125, 130–31;
original understanding of, 121–26,
141–42; to suspend habeas, 157–63;
"take care" duty, 17–18, 64–65, 75–
76; vesting clause, 123–24, 128, 130

federal courts: criticism of, 53–55; enforcement of judgments, 119, 186,
188–92, 232n. 26; enforcement
powers, 55–57, 65, 67–68, 84; injunctions against state officers, 55–
56, 211n. 29; jurisdiction, 49–53, 55,
60–61, 64–65, 67–68, 189–92,
210n. 20. *See also* Constitution, power
to interpret; judicial supremacy;
stare decisis
federal government: antebellum weakness, 16–17, 116–17, 119, 145, 196;
coercion of states, 51–52, 76, 92,
94–101; nationhood, 83, 198. *See also*
Congress; executive power; war
power

federalism. *See* sovereign immunity; sovereignty; Tenth Amendment

Federalist Papers: on compact theory, 84; criticisms of, 59, 63; on executive power, 126; on federal jurisdiction, 54, 63; on federal supremacy, 37–38, 96–97; on national defense, 98; on national power, 59, 88, 98; on ratification, 30–31, 38, 84; on sovereignty, 30–31, 217n. 7; on state authority, 89–90. *See also* Hamilton, Alexander; Madison, James

Field, Ex parte, 162

Fifth Amendment. *See* due process clause; takings clause

First Amendment: modern doctrine, 172; prior restraint rule, 173–74; violations of, 170–75

First Inaugural (Lincoln), 111–12, 113–14, 178–79

Force Act, 62

Ford v. Surget, 155

foreign policy, 67, 109, 153

Fort Sumter, 7, 13, 77, 126; decision to attack, 15; decision to defend, 15, 116, 118, 223n. 52

free speech: Alien and Sedition Acts, 45; invasion of, 17, 19–20, 170–71. *See also* First Amendment

Fugitive Slave Act, 9, 14, 104, 187

General Order No. 11, 147

General Order No. 38, 170

Gettysburg, battle of, 92

Gettysburg Address, 7

Grant, Ulysses, 146–47

habeas corpus, 84, 152; as constitutional text, 157–58; history of, 160–62, 191; suspension of, by Lincoln, 17–19, 117, 157–63, 187–92

Habeas Corpus Act, 159, 191, 194–95

Hamilton, Alexander, 37–38, 44–45,

63, 89, 96–97, 126, 200. *See also Federalist Papers*

Holmes, Oliver Wendell, Jr., 149, 162–63

Hunter v. Martin, 49–53

international law, 83, 110, 151, 154–55; and blockade, 139, 141, 222n. 43

interstate commerce, 40, 134

Iranian hostage crisis. See *Dames & Moore v. Regan*

Jackson, Andrew, 10, 44, 61, 62, 119, 136, 148, 160, 181, 199

Jackson, Robert, 125, 130–31

Jefferson, Thomas, 22, 42, 44–46, 49, 53, 68, 101, 127, 181; on necessity versus legality, 192–94, 233n. 32. *See also* Virginia and Kentucky Resolutions

judicial supremacy, 90–91, 179–88

Judiciary Act, 49–53, 64–65

Kansas-Nebraska Act, 9–10, 71, 73

Kennedy, Anthony, 28, 38, 180

laws of war, belligerent status, 23, 140–41, 145, 147–48, 151, 155, 166

legal duty, definitions of, 183–86

Lincoln: "all the laws but one," 18, 158, 179, 192–95 (*see also* rule of law); antislavery views, 11–12, 71–72, 104–5, 153–54; assassination, 2, 7; attitude toward law and courts, 176–79, 188; blockade, 19, 138–42, 222n. 45; on civil liberties, 18–20, 24, 170–71; dictatorship charge, 2, 20–21, 115, 144–46; diversion of funds, 18, 132, 137; 1860 election, 12, 74–75; 1864 election, 20; Emancipation Proclamation, 154–55; First Inaugural, 14–15, 105, 111–12, 114; and free speech, 146, 170–75; Gettysburg Address, 7; habeas suspension,

Lincoln (*continued*)
17, 157–63, 188–92, 194; July 4,
1861 address to Congress, 18–19,
24, 107, 116–18, 158–59; letter to
Corning, 171; on majority rule, 77,
102, 108–9; moral character of,
113, 152, 176, 198–200, 233–34n.
3; on national power, 94, 198; political career, 71, 106; response to
secession, 16–18, 113–14, 116–18,
138, 141, 143, 197; on right of revolution, 106; on rule of law, 176–80,
194; secession views, 78–79, 86,
102, 108–9, 111–12; on slavery,
11–12, 104–5, 153–54, 226n. 25;
on sovereignty, 19, 30; and Supreme
Court, 177–80, 199, 230n. 4; unilateral expansion of military, 15–16,
18, 117–18, 132–33, 136–38; use of
executive power, 3, 18, 19, 118–19,
132–38, 197. *See also* executive
power; secession
Locke, John, 128
Louisiana Purchase, 193
Luther v. Borden, 148–49, 160, 199

Madison, James, 22, 38–39, 46, 49, 59,
83, 94, 96, 99, 122–26, 142, 213n. 65;
on nullification and secession, 4, 36,
49, 66–69, 88–89. See also *Federalist
Papers*
Marbury v. Madison, 180, 211n. 31
Marshall, John, 39, 42–43, 50, 54–57,
158, 181
martial law, 24, 147–52, 163–70
Martin, Luther, 33
Martin v. Hunter's Lessee, 49–53, 209–
10n. 17
McClung v. Silliman, 56
McCulloch v. Maryland, 39, 42–43, 99
Merryman, Ex parte, 17, 119, 157–63,
179, 188–92, 199
Mexican-American War, 9, 106

Midwest Oil. See *United States v. Midwest
Oil Co.*
military, expansion of, 15–16, 18, 117–
18, 136–38
military arrests/detention, 19–20,
203n. 32, 223–24n. 1, 226n. 35; constitutionality of, 148–49, 157–63,
194–95, 227–28n. 46
military trials, 20, 144, 147–48, 163–70;
of Confederates, 164; constitutionality of, 149–52, 163–70; due
process, 164
militia, 15
militia clauses, 95, 98
Miller, Samuel, 133–34
Miller v. United States, 155
Milligan, Ex parte, 164–69, 228–29n. 60
Milligan, Lambdin, 164–65, 228n. 55
Missouri Compromise, 9, 71, 73. *See also*
slavery
Mitchell v. Clark, 195
moral character, 198–201, 233–34n. 3
Moyer v. Peabody, 149, 162–63

Near v. Minnesota, 174
necessary and proper clause, 48, 99
New Jersey plan, 95–96
New Orleans v. The Steamship Co., 155–56
New York v. United States, 95–96
Nixon, Richard, 127
Northwest Ordinance, 9, 103
nullification: crisis, 58–62; critique by
Madison, 66–69; Jackson proclama-
tion, 61–62; theory of, 47, 60, 65–
66, 69, 189

oath clause, 128. *See also* Article II
occupied Southern territory, 147–48,
151
O'Connor, Sandra Day, 95–96
ordinance of nullification. *See* nullification
Osborn v. Bank of United States, 55–56

Planned Parenthood v. Casey, 180–81

Preamble (to Constitution), 27, 30, 37, 52, 64, 79, 86–87, 183

precedents (stare decisis), 178–79, 182

presidential oath of office, 128, 159, 179, 194. *See also* Article II

press, restrictions on, 173–74. *See also* First Amendment

Printz v. United States, 96, 217–18n. 14

prisoners of war, 142–43. *See also* military arrests/detention

private property, 141. *See also* takings clause

Prize Cases, 138–41, 155. *See also* blockade of South; war power

property ownership, analogy to sovereignty, 29–30, 205n. 12

protective power of president. *See* emergency powers

Quirin, Ex parte, 167–68

Randall, James, 5

Reconstruction era, 2, 5, 216n. 1

Rehnquist, William, 131–32, 228n. 55

republican form of government clause, 40, 98, 144

Republican party, 9, 11–12, 71–72, 77–78, 102–3, 105

revolution, right to, 101–5

Roe v. Wade, 180

rule of law, 21–24, 91; definition of, 21; Lincoln and, 176–95; threats to, 22–23

Scalia, Antonin, 96, 217–18n. 14

Schenck v. United States, 172

secession, 12–16, 69, 71–77, 215n. 27; causes of, 12; and compact theory, 49, 81–85; democratic theory, 79, 90, 106–12; legality of, 3, 13, 36, 49, 61–62, 65, 75–76, 85–91; moral arguments, 92–94, 101–5; original un-

derstanding, 31, 83, 87–89; Quebec case, 110–11; structural arguments, 88–91; threats of, 109

secession crisis, 12–15, 74–77, 107, 116–21, 196

seizure of property, 144, 154–56. *See also* blockade of South

self-government, right to, 24, 106–12

Senate, U.S., 83, 90, 126. *See also* Article I; Congress

separation of powers. *See* Congress; executive power

Seward, William, 20, 157, 159

Shay's Rebellion, 98, 160

Sherman, William, 20, 23

Shiloh, battle of, 92–93

Sixth Amendment, 144, 229n. 66

"slave power" conspiracy theory, 72, 178, 230n. 6

slavery, 53, 152–57; as cause of Civil War, 12, 102–5; Southern views, 10, 73, 103–4; in territories, 9–11, 71–77, 103, 105, 185

South Carolina: Democratic presidential convention, 74; nullification by, 58–62; secession by, 13, 74, 76, 107

sovereign immunity, doctrine of, 28–29, 53–56, 65, 210n. 23

sovereignty, 26–38, 42–44, 152–54, 205n. 11; definition of, 26–27, 29; modern views, 27–28, 33; national, 27–28, 31, 41, 52, 54, 57–58; state, 19, 27–28, 30–36, 78; transformational theory, 42, 207–8n. 34. *See also* compact theory

Spotsylvania, battle of, 93

Stanton, Edwin, 2

stare decisis (precedents), 178–79, 182

state constitutions, 30, 35

Steel Seizure Case (Youngstown Sheet & Tube Co. v. Sawyer), 120, 130–32, 156–57

Stephens, Alexander, 78, 102–3

Sterling v. Constantin, 150–51
Stevens, John Paul, 27
Stone, Harlan, 150
Story, Joseph, 50, 52–53
Sumner, Charles, 73
supremacy clause, 41, 51–52, 58, 68, 87
Supreme Court, jurisdiction over state
  appeals, 49–53, 63, 68
suspension clause. *See* habeas corpus

"take care" clause, 17–18, 64–65, 128–
  29, 195. *See also* executive power
takings clause, 144, 156. *See also* blockade of South; Emancipation Proclamation; private property
Taney, Roger, 3, 10, 133, 141, 148, 161,
  178, 199–201. See also *Merryman*
tariff controversies, 58, 75, 102
tax power, 41–42
Tenth Amendment, 43–44, 80. *See also*
  compact theory; sovereignty
Term Limits. See U.S. Term Limits, Inc. v.
  Thornton
Thirteenth Amendment, 144. *See also*
  Emancipation Proclamation; slavery
Thomas, Clarence, 27, 64, 79–80, 204–
  5n. 7
Toombs, Robert, 15
treason, 58, 100
treaty clause, 123. *See also* foreign policy

unauthorized disbursements, 18, 118,
  137

United States v. Midwest Oil Co., 135, 137
unlawful combatants, 159, 164, 167–
  68, 228n. 52
U.S. Term Limits, Inc. v. Thornton, 27–28,
  33, 38, 79–80, 84–85

Vallandigham, Clement, 146, 171, 174
Vallandigham, Ex parte, 170–75, 229n.
  68
vesting clause, 123–24, 128, 130. *See also*
  Article I
Virginia and Kentucky Resolutions:
  drafting of, 47; impact of, 3, 47, 50–
  52; interpretation of, 66–67; response to, 48. *See also* compact theory

war power, 18, 92, 94, 138–43, 154–56,
  166. *See also* emergency powers; exec-
  utive power
War Powers Resolution, 142
Washington, George, 37–38, 127, 193
Webster, Daniel, 27, 57–58
Welles, Gideon, 174
Whig party, 119
Wilderness, battle of, 93
Wilmot Proviso, 8–9
Wilson, James, 33, 36, 160
Wilson, Woodrow, 127

Youngstown Sheet & Tube Co. v. Sawyer
  (*Steel Seizure Case*), 120, 130–32,
  156–57